AUDIO/VIDEO PRODUCTION
Theory and Practice

HENRY B. ALDRIDGE
LUCY A. LIGGETT

Eastern Michigan University

PRENTICE HALL, ENGLEWOOD CLIFFS, NEW JERSEY 07632

Library of Congress Cataloging-in-Publication Data

Aldridge, Henry B.
  Audio/video production: theory and practice / Henry B. Aldridge,
Lucy A. Liggett.

  Bibliography.
  Includes index.
  ISBN 0-13-050774-1
  1. Radio—Production and direction. 2. Television—Production and
direction. 3. Sound recordings—Production and direction. 4. Video
recordings—Production and direction. 5. Audio-visual materials.
I. Liggett, Lucy A. II. Title.
PN1990.9.P76A44 1989
791.44′0232—dc19   88-19567
                  CIP

Editorial/production supervision and
  interior design: **Marjorie Borden Shustak**
Cover design: **George Cornell**
Manufacturing buyer: **Ed O'Dougherty**

©1990 by Prentice-Hall, Inc.
A Division of Simon & Schuster
Englewood Cliffs, New Jersey 07632

Printed in the United States of America

10 9 8 7 6 5 4 3 2 1

ISBN 0-13-050774-1

Prentice-Hall International (UK) Limited, *London*
Prentice-Hall of Australia Pty. Limited, *Sydney*
Prentice-Hall Canada Inc., *Toronto*
Prentice-Hall Hispanoamericana, S.A., *Mexico*
Prentice-Hall of India Private Limited, *New Delhi*
Prentice-Hall of Japan, Inc., *Tokyo*
Simon & Schuster Asia Pte. Ltd., *Singapore*
Editora Prentice-Hall do Brasil, Ltda., *Rio de Janeiro*

For Jackie, Laura and Max

Contents _____

Preface

Audio/Video Production: Theory and Practice is an introductory text for students in beginning audio/video production courses. Its contents reflect our thirty years of combined experience in teaching audio and video production and the needs of the many students with whom we have worked over the years.

Audio/Video Production: Theory and Practice is divided into two major parts. Part I is about the theory of audio communication, the physics of sound, and the writing and production of audio programs for broadcast and non-broadcast uses. Part II deals with the theory of visual communication, the physics of light and color, video equipment, and the writing and production of video programs for broadcast and non-broadcast applications.

Each of the two parts of the book contains chapters which outline the unique communication characteristics of sound and moving images, respectively. These chapters also discuss how technology, economics, and social conditions of reception influence the content of audio and video productions. They suggest theoretical principles that can be used as guides to making audio and video messages of various kinds. Each part also contains a chapter that reviews the physics of sound or light and how production equipment is used to convert this information into electrical forms. These chapters present this material clearly and non-technically. Both parts also contain chapters on production equipment and writing.

Part II, about video, has chapters on picture composition and editing. These introduce widely practiced aesthetic approaches which students can use as a guide in making their own video productions. Part II also has two chapters devoted to descriptions of studio and location production situations. Parts I and II end with a chapter describing practical production situations, so that readers can get a sense of the wide variety of applications for the theories and practices described in the book. Readers interested in acquiring more information about the subjects discussed will find a list of suggested readings at the end of each chapter. In addition, a complete bibliography is given at the end of the book.

The appendixes contain step-by-step descriptions of four different, but typical, types of audio/video productions. Some instructors might wish to use these as actual assignments for their classes or utilize them for illustrative purposes. Key terms used in the text are defined in the glossary.

Audio/Video Production: Theory and Practice contains several unique features. The first is that it combines both audio and video production into one text. One reason for doing this is that many introductory courses cover both subjects; a second reason is that audio and video are closely related and their treatment in the same text facilitates the reader's understanding of their relationship.

Another important feature of this book is that it considers theory *and* practice. We believe that an understanding of theoretical principles is a useful guide in making audio and video productions.

Finally, the text treats production equipment as a system and describes individual items of equipment in terms of their place within that system. This allows the reader to perceive general principles of equipment operation and prevents the book from becoming a catalogue of equipment items. The technology of production equipment is changing so rapidly that all descriptions of specific items are kept general; therefore, readers can readily apply the information found in equipment chapters to the types of facilities they actually use.

The organization of chapters is designed to provide a foundation of theoretical concepts before introducing students to specific pieces of equipment and how they are used in production. Individual instructors may wish to reorder the chapters to meet the needs of specific courses.

ACKNOWLEDGMENTS

We would like to acknowledge the contributions made by our students, our colleagues, and industry professionals during the preparation of this manuscript. Our students' curiosity and questions about production provided the impetus for writing the book. Our colleagues in the Department of Communication and Theatre Arts at Eastern Michigan University encouraged our efforts. Professionals working in the industry generously answered our questions and supplied photographs and other materials.

Several individuals deserve special thanks. Harold Beer, David Lau, and Steve Martin provided valuable assistance by reading and offering suggestions on the technical portions of the book. David Gore helped with decisions about illustrations and took the photos not credited to the other sources that appear in the text. Fred Bock, Melinda Bostwick, Jackie Hull, Betsy Johnston, and Leanne Young modeled for the photos. Alex Nuckols did the line drawings. Karen Sterzik created the computer designs. Professors Annette Barbier (Northwestern University), C. John Sincell (University of Maryland), and Kimberly A. Neuendorf (Cleveland State University) graciously reviewed the manuscript. At Prentice Hall, Steve Dalphin and Marjorie Shustak guided us through the production process from idea to finished book.

There were, of course, many other individuals who graciously responded to our requests for assistance and advice. To all of them we extend our thanks.

Introduction _____

One distinguishing characteristic of contemporary American society is the extent to which we rely on electronic media as sources of information and entertainment. For example, a typical weekday morning might begin when the alarm clock radio comes on in the middle of the weather report. While one member of the family heads out for a morning jog with a walkman tucked into a pocket, another slips a video cassette into the VCR and starts an aerobic workout. Breakfast is accompanied by a cable news channel. In the car, a local radio deejay provides information about traffic conditions and last night's sports events. On campus, the teenager heads for the learning lab to use an interactive video disc to complete a biology assignment. At the office, one adult finds a memo about the arrival of a new videotape explaining how to fill out and process the latest W-4 income tax form. On her way to the office, the other adult passes technicians setting up cameras, monitors, and other equipment for a satellite teleconference scheduled to begin at 10:00 a.m.

Although our family is hypothetical, it's obvious that for all of us, the use of audio and video recordings is expanding at an amazing pace. Not many years ago, we left the operation of the equipment to engineers and technicians with specialized training in electronics. Today, basic audio recorders and video cameras with built-in recorders are simple enough for any of us to use.

In addition, from constant exposure to radio and television programming, we have become very sophisticated consumers of recorded messages. However, when we pick up our audio recorders or video cameras, that sophistication does not translate easily into satisfying recordings of our own. Sometimes the problem is technical; we simply don't understand enough about the equipment or the total production process to produce clear sound and images. More often, the problem is that we have not stopped to consider that what we are trying to do is to communicate an idea. Instead of picking up pen and paper to write a letter or essay, we're picking up a microphone or camera to record our ideas so we can share them with other people.

Whether your reasons for wanting to learn audio/video production techniques are simply to satisfy your curiosity about "how it's done" or to take the first step toward a job as a camera operator or audio technician or a career as a producer, director, or editor, this book can be a useful start.

In organizing the material, we've worked from three assumptions. First, we believe that audio and video have unique characteristics and that these are more obvious when the two are treated separately. Second, we believe that the purpose of any production is to communicate with the listener or viewer and that an audio or video message is more successful when based on an understanding of the aesthetic as well as the technical dimensions of these media. Third, we believe that you will more easily adapt to the rapidly changing technology if you understand how individual pieces of equipment function within the larger storage/retrieval system.

The chapters in this text are divided into two main parts: *audio production* (Part I) and *video production* (Part II). The beginning of each part examines how sounds or images communicate and the psychological, technological, economic, organizational, and aesthetic factors that influence audio/video messages. Then the physical properties underlying technical possibilities and limitations are described. This is followed by a discussion of the equipment used and how it works together as an input-processing-output system. Based on that background, an approach to the creation of an audio/video message from idea to final recording is outlined. Each part ends with a chapter based on interviews with professionals working in a variety of settings from broadcast stations to cable companies to corporations.

We recognize that the actual facilities to which you have access will vary widely. We think you should be aware of the latest technology and current industry practice, but we also think you should realize what can be accomplished with less than state-of-the-art equipment. Therefore, throughout the text we have stressed basic principles that can be applied to solving production problems in a variety of ways. The suggested production exercises outlined in Appendixes A, B, and C can provide valuable first-hand experience in applying those principles.

Some of the terminology in the text will be new to you. The glossary at the end of the book will help you learn the new language of audio/video production. The readings listed at the end of each chapter and in the bibliography will help you explore specific areas in more detail.

chapter one _____

Audio Communication _____

INTRODUCTION

We live in a sea of sound. As I write this paragraph, I'm surrounded by sounds. The nearest is the typewriter itself, clattering as the keys hit the page or clanging when the print wheel reaches the end of a line. Outside, a breeze is rustling the leaves on the tree by my window. Somewhere down the block, children are laughing and bouncing a ball. Farther off, traffic is moving regularly down the street. Now and then, an airplane's roar grows louder as it starts its descent to the airport. I'm conscious of each of these sounds because I am trying to describe them to you. But even when I am concentrating on other ideas or other activities, these sounds are part of my environment and I remain aware of them at some level of consciousness.

As you're reading this paragraph, you too are surrounded by the sounds of your environment. Those sounds are as familiar to you as the sounds of my environment are to me. If you're concentrating on what you're reading, you're undoubtedly ignoring those sounds. But now that we've started talking about them, you are probably very aware of each sound and its source.

You'll note that when I was describing the sounds around me, I did so by identifying the actions that were creating those sounds. If you stopped to think about the sound environment surrounding you, you probably did the same thing. We are so accustomed to assigning meanings to the sounds we hear that we seldom stop to consider how this process works. But understanding this process is important in producing effective audio messages. In this chapter we'll consider how audio communicates, the role played by perception in creating meanings, and the ways in which the components and structure of audio messages are af-

1

fected by the purposes of sender and receiver. We'll also discuss how technology, production circumstances, and aesthetic judgments influence audio messages.

HOW AUDIO COMMUNICATES

Communication can be defined in many ways. For our purposes, *communication* refers to the sharing of meanings. That seems to be a simple, straightforward definition, but it refers to a complex process. Many theoretical models have been developed to explain it. One that is useful for our discussion is the Ross Communication Model.[1] Although developed to explain speech communication, this model identifies many variables affecting audio and video messages intended for mass audiences as well (Fig. 1-1).

FIGURE 1-1 Ross model of communication. (From Raymond S. Ross, *Speech Communication; Fundamentals and Practice,* 7/ed., © 1986, p. 96. Reprinted by permission of Prentice-Hall, Inc., Englewood Cliffs, New Jersey.)

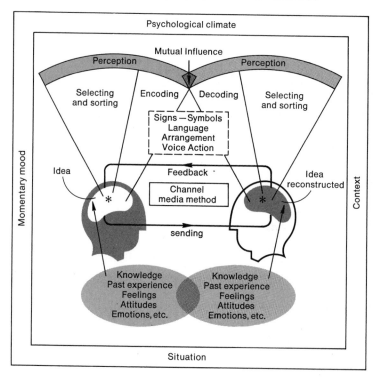

[1]Raymond Ross, *Speech Communication: Fundamentals and Practice* (Englewood Cliffs, N. J.: Prentice-Hall, 1986).

In the Ross model, the sender formulates an idea that is then encoded so that it can be transmitted via some channel, media, or method to a listener or receiver. Even this stage involves many choices. For example, suppose the sender wishes to communicate "stop." A school crossing guard may step into the intersection and hold up a red, octagonal sign with the word STOP printed on it. A parking attendant at the football stadium may hold out an arm with the palm of the hand facing the driver of the car. A lifeguard at a swimming pool may blow a whistle. Your friend may exclaim "Stop!" just as you are about to step into the street.

Although it's possible to use any of the five senses as channels for information, for our purposes in communicating via electronic media, we're most concerned with sight and sound. So in our example we've included only ways that "stop" might be communicated using verbal and nonverbal codes intended to be seen or heard. The school guard's sign has both verbal and nonverbal components: the printed word *stop* and the color and shape of the sign that we associate with the idea "stop." The parking attendant's arm gesture is a visible nonverbal signal. The lifeguard's whistle is an audible nonverbal signal. Your friend's "Stop!" is an audible verbal signal.

The receiver takes in the sensory information—in our example, the audible and visible, the verbal and nonverbal signs. Through a process of interpretation, the receiver decodes the information and reconstructs a version of the original idea. The receiver then reacts, or provides feedback on the basis of the reconstructed idea.

Important in the Ross model is the effect of the total environment, including the situation, context, mood, and psychological climate. The encoding and decoding of the message is affected by each person's knowledge, past experiences, feelings, attitudes, and emotions. In addition, the accuracy with which the listener reconstructs the original idea depends upon the degree to which sender and receiver share the same meanings for the signs and symbols, language, arrangement, voice, and action.

Thus, in encoding the idea "stop," the choice of words, gestures, objects, and tone of voice are influenced by the specific situation and the sender's understanding of the meanings that the receiver is most likely to attach to them in that situation. The closer the match between the sender and the receiver's knowledge, past experiences, and attitudes, the closer the reconstructed idea will be to the original idea.

In the Ross model, sender and receiver are depicted as sharing the situation. They are together in the same place at the same time. Thus, a wider range of cues is available to the receiver, and immediate feedback allows the sender to modify or clarify the message by providing additional information. This interaction allows sender and receiver to continue the process until they are satisfied with the meaning they share for the message.

When messages are transmitted by electronic media, the sender and receiver do not share the same situation. They are separated geographically and often by time as well. For example, the messages created by the producers,

writers, and on-air reporters for National Public Radio's "Morning Edition" origi-
nate from studios in Washington, D.C. As you listen to the program, you may be
in your car driving to campus or at home just waking up. The sender cannot use
shared-situation cues to help limit the possible meanings you may attach to the
words and sounds in the message. Nor can the sender use specific knowledge
about how you as an individual may decode particular words and sounds. In all
probability, the sender does not know you personally or that you are listening at
any given moment. The geographic and time separation make feedback difficult.
For you to share your reaction or ask a question for clarification, you would need
to go to the studios, make a telephone call, or write a letter. Even if you tried to
give immediate feedback by making the telephone call, you might find that the
reporter was not available because the report had been taped earlier.

In constructing audio and video messages, then, the sender needs to make
use of more widely shared meanings. Although each of us has had unique experiences that have helped shape our individual attitudes, values, and so on, we
nevertheless share many experiences. Living in the same country means that we
have a common cultural background.

PERCEPTION

As the Ross model illustrates, *perception* can be defined as the process by which
we take in stimuli through our sensory organs, organize that sensory information
into a pattern, and decode, or attach meaning to, that pattern. Thus, when we
talk about how audio communicates, we are concerned not only with the physical
properties of sound, but also with how people hear and interpret sounds.

Experiments designed to increase our understanding of perception have
revealed several important characteristics.[2] For example, sensory stimuli can be
ambiguous in that different perceptions of the same stimulus are possible, but
one perception usually is strongly preferred.

In addition, we tend to perceive objects as having constant properties despite differences in the stimuli reaching us. For example, when we hear the whistle of a locomotive, we form an image of the locomotive's size. The size of the
locomotive we imagine doesn't change with a change in the intensity of the
sound. It remains the same whether the whistle is loud or soft.

Context and organization are also important in understanding perception.
Our decision about whether a guitar player is only tuning her guitar or is actually
playing a melody may well depend on clues provided by the context—that is,
what has occurred just before the strumming began and what is occurring as the
sounds continue. In addition, our identification of a melody depends upon the
organization or sequencing of the individual notes.

In addition, there is evidence that we may go beyond the actual stimuli and

---

[2]For a detailed discussion of these characteristics, see Irvin Rock, *The Logic of Perception* (Cambridge, Mass.: MIT Press, 1983).

enrich or complete a perception. Perhaps you've experienced a conversation with a soft-spoken friend in which you filled in the words that you couldn't quite hear, only to discover that what you were sure he said was not what he said at all. Memory of past experiences may be influencing your perception.

Keeping these characteristics of perception in mind will help you use audio more effectively to communicate with the listener. For the receiver, perception of the audible or visible stimuli would be the first step. The receiver then decides whether this sensory information is intended as a message. If so, the decoding process will continue as the receiver attempts to reconstruct the ideas carried by that message (Fig. 1-2).

PERCEPTION OF AUDIO

Let's apply this model to examine what happens as we listen to the sounds in our environment. The first stage involves the perceptual processing we discussed earlier. Our perception of the sounds includes making judgments about the source of the sound—what it is, where it is located, how far or near it is, and so on. These judgments are influenced by our past experiences and all the associations that are evoked. They are also influenced by the present context and the expectations we have because of the situation in which we find ourselves.

A telephone's ring is a familiar sound, and you probably have no difficulty distinguishing between the ringing of your telephone and the one in the soap opera on the television set in the same room. Because you have heard it many times, you have become familiar with the sound of your telephone's ring. The pitch, timbre, duration, loudness, and quality differ from the sound being produced by the speaker in your television set. Yet the sound from the speaker is

FIGURE 1-2 The receiver's understanding of a message is affected by many variables.

similiar enough to other telephone rings you have heard in the past that you have no difficulty perceiving it as a telephone's ring. In addition, you probably relied on location cues. Remembering that the telephone was on one table and the television set was on the opposite side of the room, you would quickly assign the sound to the correct source.

The meaning you might attach to those two telephone rings would be very different. Depending upon your expectations at the moment, you might react to the ringing of your telephone by saying, "I wonder who that is," "That must be Jane," or "Those kids are probably playing pranks again," based on your predictions about the caller's identity. The ringing of the telephone in the soap opera produces a different set of interpretations. Because of your past experience with television drama and your understanding of the conventions for narrative structure, you would assume that the writer included that telephone ring as a message to you. The telephone ring was there for a specific purpose, and you would attempt to determine the intended meaning.

Because we are concerned with using sound to communicate either in audio only or as part of a video message, we must remember how the listener will respond to sounds we use. Listeners attach meanings to sounds depending on their past experiences with that sound or with similar sounds, as well as with the context created for that particular sound. Sounds evoke many associations. Some of these will be very individual. Baseball fans know that when they hear "The Star-Spangled Banner," the game is ready to begin. An individual fan may also recall the controversy created by a particular singer's last performance of the song.

Expectations created by the context within which the sound occurs also influence our interpretation of its meaning. Suppose, for example, that the story line of a situation comedy we're watching involves a glass vase someone has brought home from a garage sale because he thought it was very valuable. As the character looks around the living room for a safe place to put the vase, the camera frames a close shot of the vase being put on a table. Later, when the family's two teenagers come into the living room throwing a football back and forth and, as the football goes out of view, we hear the sound of glass breaking, we will assume that the football has knocked the vase off the table. The football might have broken a mirror or a window, of course, but our past experiences with narrative structure would lead us to assume that it hit the vase.

The meanings we attach to sounds include decisions about what produced the sound. We will arrive at conclusions about the source, including its size and location and the energy with which the sound was created. If we think that the sound was produced by a person, we will make assumptions about that person's intentions, motivations, emotional state, and personality.

THE PSYCHOLOGY OF AUDIO

Our response to sound has a physiological basis. The physical process involved in hearing sounds as well as the physical characteristics of sound waves (frequency, intensity, wave form, and time) will be discussed in Chapter 2. It's important to note here that our perception of these physical characteristics is the result of the way in which we process the electrochemical signals that reach our brains.[3]

In the process of perception, some characteristics of sound are interdependent. Pitch, for example, is our interpretation of the frequency of the sound wave. But our perception of pitch is also influenced by other factors, including intensity, wave form, and time. Loudness is our perception of the intensity of a sound. That perception may also be affected by frequency and time.

Other characteristics seem to be interpreted independently of others. Our perception of timbre, or the quality of a sound, depends on the wave form. Duration is our impression of the time length of the sound. Localization is our subjective judgment of the location of the sound.

Some of our responses to sound do not have a direct relationship to a measurable physical characteristic of the sound. Our idea of volume, or the space the sound seems to fill, has no physical correlate, but frequency and intensity seem to influence our perceptions of volume. Density, too, has no physical dimension. To us, some sounds seem to be more compact or concentrated, while others seem to be diffuse.

Since our impressions of pitch, loudness, timbre, duration, localization, volume, and density are subjective, individuals do differ in their perceptions of these characteristics. And differences will occur in various listening situations. The important thing to remember is that most of these impressions are used to help us interpret the source of the sound and the action that is occurring.

In fact, much of our response to the sounds we receive is based on factors other than the physiological. Sounds may trigger associations based on past experiences. For most of us, the sound of the bell on an ice cream truck driving through the neighborhood brings back happy memories. But the emotional response to that sound would be quite different for the person who took a part-time summer job driving the ice cream truck, only to be robbed and roughed up the first week on the job. Thus, a sound can bring back a flood of memories or associations that affect our perception or interpretation of what is happening, and these associations differ from person to person.

Our knowledge may also influence our response. To the first-time automobile owner who's had no training in auto mechanics, a change in the sound of the engine when it's idling may pass unnoticed. To the experienced auto mechanic, the sound is a precise indication of the mechanical condition of the engine.

Research indicates that sounds can produce physiological changes and affect emotions.[4] One hospital study used music to produce measurable reductions in heart rate. Another revealed that fast music with a hard beat had an overall weakening effect. One project used specific musical and rhythmic tempos in presenting information to increase learning rates. Music therapy makes use of emo-

---

[3]For a detailed discussion, see Donald A. Hodges, *Handbook of Music Psychology* (Lawrence, Kans: National Association for Music Therapy, 1980).

[4]This research is reported in a four-part *Healthworks* series written by Sheila Ritter in *The Ann Arbor News*, p. D3, March 5, March 12, March 19, and March 26, 1987.

tional responses to music and helps patients select the type of music that for them will encourage physical activity or relaxation.

To understand how listeners interpret various sounds, we need to remember that responses to the same physical stimuli will differ. These responses will be further affected by past experiences, by knowledge, and by the physiological or emotional changes produced by particular sounds (Fig. 1-3).

COMPONENTS OF THE AUDIO MESSAGE

As we have indicated, sound is the result of some action. Something sets an object in motion. The vibrations travel through the air and strike the ear. Assuming that those vibrations are within the frequency range that humans hear, they become a stimulus for the auditory system.

In creating the audio message, then, you must first analyze the action that is taking place and the sounds produced by that action. Suppose you wanted to develop a public service announcement for your local sheriff department's water safety program. You want to create for your radio listener a scene at a swimming pool. Is it a large public pool or a small backyard pool? How many people are present? Who are they—children, teenagers, or adults? What are they doing—sunning, swimming, playing water games, running, talking quietly, laughing? What action do you need to have happen in order to convey your message?

Every audio message has several components. Some of these are sounds that establish location. In our swimming pool scene, these environmental sounds might include the sound of water being pumped into the pool, sounds created

FIGURE 1-3   Our response to a police car's siren is affected by the situation we are in at the moment and by past experiences we associate with that sound.

by birds or other animals, and sounds produced by automobiles, airplanes, machinery, or equipment that might be operating nearby.

Another component would be sounds created by people. These might include voices, music, and sounds created by the activities of the people involved. We might hear people talking, laughing, crying, or making other vocal sounds. We might hear someone playing a guitar. We might hear the splash as someone jumps into the water. We might hear the thump of someone bouncing on the diving board.

A third component would be silence. It can be argued that in our usual environments, absolute silence doesn't exist. So a more precise way to talk about silence as part of an audio message would be to talk about the absence of sounds or the cessation of sound. If, for example, our scene had included the sounds of people talking and laughing and those sounds suddenly stopped, that would signal a drastic change in the action we had been imagining.

An additional component might be music that was not created as part of the action. Theme music might be used to identify a program or a character. Background music might be used to create mood or to suggest that a particular action is about to happen. Music used in this way provides important clues about how we are to interpret the other components of the audio message.

These components of the audio message have several dimensions. Many objects have characteristic sounds that help us to identify them. The airhorn on a semitruck sounds different from the typical automobile horn. Although both are reed instruments, the clarinet and the saxophone have very different sounds even when playing the same melody.

The size of the object producing the sound and the speed at which it is moving also produce auditory differences. Loudness, rhythm, and pitch may change. The sound produced by a small pebble being dropped is different from that made by a large boulder dropped from the same height. The sounds of a horse's hooves on a hard-packed dirt track are different if the horse is walking or if it is running. An electric beater sounds different when it is running at low speed and at high speed.

The location of the source of the sound, particularly in terms of its distance from us, produces other differences. Traffic sounds that are muted become louder and more distinct as we move closer to them. Even though we cannot see the bird hopping around in the trees, we can follow its movement as its song shifts from the ground to our right up into the trees and around in front of us to the left.

Because of our stereotypes of people, we read personality traits, age, and emotional state into voices. The quality of a person's voice may indicate to us whether that person is 6 years old or 60. We may assume that a high-pitched voice goes with a tense, high-strung personality. A low-pitched voice may suggest a strong, easygoing person. Anger, fear, boredom, excitement, and happiness may all be indicated by the tone of the voice as well as by the patterns of speed and rhythm we associate with these emotional states.

Two other important variables are sequence and context. The sequence, or order, in which we hear sounds, affects our impression of what is taking place. Suppose we are working with three distinct sound elements: silence, an automobile engine running, and an automobile's starter turning. We can arrange them in any order. But the order will influence the action we imagine as we listen. Silence–starter turning–engine running creates a very different image than does engine running–silence–starter turning.

The context we create for the sounds included in the message will also influence the listener's interpretation of the action. Setting up the image of a dark and gloomy night will lead us to interpret the sound created by shaking a sheet of galvanized steel as thunder. Or if we imagine we're in a cozy living room on a winter evening, the sound of crumpling cellophane helps create the impression of a blazing fire in the fireplace.

STRUCTURE OF THE AUDIO MESSAGE

The audio message itself is affected by several variables, including the purposes of the sender, the purposes of the listener, and the listening environment.

Purposes of the Sender

In planning the programming of a radio station, management's primary goal is to attract and keep listeners. More listeners mean higher ratings, and higher ratings mean more revenue from advertising. Even noncommercial or public radio stations need to attract an audience in order to get revenue from budget appropriations from university or governmental sources, grants from corporations and foundations, or contributions from individuals. Station personnel who produce news reports, cover sports stories, plan interview shows, write commercial copy, decide on music play lists, or create station promotions all may have specific goals in mind (Fig. 1-4). In an individual audio message, they may want to inform their listeners about what's happening at home and around the world, to persuade them to try a specific product or to listen to a particular program, or to entertain them with music, drama, or comedy shows.

In television programs and in film, audio is one component of the message. Although it is an important component, it serves primarily as support for the visual message. The audio track may supply information that is missing or ambiguous in the visuals. It may reinforce the visual message. Through sound effects and music, it may create an emotional climate for the visual. It may provide clues about how we are to interpret the visuals. Thus, the various elements of the audio track—dialogue, narration, sound effects, ambient sound, music—all help to carry out the purpose of the video or film message. (In music video, the opposite is usually true; the visuals support the audio.)

In corporate and educational settings, the usual purpose of audio messages is to provide information and instruction for employees and students. The major concern is to communicate clearly. At times, the public relations department may be involved in producing materials intended to project a favorable corporate image to the larger community.

FIGURE 1-4 A radio station's advertising reinforces the image created by the station's programming.

Advertising agencies are concerned with influencing consumer behavior. Radio ads or sound tracks for television ads are intended to persuade listeners to buy a particular product or to use a particular service.

All these senders have clearly defined purposes in constructing messages for their listeners. There is, in addition, another segment of the industry that provides audio recordings primarily for entertainment. Music recordings make up the bulk of this category, although books-on-tape are becoming more popular.

Historians, too, are finding audio recordings to be a useful way of preserving the sounds of important events and of collecting oral histories detailing the personal experiences of individuals. With the widespread availability of portable tape recorders, more and more people are making home recordings, ranging from letters-on-tape, from those who hate to write, to lectures-on-tape, for those who don't trust their classroom notetaking.

Purposes of the Receiver

Like the producer of the audio message, the receiver or listener has a purpose for listening to a particular message. One purpose is to get information. We turn on the radio to get news about the bus strike or the weather. We listen to ads to get information about sales or store hours and addresses. We listen to the company's corporate news tapes to get up-to-date information on developments that affect our jobs.

Another purpose for using audio messages is to help us learn. We may use language tapes to help us practice vocabulary and pronunciation. We review lecture information from a class. We may listen to the directions on a do-it-yourself demonstration tape as we try to master a home repair project.

A major purpose for listening is for entertainment. We tune into our favorite radio station to be entertained by music or talk. We play records or tapes to laugh at the comedy routines or to enjoy the music.

Listening to audio messages also fulfills other needs. Many of us use the radio or records or tapes as companions—as background sounds that make us feel less alone or less isolated. We listen to news and talk shows to help satisfy our need to think of ourselves as well-informed. Even a deejay's chatter may provide us with bits of information on sports, weather, entertainment events and entertainers, and fads and trends that help us feel in touch with our world. We may seek out programs that reinforce our deeply held beliefs, values, and attitudes. By listening to programs, we may vicariously live out experiences or explore taboo subjects in guilt-free ways. For each individual, listening to various kinds of audio messages provides a wide range of psychological gratifications. While the producers of any given audio message may understand that principle, they have no control over the actual use any given individual may make of a specific message.

Listening Environment

Because the kinds of audio messages we're concerned with are intended for mass distribution, the sender has little or no control over the situation in which the listener receives the message. Radios go with us virtually everywhere. We listen while we're reading or jogging, driving or working, waking up or shopping. The sound tracks of television programs and films-on-tape also compete for attention with normal household activities and interruptions. Even when we are in an environment designed to help us concentrate on the message, such as a conference room during a corporate training workshop or a movie theatre, our attention can easily drift to concerns about our personal problems and plans, to an awareness of what those around us are doing, or to whispered conversations among those sitting near us. In fact, we have become so accustomed to using radio and recorded music as background sound that we may have to work harder to keep our attention focused on it when we truly want to hear the message or the music.

TECHNOLOGY

Since the kinds of audio messages we're talking about are electronic messages, the technology used produces an additional set of variables. In order to send audio information over long distances, as radio does, or to store it for use at some future time, as tape recordings do, the original acoustic signals must be transduced, or changed into other forms of energy. In every step of the process, however, some of the original complexities of the acoustic energy are lost. Although the technology of the system is improving rapidly, it is limited in its ability to reproduce sounds accurately.

For example, microphones are limited in the range of frequencies to which they respond. Any given microphone responds well to some frequencies and less well to others. Thus the full range of frequencies in the original sound is not entered into the system. Speakers, too, are limited in the range of frequencies they can handle.

The system is also limited in its ability to reproduce accurately the full range of intensity or loudness that we hear. Very soft sounds may not be picked up; very loud sounds may introduce distortion. In addition, location cues normally available to us are lost. Rather than arriving from anywhere in the 360-degree spectrum surrounding us, electronic messages are confined to the location of the speaker. Although stereo and quadraphonic systems have attempted to expand the impression of space, they cannot duplicate the location cues of an actual space.

Moreover, the electronic audio system cannot separate sounds as our own aural processing system can. In a noisy room, we can isolate one voice or sound that's important to us and concentrate on that while screening out unwanted sounds. We can instantaneously shift our attention to another sound. Relative volume and location of the sounds remain the same. Our perceptual processing makes the change. Even the most sophisticated audio system is not as efficient in isolating individual sounds.

The electronic system also adds its own noise to the final message. Because of the way electronic equipment works, electrical signals unrelated to the original audio information may be added onto the message. New developments, such as improved audio tapes, compact discs using laser technology, and noise-reduction systems, attempt to minimize the extraneous sounds that reduce the accuracy of the sound reproduction (Fig. 1-5).

FIGURE 1-5 Over the past 100 years, recording technology has evolved from wax cylinders used to record sound to compact discs and video discs which record both sound and image.

In processing the electrical signal, the original sound may be altered. The relative volume levels of frequencies can be changed by lowering or increasing selected frequencies so that the overall timbre we hear differs from the original. A sound may be repeated at a delayed time interval so that we hear added reverberation, or echo. Synthesizers can create original, artificial sounds.

PRODUCTION SITUATION

Production circumstances create other variables. As we've discussed, most electronic messages are created as part of a profit-oriented system. They are the products of commercial enterprises. Thus, considerations about ratings or sales or cost-effectiveness influence many decisions. And because these decisions are made within complex organizations, most are group or multilevel decisions rather than the decision of one person. In addition, these organizations exist within the larger society, so legal and regulatory constraints apply. Decisions about the content of messages are influenced by laws, court rulings, and regulations related to such matters as obscenity, libel, national security, and false and misleading advertisements. Social standards of good taste and offensive language also affect decisions about content.

Most audio messages are also produced under circumstances in which time and money are crucial factors. Although some production situations are more leisurely than others, time deadlines for the completion of projects enter into practical decisions about the actual content and the production techniques to be used. Money, too, is a consideration in decisions about hiring talent and buying or renting equipment and production facilities.

Ultimately, the creativity and skill of the production personnel affect the final audio message. As we've noted, audio messages are created with a specific purpose in mind. They are heard by receivers who are listening for a number of reasons in circumstances that may or may not encourage concentration on the message. While the technology does not permit exact duplication of natural sound, it does permit manipulation of sounds and even creation of sounds. Rather than attempt to simply reproduce reality, the person who understands the capabilities of the technology attempts to create an aural environment that will suggest to the listener a "reality" that carries the intended meanings. Moreover, the creative person attempts to communicate clearly in an aesthetically pleasing way.

AESTHETIC CONSIDERATIONS

Before beginning a consideration of aesthetic principles that influence audio production, we need to point out two problems. One is the difficulty of defining what we mean by aesthetic principles. Generally, *aesthetics* refers to those characteristics that make a painting or a novel or a movie or a radio drama beautiful in the sense that we find pleasure and satisfaction in simply looking at it or reading it or watching it or listening to it even if the content is troubling or unpleasant. The second problem is the difficulty in agreeing on what is beautiful or satisfying. Because we all experience these things differently, it may be possible to talk about general principles but impossible to reach agreement on absolute rules or guidelines.

Thus, in talking about what makes one audio production more aesthetically satisfying than another, we can try to identify general principles that seem to be operating in those that are successful and missing in those that are not. Many of these principles were suggested in earlier sections of this chapter.

In creating audio messages, for example, we are attempting to evoke mental images for our listener. Each sound is carefully chosen to help construct those images. We don't duplicate every detail of an actual scene: We select only those elements that are most suggestive of the scene. Then we choose sounds that will represent those elements and carry the specific connotations we intend.

We use the capabilities of the technology to create those mental images and to direct the listener's attention to specific sounds. For example, we can suggest distance by altering the placement of the microphone, or suggest the size of the space by changing the acoustics of the recording studio. We can vary the relative importance of sounds by manipulating their volume levels. With stereo, we can suggest placement and movement from left to right by assigning sounds to left and right channels. In the following chapters, we'll discuss in more detail how audio equipment is used to achieve specific effects.

Technology also imposes limitations, however. Although improvements continue to be made, the equipment used to change sound into electrical signals, process the signals, and change them back into sound cannot reproduce all the qualities of the original sound. Much is lost, and noise is introduced from the system itself. Extremes in volume are deliberately modified to prevent distortion. Subtle changes in pitch and volume may disappear. Indeed, pitch may be altered by the characteristics of the microphone or playback system.

The elements chosen are arranged in predictable patterns. In radio, stations as well as individual programs have a characteristic sound created by theme music or station jingles, standardized verbal introductions to programs and participants, and sequence of program elements, as well as the vocal style of the on-air personalities. The structure of individual programs is influenced by the format of the station, by the genre, or type, of program, and by the time constraints imposed by the program schedule. Because listeners are accustomed to the patterns created by radio programming, other types of audio messages make use of them also.

Both verbal and vocal delivery styles in radio or in audio production are personal and conversational. Language tends to be simple and easily understood. Words are chosen for their meaning and for their sound. Sentence structure is uncomplicated. Messages are often organized as narratives, with speakers acting as storytellers speaking directly to the listener. The performers' manner of speaking is different from that of the stage actor or public speaker. The rhythm of the voice, the manner of emphasis and inflection, the range of pitch and volume are all carefully controlled to support the impression that the deejay or newscaster is speaking directly to us.

SUMMARY

In this chapter, we've described how audio communicates. If we think about communication as a process of sharing meanings, then we can identify the elements that go into the making of effective audio messages. The process begins when the sender or producer identifies the purpose of the message. Is it to entertain the listener, to provide information or instruction, to change attitudes, or to influence behavior? What ideas will be effective in accomplishing that purpose? What sound elements, alone or combined with visuals, will represent those ideas?

To increase the probability that the receiver or listener will reconstruct the sender's original idea correctly, it's important to keep in mind the process of perception by which we organize sensory information into patterns and attach meanings to the patterns. The actual physical process of hearing, of course, provides sensory information about the frequency of the sound wave, its intensity and wave form, as well as its time and location. Our interpretation of that sensory information is influenced by our past experiences, by associations evoked by particular sounds, by our knowledge and attitudes, and by our emotional or physiological responses. Our re-creation of the message is also affected by the situation in which we find ourselves, by the context that is established for the message, and by the expectations we have in a given listening situation.

The components of the audio message may include environmental sound, sounds created by people, silence, and music. These have several dimensions. Objects may produce characteristic sounds. An object's size, speed, and location will produce differences in its sound. We may judge age, emotional state, or personality from the quality of a person's voice. The sequence of sounds and the context created for them affect our interpretation of what is taking place.

The structure of the audio message depends on many variables. One is the purpose of those creating it; another is whether the audio message is to stand alone or to accompany visuals. The listener's purpose is also a consideration, as are the needs listening may satisfy for any individual. Since electronic messages are intended for mass distribution, with little control over the final listening situation, they usually compete for attention with a multitude of potential distractions.

The technology of the system is limited in its ability to reproduce the full complexities of natural sounds. In addition, it introduces extraneous noise. However, it also makes possible a variety of ways to manipulate sound and to create artificial sounds. Thus, electronic audio messages attempt to suggest, rather than rigidly duplicate, the actual sounds produced by the actions of people and objects around us.

Production circumstances are also important in shaping the audio message. Concerns about profitability, legal and social considerations, time constraints, and budgets become factors in decisions about any audio production. And, of course, the creativity and skill of the production personnel are crucial in determining the final effectiveness with which the sender can communicate the desired message in an aesthetically pleasing way.

While aesthetic judgments are subjective, it is possible to identify general principles that are common to successful audio messages. Sound elements are carefully selected to evoke specific mental images. Technology is used to manipulate the sounds to help create those images and direct listener attention. Sounds are arranged in predictable patterns. Verbal and vocal delivery styles are personal and conversational.

FOR FURTHER READING

DeFleur, Melvin L. and Sandra Ball-Rokeach. *Theories of Mass Communication,* 4th ed. (New York: Longman, 1982).

Schwartz, Tony. *The Responsive Chord* (New York: Anchor Press, 1973).

chapter two _____

The Physics of Sound _____

INTRODUCTION

In Chapter 1, we considered the ways in which listeners attach meaning to sounds and the ways in which sounds used in audio productions differ from those in the real world. The production of audio messages for broadcast or recording involves a special selection and arrangement of sounds. That process requires an understanding of how sounds are produced, how they are influenced by the surrounding space, how they are perceived, and how audio equipment reproduces them.

DEFINITIONS OF SOUND

There are two general definitions of sound. The first describes it as a physical phenomenon in which pulses of energy are transmitted through a medium (gas, liquid, or solid) by the movement of molecules within that medium. The second describes it as the perception of that physical phenomenon by humans or animals. The answer to the question "If a tree fell in the forest and there were no one to hear it, would there be a sound?" is both "yes" and "no." There would be sound in a physical sense, but no perception and recognition of it.

Sound as a Physical Event

Molecules within a medium are not tightly packed together. They are free to move about, and they usually do so in random fashion, bumping into one another on occasion. They are similar to individuals in a huge crowd who jostle one another this way and that but maintain their relative positions.

Just as a person in the crowd pushes against a neighbor, so an object moving within this environment pushes on the molecules nearest it. These in turn jostle their neighbors and pass on the energy of the original movement. Let us say that the clapper of a doorbell strikes a metal resonator. The resonator vibrates against the air molecules around it, and they pass the movement on in a series of pressure waves radiating out in all directions (Fig. 2-1). This action would exist even though there might not be anyone to hear it. These pressure waves travel through the air and through liquids and solids.

Sound as Perception

The clapper strikes the bell, and the energy radiating out from the resonator finally reaches your ears. You recognize the sound and interpret this to mean that someone is at the front door. The physical phenomenon has been recognized by means of a particular kind of sound.

This is a complex process, and it begins with the mechanisms of the human ear. This organ consists of three main parts: the outer ear, the middle ear, and the inner ear (Fig. 2-2). As the sound vibrations reach us, the outer ear channels the acoustical signal through the external ear canal to the eardrum, or tympanic membrane, which is stretched across the end of the canal. The shape and folds of the outer ear, along with the ear canal, serve to amplify sounds and help us to detect their location. The changes in air pressure produced by the sound vibrations cause the eardrum to move.

The movement of the eardrum sets the tiny bones of the middle ear in motion. These bones (the hammer, anvil, and stirrup) transfer the movement of the eardrum to the oval window of the inner ear. These bones act as a lever,

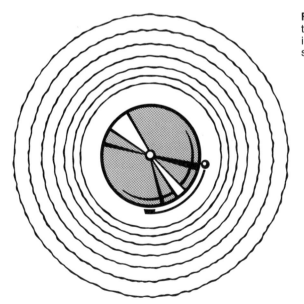

FIGURE 2-1 A clapper strikes the resonator of a doorbell, sending out concentric waves of sound in all directions.

FIGURE 2-2 The outer, middle, and inner ear.

converting a slight movement at the eardrum to a greater movement at the oval window. This action serves to amplify faint sounds.

Unlike the middle ear, which is filled with air, the inner ear is filled with fluid. When the stirrup presses against the oval window, it creates waves in the fluid that travel through the cochlea, a spiral-shaped structure, to the round window, where the pressure is transferred back to the air of the middle ear.

In the cochlea is the organ of Corti. It is a membrane containing sensitive hairs attached to nerves. When the hairs sense changes in the fluid, they excite the nerves to which they are connected. The nerves generate electrochemical signals, which are sent along the auditory nerve to the brain. The slightly different signals from each ear help us to sense the sound's location. Differences in phase, pitch, and loudness at the two ears help the brain to determine the direction of the sound.

As you can see, the physical process involved in hearing is quite complicated and remarkable. Humans are able to hear sounds over a wide range of frequencies and intensities, to determine their location, and to recognize them with great speed and accuracy. Individual differences, damage to the physical structures of the ear or to the auditory nerves, and changes due to aging can affect how accurately the auditory stimuli that reach our ears are relayed to the brain.

THE CHARACTERISTICS OF SOUND

The transmission of sound energy is a three-dimensional phenomenon, but it is customary to reduce it to a two-dimensional model, called a *wave form*. In this model, the pressure waves in the transmitting medium are represented as vertical disturbances like ripples on the surface of a pond. The wave's height represents the sound's strength, or amplitude. We hear this as loudness. The number of waves per unit of time (customarily 1 second) represents the frequency of the sound. We hear this as pitch.

The wave-form model shows that sound is periodic. For every wave crest, there is a trough of equal size. The molecules of the air (or other transmitting medium) briefly return to a position of rest before passing along the next pressure wave (Fig. 2-3).

You will note that the wave form in Figure 2-3 is very simple. It is clean, smooth, and quite symmetrical. Such a configuration is called a *sine wave*. It is produced by the sounds of tuning forks and electronic signal generators. Natural sounds create much more complex wave-form patterns than these. They differ from pure sine waves by the presence of overtones and varying degrees of attack and decay.

Overtones

A tuning fork labeled *A 440* produces a pure tone with a frequency of 440 Hz. (*Hz* is the abbreviation for *hertz*, which is the same as cycles, or oscillations, per second.) This is its *fundamental pitch*. The A above middle C on the piano also produces a tone of 440 Hz, but it also generates sounds at several other frequencies. This happens because the string vibrates along its entire length and at shorter intervals as well. The longest vibration produces the *fundamental*, and the shorter ones generate *overtones*, or upper harmonics. These sound at frequencies that are mathematical multiples of the fundamental. The octave above A 440 would have a frequency twice as great as the fundamental; it would sound at 880 Hz. Two octaves above the fundamental would sound at 1,320 Hz., or three times the frequency of the fundamental. Pitches between the octaves, such as thirds, fifths, sevenths, and so on, sound at fractional multiples of the fundamental. The fifth above A 440 (this would be D above the A) sounds at a frequency 1.5 times that of the fundamenal, or 660 Hz. (Fig. 2.4).

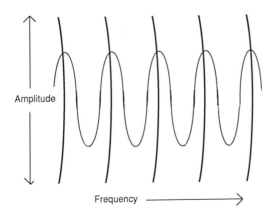

FIGURE 2-3 Concentric pressure waves of sound matched to a linear representation (a wave form model). Every crest in the wave form model corresponds to an actual sound wave. Every trough corresponds to the moment of rest between the sound waves.

FIGURE 2-4 This shows a string vibrating at full length, which produces the fundamental; at half length, which sounds an octave higher; and at quarter length, which sounds another octave higher.

Overtones are usually softer than the fundamental, but they add an important quality to the sound. Every natural sound source has its own unique pattern of overtones. These overtone patterns enable us to distinguish between two different musical instruments that are playing the same fundamental. A flute has relatively few overtones and sounds very pure. An oboe has more overtones and sounds rather piercing.

Since overtones occur at higher frequencies, they cannot all be heard with poor-quality recording and reproducing equipment. An inexpensive radio can reproduce fundamental tones, and so we can distinguish the melodies of a Beethoven symphony easily enough. Only well-made high-fidelity equipment can reproduce the vast range of overtones generated by a symphony orchestra, however. These overtones provide the clarity and richness that we associate with high-quality sound reproduction. When age or ear damage causes a deterioration of high-frequency hearing, persons lose their ability to distinguish among different types of sounds because they can no longer hear the unique patterns of overtones.

Audio engineers are aware of this need to record overtones when they select equipment for recording sessions. Equipment with a wide frequency range is necessary for recording a symphony orchestra so that the important overtones can be captured. Recording a lecture would not require such high-quality equipment because the human voice has a much more limited range of frequencies. Engineers try to select the equipment that is adequate to do the job.

Attack and Decay

Sounds differ from one another not only by the overtones they produce but also in terms of attack and decay. *Attack* describes the rate at which a sound reaches its full intensity. *Decay* refers to the rate at which a sound dies away. Some sounds, such as drums, pianos, and trumpets, have a very fast attack. You can sense the percussive impact at the beginning of the sound. Other sounds, such as violins, flutes, and harps, have a slower attack. Generally, when a sound source is struck or blown sharply, it produces a sound with a fast attack. Objects that are plucked, bowed, or gently blown have a slower attack.

Some sound sources vibrate for a long time after they are originally set in motion, while others stop vibrating rather quickly. Long elastic materials, like piano strings, produce a sound with a slow decay. Short, brittle objects, like the wooden bars of a xylophone, have a quick decay. To accurately reproduce attack, audio equipment must have a very quick response. Some inexpensive audio speakers do not move quickly enough to reproduce a fast attack, so the sound becomes muddy.

Phasing

The waves from two or more sound sources can reinforce or cancel each other by being in or out of phase with each other. Figure 2-5 shows two sine waves. They have slightly different frequencies. Where the wave crests coincide, they reinforce each other. At other points, they can partially or completely cancel each other out. This drifting in and out of phase is heard as a series of throbbing beats. Phase differences are used to tune pianos because the string will "beat" against the true pitch of the tuning fork until it is brought in tune.

Phasing can also cause dead spots in a room because waves reflected from a wall can arrive at a spot out of phase with those from the source. An audio engineer needs to avoid placing a microphone in such a dead spot. (See discussion of standing waves.)

When two microphones are being used for recording stereo (that is, two audio channel) information, it is possible to place the microphones so that the signal is in phase at one microphone and out of phase at the other. If this happens, the microphones will work against each other to produce a very weak composite signal. Care must be taken in the positioning of the microphones to avoid this problem.

THE MEASUREMENT OF SOUND

Over the years, standard measurements have been adopted for quantifying the various characteristics of sound. *Frequency* is measured by counting the number of periodic waves within a given unit of time, such as 1 second. A tuning fork that vibrates at a rate of 440 times per second generates a sound wave with a frequency of 440 cycles per second. The term *cycle* has been replaced by the unit

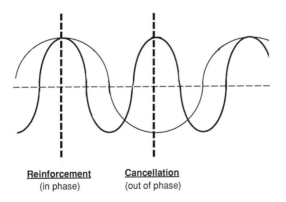

FIGURE 2-5 Two wave forms of different frequencies alternately reinforce and cancel each other.

<u>Reinforcement</u>
(in phase)

<u>Cancellation</u>
(out of phase)

hertz (Hz) in honor of Heinrich Hertz, a nineteenth-century scientist who experimented with electromagnetic energy. One cycle per second is the same as 1 Hz. A sound of 440 cycles per second has a frequency of 440 Hz. For the sake of convenience, we can add the prefix *kilo* (k), which means thousand, and the prefix *mega*, which means million. Thus, 15,000 Hz is 15 kilohertz, and 15,000,000 Hz is 15 megahertz.

Frequency Response of Receiver

Frequency response is the term used to describe the sensitivity of human ears, animal ears, and audio equipment to different frequencies. Humans are capable of hearing sounds with frequencies of between approximately 20 Hz and 20,000 Hz (20 kHz), although most of us don't hear above 12 kHz. As we get older, our ability to hear high frequencies drops off dramatically, to around 8 to 10 kHz. Fortunately, human speech and the fundamental tones of musical instruments are at much lower frequencies, so our ability to hear them is not markedly affected by high-frequency hearing loss. We do lose our ability to hear overtones, however, and thus have more difficulty distinguishing one type of sound from another.

High-quality audio equipment strives to reproduce the entire range of frequencies that the human ear can hear. A response of 20 to 20,000 Hz is standard for most high-quality amplifiers and speakers. Inexpensive equipment has a much more limited frequency response, and that is one of the reasons it doesn't sound full and bright.

Frequency Range of Source

Frequency range is the term used to describe the range of frequencies produced by different sound sources. This is particularly valuable information to have when recording music. The pipe organ has the widest frequency range of any acoustical instrument. It can produce frequencies below 100 Hz and as high as about 8,000 Hz. In contrast, a clarinet can produce sounds only between 75 Hz and 1,800 Hz. A microphone with sufficient frequency response for a clarinet might not be able to record the entire range of the pipe organ.

Measures of Loudness

Human ears are very sensitive to the loudness, or intensity, of sound, and some very loud sounds can actually damage the ear. Loudness can be measured in two ways. One measure indicates the actual strength of the sound. The other indicates our perception of that strength. Objective measurements of sound can be calculated in terms of *watts* of sound power, but this does not give a clear indication of how loud the sound seems to us. For example, a sound with a slight power of .000001 watt could be very loud. An increase to .001 watt would produce a sound of intolerable loudness. Yet, because the numbers are small, we might not think that the sounds would be very loud.

A more useful measurement of sound is its relative loudness—that is, how loud it seems to the hearer. The standard measure of relative loudness is the *decibel* (dB). *Deci* means one-tenth, and *bel* is a tribute to Alexander Graham Bell. A sound at the threshold of hearing would be rated at 0 dB. A sound with ten times the intensity would have a rating of 10 dB. Each tenfold increase in the sound intensity would cause a 10 dB increase.

As the actual intensity of a sound increases by 10 dB, we perceive the sound as being approximately twice as loud. Therefore, the decibel system provides us with a means for expressing perceived increases in loudness. This means that the ear does not hear increases in intensity at the rate at which they actually occur. This is due in part to the fact that small muscles restrict the movement of the middle ear bones when sounds become very loud. This action protects the ear from damage by making it less sensitive.

Standard decibel ratings can be confusing (Fig. 2-6). We might expect a very quiet room to have a 0 dB rating, but actually there is nearly always some ambient noise present. A quiet room might have a rating of 30 dB, and a subway train might be rated at 100 dB. Jet airplanes, artillery, and rockets taking off produce sounds higher than 100 dB. At around 130 dB, the sound becomes quite painful to hear. Very loud sounds, such as music at a rock concert, can produce physiological changes such as an increase in blood pressure, a loss of equilibrium, and even nausea.

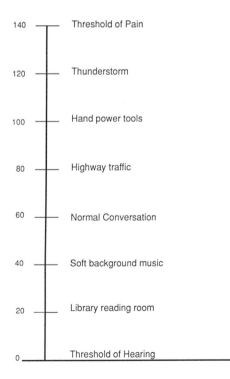

FIGURE 2-6   The decibel scale with sounds at those intensities.

THE SOURCES OF SOUNDS

Sounds are produced by a large number of sources, including moving elements in the environment, human and animal vocalizations, musical instruments, manufactured objects, and electrical generators such as synthesizers and computers. Our world is filled with sound at all times.

Human Speech

The sound with which we are most familiar is human speech, both our own and that of others. The sounds emitted by humans can be shaped in very complex ways to carry a wide variety of specific meanings.

The process of speech begins when air is expelled from the lungs. It passes through the larynx and then through the mouth and nose. Some of the air passes directly from the lungs without being shaped by the larynx, tongue, or lips. This air forms what we call *unvoiced* speech sounds. Other air may be set in motion by the vocal cords to produce *voiced* sounds.

The vocal cords are not cords at all but pieces of muscle tissue attached to the inside of the larynx. As the air passes them, the "cords" vibrate and set the air around them in motion. These vibrations are then shaped by the resonant chambers of the throat, mouth, and nose. This process creates a complex pattern of fundamental pitches and harmonics that is unique for each person. The action of tongue and lips, speed of delivery, intonation, and accent also help to differentiate one voice from another.

Animal Sounds

Humans are not the only animals with vocal cords. Cats, dogs, lions, tigers, and many other animals emit sounds produced in a manner similar to that by which humans vocalize. Other animals emit sounds by different methods; the frequencies of some of these sounds are well beyond the limits of human hearing.

Musical Instruments

Musical instruments are a familiar source of sound. They are traditionally divided into four families: percussions, winds, reeds, and strings. The ways in which the sounds are produced and the materials from which the various instruments are made help to give these families their distinctive characteristics.

Percussions.   Drums, rattles, bells, castanets, tambourines, gongs, and several other struck or scraped instruments make up the percussion family. Some of these instruments produce a definable pitch, while others do not. The sounds of these instruments are the result of the shape, size, resonance, and composition of the materials from which they are made. When struck, these instruments vibrate in unique ways to set up their own particular patterns of sound.

Winds.   Wind instruments produce their sound when air is passed over a sharp edge or by the vibrations from the lips of a player. Wind instruments include flutes, tubas, French horns, trumpets, trombones, and pipe organs. The moving air passes into a tube, where it resonates. The length of the tube determines the instrument's pitch. The shorter the tube, the higher the pitch. The length of the tube can be changed by connecting additional sections by means of valves, as is the case in the trumpet and French horn, or by a slider, as in the trombone. The pipe organ generates different pitches by means of a pipe of a different length for each note of the scale (Fig. 2-7).

Reeds.   The reed instruments, such as the oboe, clarinet, and bassoon, generate sound as air passes over a reed and sets it in motion. The reed can be a single one, as it is in the clarinet, or a double one, as in the oboe. The air then passes into a tube, the length of which determines the instrument's pitch. As is the case with wind instruments, the length of the tube can be varied by valves.

Strings.   The string family of instruments generates sound when the strings are set in motion by striking (piano, hammered dulcimer), plucking (the harp and harpsichord), or scraping (the violin). Pitch, which is determined by the length of the string, can be varied by stopping the string with the fingers, as it is on the violin or guitar, or by having an array of strings of different lengths, as in the harp and piano.

The unique sounds of all these instruments result from different methods of sound production, the shape and construction, and different playing tech-

FIGURE 2-7   The pitch of organ pipes is determined by their length. The shorter the pipe, the higher the pitch.

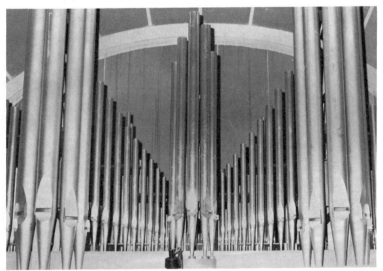

niques. All these factors in combination cause each instrument to produce a different pattern of fundamental and harmonic tones that can be identified by the human listener.

Environmental and Artificial Sounds

Another important source of sound is the environment. Anything that moves, scrapes, strikes, or vibrates will produce a sound. There are natural sounds, such as the wind blowing through the trees and water roaring down a river, and artificial sounds, such as airplanes, typewriters, and automobiles. Our world is so filled with sounds that it is virtually impossible to find a really quiet place. Some people are concerned about the psychological and physiological effects of the high noise levels in our modern environment.

Electronic Sounds

In the past few years, there has been an increasing number of electronic devices that can produce sounds artificially (Fig. 2-8). We have already mentioned the tone generator, but it is now possible to produce much more complex wave forms by artificial means. A synthesizer can mimic the wave form of any musical instrument by reproducing amplitude, frequency, harmonics, attack, and decay. Some synthesizers can give a good approximation of the human voice. The synthesizer can also produce sounds that are totally unlike any found in nature. These electronic devices open up a whole new world of sound to composers, performers, and listeners.

FIGURE 2-8 An electronic musical instrument capable of artificially reproducing natural sounds and many unique sounds not found in nature. (Courtesy of Yamaha Music Corporation, USA)

THE ACOUSTICAL SPACE

The environment in which a sound is produced has a marked effect on its quality. This is because some of the sound produced by a source does not reach our ears directly but is reflected from nearby surfaces. The number, shape, size, place-ment, and sound-absorbing characteristics of these surfaces all affect the nature of the reflected sound. It is the acoustical space that causes a college glee club to sound different in a high school auditorium, a cathedral, and a recording studio.

Sound energy travels out from its source in all directions, and it continues to do so unless it strikes a surface. Some of the sound is then reflected back, and some is absorbed. The angle of this reflection is equal to the angle at which the sound approaches the reflecting surface, so not all of it bounces back directly to its source. The variations in the angle of reflection cause sound to be scattered in many different directions within an acoustical space (Fig. 2-9).

Echo and Reverberation

A listener in a concert hall hears first the sound from its source, then the sounds reflected from nearby surfaces, and finally a series of rapidly repeated reflections as the sound travels around the hall, bouncing from many different surfaces. The early reflections are called *echo*, and if the delay is short, the listener might only *sense* them and does not actually *hear* separate sounds.

Reverberation is the series of quickly spaced echoes that come later (Fig. 2-10). Some reverberation is desirable because it gives richness and character to sounds. The time it takes for the reverberating sound to drop to the level of audibility from the moment the original sound stops is called the *reverberation time.*

Echo and reverberation present challenges for recording engineers in the postproduction editing of recorded materials. They must be careful to edit only after a sound's reverberation has completely died away. It is sometimes necessary to rerecord materials in a location different from the original one. This could require the use of artificial reverberation units to match the reverberation time of the new space to that of the old one.

Original waves ⟶

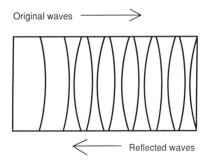

← Reflected waves

FIGURE 2-9 A simplified diagram of sound waves reflected in acoustical space.

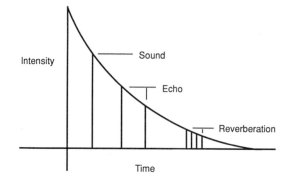

FIGURE 2-10 The relationship in time among the original sound, echo, and reverberation.

The reverberation time for different acoustical spaces varies considerably. In a large auditorium, a sound might take two or three seconds to die away, while in a television studio this time might be less than half a second. If a room is used for a speech or a play, the reverberation time should be relatively short because too much echo and reverberation can blur the spoken word. If a space is to be used for music, on the other hand, there should be more reverberation time so that the musical instruments can blend together and achieve a richer sound.

Some music is written to take advantage of particular kinds of acoustical spaces. Most organ music depends upon the long reverberation time of large churches and concert halls. In these environments, the organ can achieve great sonority. In a small, acoustically "dead" room, it loses much of its fire and color.

Within limits, echo and reverberation are beneficial, but if delay is so great that the listener is conscious of hearing many different sounds, it can become an annoyance. Sound-absorbing materials, such as sheets of cork or carpet, often have to be placed on the walls or hung from the ceiling of an acoustical space to reduce the reverberation time.

Interference and Resonance

Two other characteristics of acoustical spaces are interference and resonance. At some areas in an auditorium or concert hall, reflected sound waves reach the ears slightly out of phase with waves from the source. The phase differences can cause cancellation of some frequencies and exaggeration of others. Some halls have "dead spots" in which voices become hard to understand or in which some groups of instruments cannot be heard clearly. At other spots, the reflected wave reinforces the direct wave, and the overall sound is stronger. If these alternating positions of cancellation and reinforcement do not change, we have "standing waves."

Many objects have a particular frequency at which they begin to vibrate. This is called the *resonance point*. At a particular pitch, a chandelier in an auditorium can begin to vibrate and add unwanted sounds. Singers use this principle to shatter drinking glasses. They sing at the resonant pitch of the glass, which sets it in motion until it breaks. Concert halls and listening rooms also have resonance points, and sounds at these frequencies are reinforced.

Shaping the Acoustical Space

Before the science of acoustics was developed, architects tried to build good acoustical spaces by copying the characteristics of existing ones. Thus one ornately decorated auditorium led to another with similar features. Today, architects apply more scientific methods and use mathematical measurements and actual models to test for echo, reverberation, standing waves, and resonance points.

Sometimes even the best preparation cannot prevent an acoustical disaster. Some modern auditoriums have very poor acoustics even though they were designed according to scientific principles. In some cases it has been necessary to correct these problems by installing sound-absorbing wall materials, reflecting baffles, and amplifying systems. It seems that the smooth walls of some modern concert halls reflect sound *too* well. The ornamentation, drapes, chandeliers, and odd shapes of older concert halls actually helped to create good acoustical spaces (Fig. 2-11).

Many modern halls are designed to be used for several purposes. A concert on one evening might be followed by a play on another. Because different events require different reverberation times, these halls can actually be "tuned" until they are just right. This is accomplished by raising or lowering ceiling or wall

FIGURE 2-11 The ornate decorations and uneven surfaces inside Yale University's Woolsey Hall make a reverberant acoustical space. (Courtesy of Yale University.)

reflectors, altering the area of sound-absorbing materials, and adding baffles. Amplification and artificial reverberation are sometimes employed (Fig. 2-12).

The Ideal Acoustical Space

Good acoustical spaces have several things in common. They are quiet and well isolated from outside noises. They are relatively free from unwanted resonance and "dead spots." All frequencies can be heard clearly from every location, including the stage. (In some halls, performers have difficulty hearing themselves clearly.) The space should generally enhance the quality of sounds and should retain their stereophonic separation. The space should also have some reverberation but not too much.

THE FUNCTION OF AUDIO EQUIPMENT

Millions of people attend "live" concerts every year, but millions more hear music over the radio or a stereo system. Audio equipment gives us access to audio information from around the world and also permits us to store and retrieve it later. Audio equipment is an extension of our ears and our memories. In Chapter 3,

FIGURE 2-12   The movable baffles in Toronto's Roy Thomson Hall make an adjustable acoustical space with changeable reverberation time. (Courtesy of Roy Thomson Hall, Toronto, Ontario; Shin Sugino, photographer)

we will talk about specific items of audio equipment, but we'll consider some of its general functions and limitations here.

Audio equipment has several basic functions, including detection, amplification, mixing, storage, and reproduction. The process of recording and reproducing sounds begins with the detection of sound impulses by microphones. Microphones convert the sounds into electrical energy, which is boosted by amplifiers. Several different signals can be mixed together, and the composite signal is then stored either on magnetic tape or disc. The stored information is extracted from the tape or disc and is amplified again. This signal is used to drive loudspeakers, which convert the electrical energy into audible sounds. In addition to microphones and speakers, this process requires amplifiers, mixers, reverberation units, signal enhancers, noise-reduction systems, tape recorders, cutting lathes, styluses, cartridges, turntables, and a host of other equipment.

LIMITATIONS OF AUDIO EQUIPMENT

Ideally, audio equipment would reproduce a sound that is indistinguishable from the original signal, but this is not yet possible. Every element in the chain of events, from detection to reproduction, adds a slight coloration to the signal, so that what we finally hear is slightly different from the original signal. The coloration exists as noise and distortion. *Noise* is information that is added by the system. *Distortion* is an alteration of the original signal. Since you will be using audio equipment in production, you should be familiar with the ways in which it changes an audio signal.

Transducers

Transducers are devices that convert energy from one form into another. A recording and reproducing system employs several different transducing elements. Microphones convert sound into electricity, and speakers convert electricity into sound. In between, tape recorders convert electricity into electromagnetic fields, which create patterns on the oxide coatings of audio tape, and cutting lathes convert electricity into physical movement as they cut grooves onto the surface of vinyl discs. Tape players, styluses, cartridges, and turntables convert magnetic fields and grooves back into electrical energy.

Microphones. Most professional microphones are able to detect the entire frequency and amplitude ranges of an original sound and generate an electrical signal that contains all of that information. Unlike the ear, however, microphones do not have the ability to discriminate between important and unimportant sounds. Humans are able to block out background noises and focus on a conversation in a crowded room. They can concentrate on a favorite instrument during a concert. Microphones, on the other hand, hear everything equally well.

Recording engineers are well aware of this limitation and try to overcome it in several ways. Some microphones are designed to be sensitive in just one direction (see discussion in Chapter 3). Engineers also use wind screens and shock mounts to isolate microphones from unwanted sounds. They sometimes place a microphone closer to a sound source in an effort to hear it better. Engineers also isolate important sound sources behind screens or soundproof booths and mike each of them separately.

Speakers.   Loudspeakers are also subject to a number of limitations. For one, they do not reproduce all frequencies equally well. To overcome this problem, speaker enclosures usually have two or more speakers of different sizes. A large speaker reproduces low frequencies, and smaller speakers handle higher frequencies. The enclosure contains a crossover network which switches the incoming signal to the appropriate speaker.

Speakers also do not radiate all frequencies equally well. Low frequencies travel out in all directions, while higher ones travel in straight lines. Speakers must be carefully placed in order to minimize this problem. The materials out of which cones are made are subject to varying kinds of limitations. They are expected to respond instantly to an incoming signal and then immediately return to rest when the signal stops. Because this is virtually impossible, some coloration of the sound results. Speaker enclosures are also subject to resonance, and will vibrate at certain frequencies. These too will alter the sound. Engineers have come up with many different speaker designs to correct these problems, but speaker performance remains subject to many imperfections.

Tape recorders.   The process of transferring an electrical signal to tape involves moving a plastic tape past recording heads at a steady speed. The tape is coated with a metal oxide, which is affected by magnetic information from the record head. The tape transport mechanism is subject to slow variations in speed, called *wow,* and rapid fluctuations, called *flutter.* Both can be induced by a number of factors, including variations in voltage, wear on moving parts, and tape imperfections. Wow and flutter can also be present in the playback process, and this can be added to the wow and flutter already present on the recorded tape.

An annoying problem with tape recording is tape hiss. *Hiss* results from an incomplete realignment of oxide particles on the tape during the recording stage; these unaligned particles produce a hiss as they move past the playback head. Engineers try to overcome tape hiss by recording the program signal at a high level, which produces a high signal-to-noise ratio. During playback, the signal is lowered to normal levels, and in the process, the tape hiss is also reduced. Because hiss is most noticeable at high frequencies, these frequencies are often boosted at the recording stage and then "rolled off," or attenuated, during playback. This is the basic principle behind several noise-reduction systems now on the market.

Phonographs.   The moving parts of a cutting lathe or playback turntable can introduce speed variations and a very low-frequency rumble to the signal information. As the playback stylus slides over the grooves on a record, it picks up background noise and reproduces every surface imperfection as a clicking or popping sound. Stylus wear also causes distortion of the signal. A low-level signal can disappear into all this background noise. Loud passages can occasionally overmodulate a record groove and distort the shape of adjacent grooves, causing a worn or poorly adjusted stylus to jump out of the groove.

Engineers attempt to overcome these problems by boosting weak signals and suppressing strong ones. The result is that the dynamic range on the recording is not as great as that of the original signal.

Electronic components. Amplifiers and other electronic components introduce both noise and distortion. Noise can be present in the form of hum, and distortion can occur whenever the incoming signal is altered. Strong signals can sometimes overload an amplifier so that it cannot accurately reproduce them. An amplifier can clip off the tops of incoming waves, producing an unpleasant sound. Some amplifers have a circuit that causes the extremes of the waves to be suppressed or limited, thus reducing distortion.

ANALOG AND DIGITAL TECHNIQUES

Since the phonograph's invention in 1877, it has used the *analog method* of signal storage. This means that the incoming sounds are converted into an electrical or mechanical form that bears a resemblance to the original sound. A diaphragm on Edison's original machine moved up and down in response to the pressure of the sound waves hitting it. A stylus cut a pattern of hills and dales in grooves on the surface of tinfoil wrapped tightly around a cylinder, which was turned by a crank. These vertical undulations in the grooves were a physical representation (or analogy) of the fluctuations in loudness and frequency of the original sound. A few years later, the "hill-and-dale" method was replaced by the side-to-side cutting pattern now in use on phonograph discs. Later, microphones and amplifiers, which converted the incoming sounds into fluctuations in electrical current, were introduced. Once amplified, the electrical signal was used to drive a lathe which cut an analog representation of the signal in the grooves of a record.

A major problem with the analog method is that signal information cannot be separated from the background noise. The surface noise of a record or the hiss of a tape is reproduced along with the music or voice. We have already mentioned that engineers boost a signal to overcome this background noise, and suppress strong signals to prevent overmodulation of grooves.

The audio industry has recently begun to use digital technologies to replace the analog method, and this new approach offers a dramatic improvement in the quality of tape and disc recordings.

In the digital method, a microphone converts sound into an analog electrical signal; this signal is fed into a converter which transforms it into mathematical information. The process uses the binary system, in which any quantity can be represented by a combination of ones and zeros. Instead of being represented by continuous fluctuations in a magnetic field or lateral movements in a record groove, the original sound is thus converted into a stream of numbers. These discrete on-and-off "bits" of information can be recorded on tape or in the grooves of a disc. This mathematical representation bears no physical resemblance to the original sound, and there is no analogy (or analog representation) of it.

To understand how the digital system works, we must return to the waveform model of audio signals. Every point on the wave represents continuously varying information about the original sound. The first step in converting this information into numbers is to sample the wave at an instant in time. This is done by taking a vertical slice through the curve to determine its value at a particular moment. A few samples will give us only a crude approximation of the shape of the original curve. As the number of samples increases, the more closely our representation approaches the shape of the original wave. It turns out that the sampling rate must be approximately twice the highest frequency we wish to reproduce. If we want to have fidelity up to 20,000 Hz, our sampling rate must be at least 40,000 times per second. At this rate, our mathematical model will be indistinguishable from the original wave up to 20,000 Hz (Fig. 2-13).

Quantizing is the next part of the process. It involves establishing a scale and assigning numerical values to each of the sampled points. This is done by converting the wave form into a series of discrete steps, each of which has a precise mathematical value. The more steps we use, the more accurate numerical representation of the wave will be. Currently, the scale from 0 (no signal) to 100 (maximum signal strength) is divided into approximately 4,000 separate steps (Fig. 2-14).

Because the signal information is encoded mathematically, it is unaffected by the medium that carries it, just as the word *bit* has the same meaning whether written on high-quality bond paper or on the side of a grocery sack. The digital

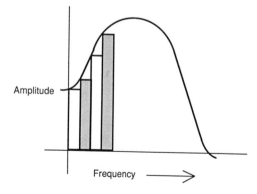

FIGURE 2-13 Digital sampling. Rectangular slices approximate area under the curve. More slices increase accuracy of the approximation.

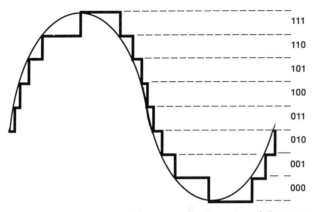

FIGURE 2-14 The quantizing process. Samples of the wave form's height are assigned binary numerical values.

information is read from the tape or disc, and extraneous data, such as surface noise or tape hiss, is ignored.

If the mechanics of digital audio are difficult to understand, its benefits are not. Because there is no surface noise, a digital recording is very quiet. Soft passages can be heard clearly at their correct volumes. There is no need to artificially boost them above background noise. Since there is no physical modulation of the record groove, it can carry a high quantity of signal information without overmodulation. Thus a digital recording can reproduce the entire dynamic range of an original sound without boosting the soft passages and compressing the loud ones.

Another advantage of digital audio is that there is no discernible difference between a master and a copy. There is no deterioration of sound with multiple generations of copying. Finally, digital discs are not subject to appreciable wear. A laser, rather than a stylus, reads the information from the grooves without physically contacting the disc's surface. This means that a digital compact disc can be played an infinite number of times without deterioration of sound quality.

THE PLAYBACK SITUATION

Even the finest digital audio system cannot re-create the sound of an orchestra as it is heard in a concert hall. This is partly because of the various alterations of the signal during recording and playback and partly because the listening situations are very different. The standard playback situation is often compared to that of sitting in a soundproof box constructed in the middle of a concert hall. If you cut two holes in the box, you have an approximation of how the orchestra might sound through a pair of speakers. In the concert hall, the sound comes from many different directions, while at home, it comes from localized speaker sources.

One way to make the typical listening situation more lifelike would be to add more speakers, but each one would have to be fed by a signal separately recorded with its own microphone and amplifier. The more speakers you added, the more lifelike the sound would be. A few years ago, the audio industry introduced four-channel sound, which added two speakers behind the listener. The speakers were fed separately recorded signals and reproduced the sounds that reflect from the back walls of concert halls. Quadraphonic (four-channel) sound did enhance the sense of realism, but not enough to justify the added cost of new amplifiers and more speakers. People seemed content with stereo as it was. Another drawback to quadraphonic sound was that the listener had to remain in a midpoint position in order to hear the full effect of the four speakers.

Binaural recording and playback offer a solution to the limitations of the standard listening situation. In binaural recording, microphones are placed on a dummy head where the ears would be. This approach produces a very lifelike sound, but requires the use of headphones in playback.

APPLICATIONS FOR PRODUCTION

In this chapter, we have touched on some of the ways in which recorded sound is different from "live" sound. Making a good recording is not simply a matter of placing a few microphones and hoping for the best. It involves a consideration of equipment performance characteristics, frequency ranges of sound sources, and the influence of acoustical spaces.

There are two basic approaches to the making of audio recordings. One involves a careful selection and adjustment of equipment prior to the recording and then a minimum amount of adjustment during the actual recording session. During the 1950s, some record companies used this approach with great success. One microphone (two for stereo) would be hung above the conductor's podium, levels would be set for the loudest passages, and then the recording would be made. The result was a natural, balanced, dynamic sound. There is currently a resurgence of interest in this "minimal-miking" approach.

Another approach is to place separate microphones for different sections of the orchestra, and sometimes for individual instruments, boost the gain on soloists, and then adjust audio levels throughout the recording session. Instruments are sometimes isolated from one another in soundproof booths, reverberation added, frequencies adjusted, and separate signals mixed at an audio console. Often, performers do not even record their parts at the same time but add their performances to tapes made during previous sessions. Thus a recording can be built track by track, with every element carefully controlled. Many popular music recordings are made this way, while classical recordings tend to be made with less interference. The approach you take is dictated by the kind of recording you wish to make. Is it to be a close reproduction of the original sound or something quite different?

SUMMARY

Sound is both a physical phenomenon and a perception. A vibrating object generates disturbances in the medium surrounding it. These disturbances, traveling out in all directions through the medium, are perceived as sound. The most common medium of transmission is air, but sounds also travel through liquids and solids. The ear converts these physical disturbances into electrical impulses, which travel along the auditory nerve to the brain.

We use the wave-form analogy to study the characteristics of sound. In this model, the amplitude (loudness) of the sound is rendered as the height of the wave from rest. Frequency (pitch) is shown as the number of wave crests per given unit of time. Amplitude is usually measured in decibels, and frequency is measured in hertz. The wave forms of most sounds are quite complex. They have unique amplitude, frequency, harmonics, attack, and decay characteristics.

Sounds are emitted by humans and other animals, objects in the environment, and musical instruments. Each source produces a unique sound. It is also possible to generate complex wave forms by electronic means. These sounds can either mimic those of the real world or be entirely different. Electronic sound generation has opened up many new possibilities for composers.

The acoustical space in which a sound occurs contributes echo, reverberation, resonance, interference, and standing waves. Some acoustical spaces are "live," with a long reverberation time. Other spaces are relatively "dead," with a short reverberation time. Some acoustical spaces can be tuned to alter the reverberation time for different uses. An ideal acoustical space would provide some reverberation, good sound dispersion to all locations, and an enhancement of the sound's directional characteristics.

Audio equipment is an artificial hearing device. Its job is to capture sound information, translate it into electrical energy, amplify, mix, and store it until a later time. Audio equipment is subject to noise, distortion, and other limitations. Digital recording techniques have overcome many of the limitations of older analog methods.

To make good recordings, it is necessary to understand audio equipment, the nature of the sounds being recorded, and the effect of acoustical spaces. Some recordings are made with little alteration of the original sound, and others are made with considerable balancing, adjusting, and mixing during the recording process.

FOR FURTHER READING

STEVENS, S. S., FRED WARSHOFSKY, and the editors of Time-Life Books. *Sound and Hearing* (Alexandria, Va.: Time-Life Books, 1980).

WORAM, JOHN M. *The Recording Studio Handbook* (Plainview, N. Y.: ELAR, 1982).

chapter three

The Audio System

INTRODUCTION

Now that you have an understanding of the physical properties of sound and an appreciation for the complexities involved in how we attach meanings to the sounds we hear, it's time to consider the equipment used to collect, process, store, and retrieve those sounds. Knowing what equipment is available, what its capabilities are, and how to use it to achieve the effects you want is critical in constructing an audio message that means to the listener what you want it to mean.

Of course, decisions about what equipment to use depend upon the specific production situation. Suppose, for example, that you are assigned to produce an audio feature on the top-scoring players in the women's basketball championship playoff. You decide that you want to include interviews with the players, their coaches, perhaps teammates, friends, and fans. Some of the interviews will be conducted in the stands during the tournament, some in offices or locker rooms, and some in the studio. You also want to mix in background sounds from the game and other locations. Or, suppose that a friend who's a music major has asked you to record his senior piano recital. Which equipment—microphones, mounts, tape, recorders, and so on—would be the best choice? Would the same equipment give you equally good results in all these situations? Helping you make appropriate technical choices is what this chapter is about.

Although we are concerned with specific pieces of equipment and how they work, it's also important to remember that these individual pieces of equipment work together as a system. The audio system includes inputs, a means of processing the signals provided by the inputs and of routing them to various outputs, and ways to store and retrieve the signals.

INPUTS: MICROPHONES

The first step in audio production is to collect the sounds and convert them into a form we can manipulate. It is for this reason that the microphone is basic to any audio production. As an input, the microphone acts as a transducer, converting acoustical energy into electrical energy that can be processed and stored. Microphones differ in several important ways, and choosing the best microphone for a specific use involves understanding their performance characteristics.

Classification of Microphones: Generating Elements

All microphones have a vibrating element that responds to the waves of acoustical energy reaching it. One way of classifying microphones is by the type of vibrating element, or diaphragm, they use. The microphones you are most likely to find in audio production today are the dynamic and the condenser microphones.

Dynamic microphones. Dynamic microphones use a conductor moving in a magnetic field to produce the electrical signal. The vibrating element in some dynamic microphones is a diaphragm to which a coil of wire is attached. The coil of wire is suspended in a magnetic field so that when sound waves strike the surface of the diaphragm, the coil of wire vibrates in a magnetic field. This creates an electrical signal that varies in strength with the variations in the movement of the diaphragm. This dynamic moving-coil microphone is commonly referred to as a *dynamic* microphone (Fig. 3-1).

Other dynamic microphones have a thin "ribbon" of metal foil suspended within a magnetic field. The sound waves striking the ribbon create vibrations in the magnetic field, which, in turn, sets up the flow of the electrical current. The dynamic ribbon microphone is usually referred to as a *ribbon* microphone (Fig. 3-2).

Condenser microphones. In condenser microphones, the diaphragm and a stationary plate are arranged to form a capacitor (Fig. 3-3). When the capacitor is charged with a polarizing voltage, a difference in electrical potential is created between the diaphragm and the stationary plate. As the diaphragm moves toward and away from the stationary plate, the capacity changes, causing the electrical signal to change in strength.

The signal produced by the condenser microphone is relatively weak and needs to be amplified before it travels through the microphone cable, so the condenser microphone requires an external power supply (Fig. 3-4). This power can be provided by batteries within the microphone housing or in the cable connector, by an outside power source, or by phantom power (electrical power fed from the audio console to the microphone via the same cable that carries the audio signal).

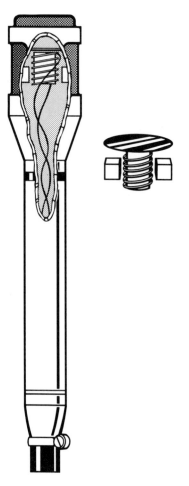

FIGURE 3-1   Dynamic moving coil microphone.

Classification of Microphones: Pickup Pattern

Microphones are also classified by their pickup pattern, or directional characteristics.

Omnidirectional.   The omnidirectional microphone responds with equal sensitivity to sounds coming from all directions (Fig. 3-5).

Bidirectional.   Bidirectional microphones are equally sensitive to sounds coming from directly in front or directly behind (Fig. 3-6). They are least sensitive to sounds coming from the sides.

Unidirectional.   Unidirectional microphones are most sensitive to sounds coming from directly in front. Because the pickup pattern of these microphones

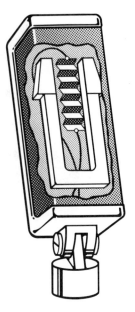

FIGURE 3-2   Dynamic ribbon microphone.

FIGURE 3-3   Condenser microphone with cross section of the capacitor.

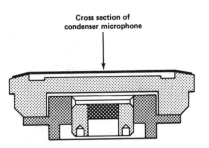

Cross section of
condenser microphone

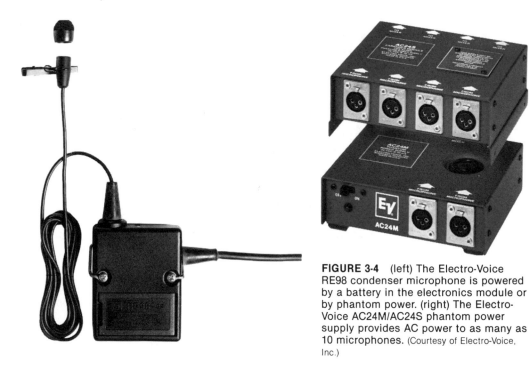

FIGURE 3-4   (left) The Electro-Voice RE98 condenser microphone is powered by a battery in the electronics module or by phantom power. (right) The Electro-Voice AC24M/AC24S phantom power supply provides AC power to as many as 10 microphones. (Courtesy of Electro-Voice, Inc.)

resembles a flattened heart shape, they are often referred to as *cardioid* microphones. As the pickup pattern becomes narrower, they may be referred to as *supercardioid* or *hypercardioid* (Fig. 3-7). The shotgun microphone is ultradirectional, with a very narrow pickup pattern.

Multidirectional.   Some microphones have either a switchable diaphragm or two diaphragms. This feature allows the microphone's pickup pattern to be changed.

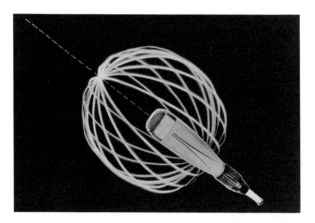

FIGURE 3-5   Omnidirectional pickup pattern. (Courtesy of Sennheiser Electronic Corporation)

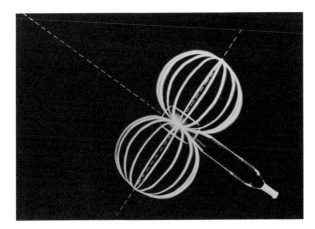

FIGURE 3-6 Bidirectional
pickup pattern. (Courtesy of
Sennheiser Electronic Corporation)

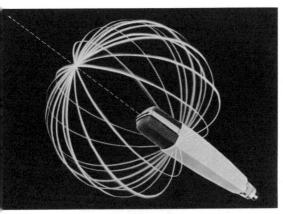

A

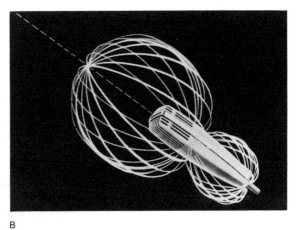

B

C

FIGURE 3-7 (a) Cardioid
pickup pattern. (b) Supercardioid pickup pattern. (c) Ultra-
cardioid pickup pattern. (Courtesy
of Sennheiser Electronic Corporation)

A microphone's polar response pattern, using circles to represent sound levels, provides a visual reading of a particular microphone's sensitivity to sounds reaching it from various directions.

Stereo.   The stereo microphone is actually two microphones in one case. The two microphones are positioned so that the axis of one pickup pattern is rotated 90 degrees or more from the other. One microphone's output is fed to the left channel, while the other microphone is fed to the right. A similar effect can be achieved by using two separate microphones positioned on the X-Y axis, as illustrated in Figure 3-8.

Other techniques, such as M-S (middle-side) or Blumlein (coincident), use a matrix to add and subtract the output of the two microphones to produce the left and right channels (Fig. 3-9).

Performance Characteristics: Frequency Response

A microphone's performance is often described by adjectives such as *crisp* or *bright* or *mellow* or *muddy.* These differences occur because of differences in the microphone's response to a specific range of frequencies. The term *frequency response* refers to the range of frequencies to which a particular microphone is designed to respond.

Although the manufacturer's specifications can serve as a guide, listening carefully to how each microphone sounds will help you decide which is best for various musical instruments and voices. Some microphones have a bass roll-off switch that can be used to help eliminate low-frequency sounds such as room noises from fans or the low vocal pitches that are accentuated when the speaker works very close to the microphone.

Performance Characteristics: Sensitivity

Sensitivity is an important consideration in choosing a microphone for a particular production situation. In general, dynamic moving-coil microphones are less sensitive to strong sound levels. The older ribbon microphones can be

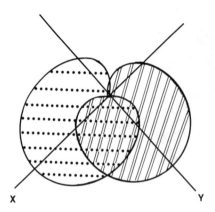

FIGURE 3-8 Two cardioid microphones positioned on the X-Y axis.

X   Y

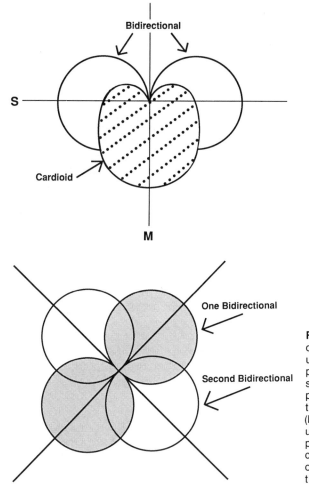

FIGURE 3-9 (top) The M-S microphone placement technique uses a cardioid microphone to pick up sounds from the middle section and a bidirectional microphone to pick up sounds from the extreme left and right sides. (bottom) The Blumlein technique uses two bidirectional microphones placed on the same vertical axis with the pickup pattern of one rotated 90 degrees from the other.

damaged by strong sound pressure levels; the newer ribbon microphones are more durable. Condenser microphones, too, can be overloaded at very high sound pressure levels so that sounds are distorted.

Distortions can be created by the rush of air from wind or from the explosive speech sounds, such as *p, t,* or *b*. Omnidirectional microphones tend to be less sensitive to these than are cardioid or bidirectional microphones. Wind screens or foam covers can minimize these noises (Fig. 3-10).

Microphones may also pick up vibration noises from surrounding movement or from being moved when held. Shock mounts of various types can lessen the vibration carried to the microphone (Fig. 3-11). Again, omnidirectional microphones are less sensitive to mechanical shock and vibration than are cardioid microphones.

A microphone's generating element is sensitive enough to respond to the slight changes in air pressure produced by a quiet conversation; therefore, micro-

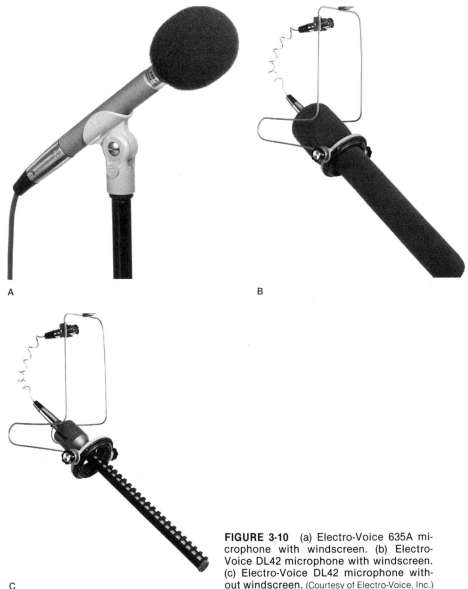

A

B

C

FIGURE 3-10   (a) Electro-Voice 635A microphone with windscreen. (b) Electro-Voice DL42 microphone with windscreen. (c) Electro-Voice DL42 microphone without windscreen. (Courtesy of Electro-Voice, Inc.)

phones must be handled with care. In general, dynamic moving-coil microphones are more rugged and durable, but all microphones can be damaged by physical shock (such as being dropped or knocked against hard surfaces), and their pre-amplifiers can be overloaded by strong bursts of sound pressure (being placed close to very loud sounds, for example).

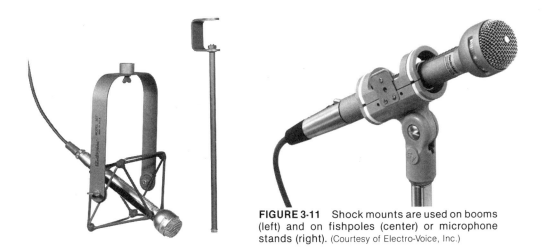

FIGURE 3-11 Shock mounts are used on booms (left) and on fishpoles (center) or microphone stands (right). (Courtesy of Electro-Voice, Inc.)

Performance Characteristics: Placement

The placement of a microphone depends upon both the specific characteristics of the microphone and the effect you want. Some microphones, such as the headset microphones used by sportscasters, are intended to be placed very close to the mouth. Other microphones, such as those mounted in parabolic reflectors, can pick up voices from long distances. Knowing the optimum pickup distance for the particular microphones you use will help you get optimum performance from them.

The placement of the microphone can also suggest the spatial relationship between the listener and the source of the sound. Placing the source of the sound "on beam," or directly in the most sensitive area of the pickup pattern of the microphone, creates a sense of "presence," or closeness. Distance can be suggested by moving the source of the sound "off beam," or into a less sensitive area of the pickup pattern. Thus, changing the placement of the microphone relative to the sound source can be used creatively to establish an aural foreground and background, to suggest movement within the scene, to involve the listeners intimately in the scene, or to let them listen in from a distance.

As we discussed in Chapter 2, the physical location of a scene can be suggested by the ambiance created by the acoustical characteristics of the space used for the audio production. A room with many hard, reflective surfaces will provide echoes that suggest an immense, cavernous space. A room with surfaces that absorb, rather than reflect, sound waves, seems "dead," as if everything were muffled and stifled. Often you may want to maintain a sense of continuity of space even though some recording is done on location and some in the studio. One way to accomplish that is to record several minutes of on-location ambiance, or natural sounds, to mix with the in-studio voice segments.

Mounting Devices

The choice of mounting devices to hold the microphone also depends on the production situation and the effect desired. As illustrated in Figure 3-12, there are many different mounting devices available. In making your selection, you need to know whether the talent will be seated or standing, working at a desk or moving around. You should also consider whether more than one person will be using the microphone and, in television, whether the microphone should be concealed or visible.

Special-purpose Microphones

Special-purpose microphones have been developed to meet the needs of particular production situations.

Cables and Connectors

The signal from a microphone travels to the audio console via a cable. In professional studios, this cable will be a *balanced line*—a cable that uses two conductors plus a shield (Fig. 3-14). With two conductors, noise signals induced by other electrical signals in the area are canceled out. Unbalanced lines, with only one conductor, are more likely to transmit the noise signal along with the signal from the microphone.

A three-pin XLR connector is used to connect the microphone to the microphone cable. The cable is then plugged into the connector box located in the studio or directly into the audio console. A locking device prevents accidental disconnection, so you must remember to push the release catch when disconnecting the cable.

Some connections require other types of plugs, as illustrated in Figure 3-15. If a cable is not fitted with a compatible connector, an adaptor can be used.

Damaged audio cables can produce annoying hums or loss of sound, so it's wise to treat them with care. When setting up for a production, run the microphone cables where they won't be in the path of traffic. Tape them down securely at any point where someone might trip over them. Bending or twisting can break the fine wires inside the cable, so follow the natural curve when coiling the cable.

On location, unless a portable audio board is used, the microphone is plugged directly into the audio or video tape recorder. Check to make sure that the microphone cable has a compatible plug.

INPUTS: ELECTRONICALLY GENERATED SOUNDS

In addition to inputs provided by microphones, synthesizers can be used to generate audio signals. Unlike microphones, which convert acoustical energy into electrical signals, synthesizers create electrical signals directly without using ac-

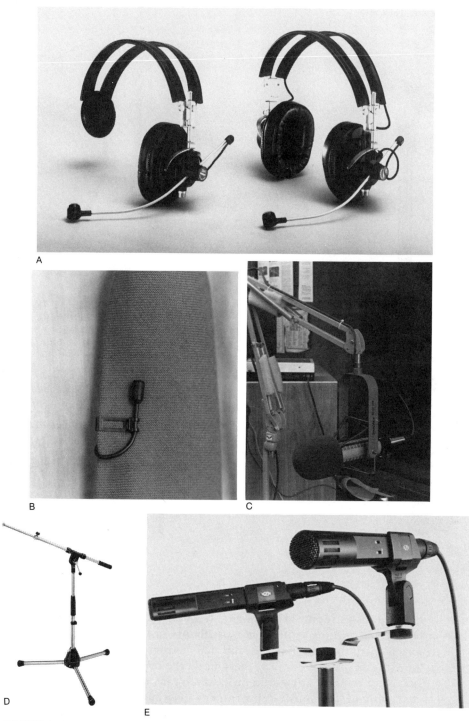

FIGURE 3-12 Microphone mounting devices. (a) Headset microphones. (Courtesy of Shure Brothers Incorporated, Evanston, IL) (b) Clip for lavalier microphone. (Courtesy of Sennheiser Electronic Corporation) (c) Adjustable arm commonly used in radio studios. (d) Microphone stand with adjustable boom. (Courtesy of Sennheiser Electronic Corporation) (e) Stereo mount. (Courtesy of Sennheiser Electronic Corporation)

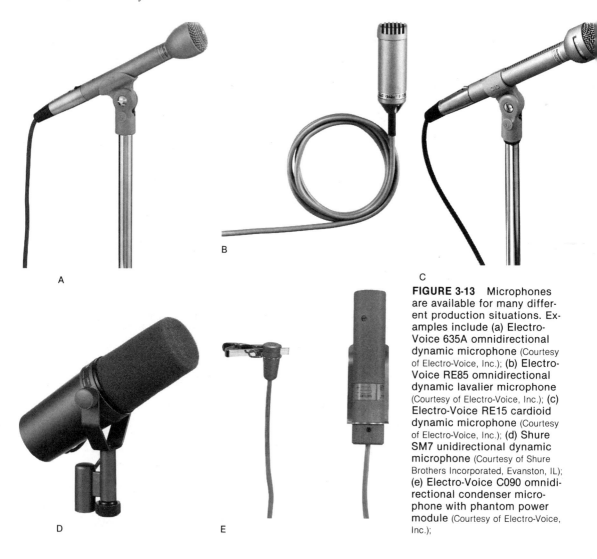

A

B

C

D

E

FIGURE 3-13 Microphones are available for many different production situations. Examples include (a) Electro-Voice 635A omnidirectional dynamic microphone (Courtesy of Electro-Voice, Inc.); (b) Electro-Voice RE85 omnidirectional dynamic lavalier microphone (Courtesy of Electro-Voice, Inc.); (c) Electro-Voice RE15 cardioid dynamic microphone (Courtesy of Electro-Voice, Inc.); (d) Shure SM7 unidirectional dynamic microphone (Courtesy of Shure Brothers Incorporated, Evanston, IL); (e) Electro-Voice C090 omnidirectional condenser microphone with phantom power module (Courtesy of Electro-Voice, Inc.);

tual sounds as inputs. The tone or frequency of the desired output sound can be selected and the synthesizer's oscillators instructed to generate the electrical waveform of that frequency. Additional instructions can be given about the envelope (the attack and decay of the sound), the overtones or timbre, and the intensity. Thus, virtually any sound produced by any musical instrument can be generated without the musical instrument, as can an entire spectrum of purely electronic musical tones and sounds. Advances in computer technology have increased the range and sophistication of the synthesizer as a source of audio inputs.

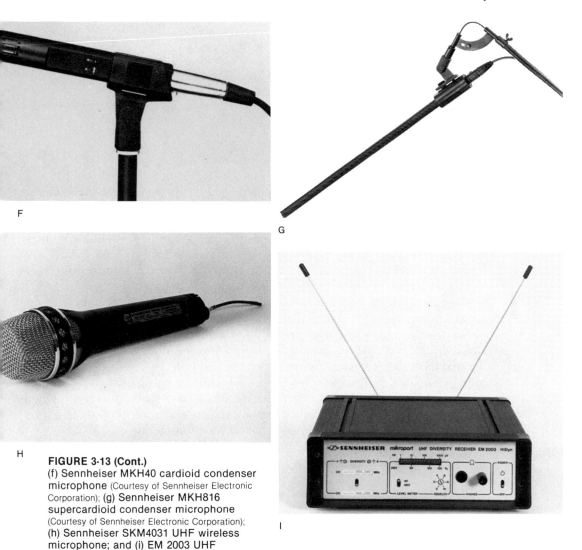

FIGURE 3-13 (Cont.)
(f) Sennheiser MKH40 cardioid condenser microphone (Courtesy of Sennheiser Electronic Corporation); (g) Sennheiser MKH816 supercardioid condenser microphone (Courtesy of Sennheiser Electronic Corporation); (h) Sennheiser SKM4031 UHF wireless microphone; and (i) EM 2003 UHF wireless microphone receiver. (Courtesy of Sennheiser Electronic Corporation)

PROCESSING

After the audio signal is generated by the microphone or electronic synthesizer, it is sent to an audio console. At this point in the system, the audio signal is amplified, processed, mixed with other audio signals, and routed to various monitoring devices and outputs, including tape recorders or a transmitter. Consoles can range from simple to complex in appearance, but they all use the same basic principles in operation. Therefore, understanding what happens to the audio signal as it flows through the console will let you adapt to different consoles.

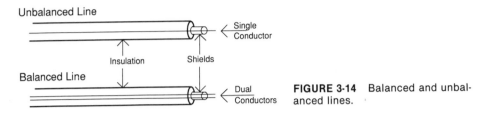

Unbalanced Line

Single Conductor

Insulation   Shields

Balanced Line

Dual Conductors

FIGURE 3-14 Balanced and unbalanced lines.

Input Section

The first section of the audio console is the *input section,* where incoming signals are fed through preamplifiers. As mentioned earlier, the signal generated by the microphone is relatively weak and needs to be amplified. As the signal passes through a mic-level preamplifier, it is boosted to line levels. Turntables, compact disc players, and tape recorders can also be used as inputs. Although the signal levels they generate are stronger, they still need amplification. These inputs are routed through line-level preamplifiers.

Since mic-level and line-level preamplifiers differ, it's important that the various inputs are connected to the correct input circuit. The signal from a microphone fed through a line-level preamplifier would still be relatively weak. The signal from a tape recorder put through a mic-level preamplifier would be boosted too much, so that the sound would be distorted and the mic-level preamplifier could be damaged. In some facilities, the inputs may feed directly into the audio console (Fig. 3-16). In other facilities, the inputs may be routed through a patch bay (Fig. 3-17). Some consoles allow you to select mic-level or line-level preamplification for the individual input module (Fig. 3-18).

As the signal flows through the input module, it can be modified in several

FIGURE 3-15 Commonly used connectors include (from left to right) XLR pair, RCA phono, balanced 1/4-inch phone, unbalanced 1/4-inch phone, 1/8-inch mini, BNC.

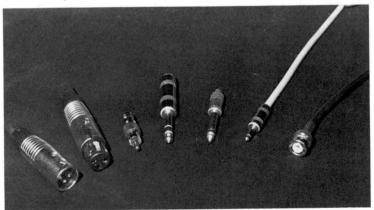

FIGURE 3-16 Lines run directly from inputs into the individual channels of the audio console. Other lines carry signals out of the channels.

ways. Volume can be controlled by the potentiometer, a rotary knob or slider (Fig. 3-19).

The volume of specific frequencies can be *boosted* (increased) or *attenuated* (decreased) by an equalizer. For example, the effect of someone talking on the telephone can be achieved by attenuating or decreasing the volume of the high and low frequencies and leaving the midrange between 400 Hz and 4,000 Hz.

The frequency range of the signal can also be changed by passing it through a filter. The filter is designed to allow only certain frequencies to pass through.

FIGURE 3-17 Signals can be routed through a patch bay.

FIGURE 3-18 Each channel can be assigned to line-level or mic-level inputs. The strength of the incoming signal can be increased or decreased using the trim control.

Thus a high-pass filter would eliminate any frequency below a set level; a low-pass filter would eliminate those above a set level; and a band-pass filter would eliminate all but a narrow range of frequencies.

Echo and reverberation can be added by routing the signal out to signal delay and reverberation systems, then back into the console. For example, the size and acoustical characteristics of a room can be suggested by the amount of reverberation added to a recorded conversation.

Stereo consoles also have pan controls that allow you to assign the audio signal to the right or left channel or to divide it between the right and left channels.

FIGURE 3-19   Potentiometers.

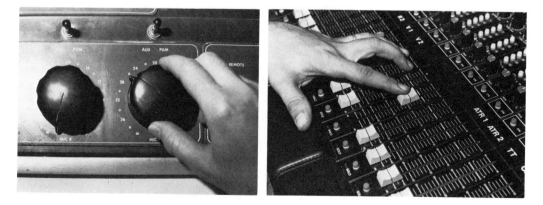

Output Section

The output section routes the audio signal to the tape recorders or to the transmitter. At this point, a master potentiometer allows you to control the output level of the outgoing signal (Fig. 3-20).

Monitor Section

Audio consoles provide several ways to monitor the audio signals. Volume-unit (VU) meters give a visual readout of the signal strength measured in decibels. The program, or line, VU meter measures the average strength of the signal going to the outputs. Because it measures the combined level of all inputs being mixed, it won't give you information about the level of the individual inputs or their relative strength or balance in the final mix.

To monitor the individual inputs, some consoles are equipped with light-emitting diode (LED) displays, VU meters for individual inputs, or a solo switch, which isolates one input by feeding only that input to the control room loudspeakers (Fig. 3-21).

The output from the console is normally sent to the loudspeakers in the control room. The volume control for these speakers has no effect on the level of the signal flowing to the outputs.

It is also helpful to be able to listen to an input before sending it out on line. For example, you may want to cue a record or a tape before using it. Some potentiometers have a cue position which, when selected, lets you listen to that

FIGURE 3-20 The input and output sections of some portable audio mixers are similar to larger audio consoles. (Courtesy of Panasonic Industrial Company)

FIGURE 3-21 The audio signal can be monitored visually using LED displays and VU meters or using the solo switch to send the signal from one channel to the loudspeaker.

input on a cue loudspeaker. Other consoles have a switch to allow you to direct the signal to an audition loudspeaker rather than to the program line (Fig. 3-22).

Earphones can also be used to monitor the audio signal (Fig. 3-23).

Using the Console

Before a recording session or a broadcast, you should test each sound source and set the levels. After the microphones are positioned, connected, and assigned to specific inputs, have the talent talk through the script as it will be performed during the production. (Counting or repeating "testing" may tell you that the microphone is working, but it doesn't give you accurate levels.) Check the sound quality for proper microphone placement. Note the potentiometer readings that give you the desired VU meter levels. Ideally, the signal feeding the outputs would read 0 VU on the VU meter. In reality, people do not speak at a constant volume, so a level that produces peaks at 0 VU is generally satisfactory.

To set levels for recorded material, play parts of the records and tapes that will be used in the production and again note the readings that give you the effect you want. If the music is to be used as background under the voice, the

FIGURE 3-22 Cue circuits and audition circuits are used to monitor the signal before it is sent to the output section.

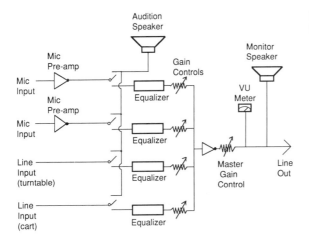

FIGURE 3-23 Earphones provide another way to monitor the audio signal.

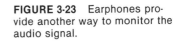

FIGURE 3-24 Signal flow through an audio console.

volume level will be quite low. If the music is to serve as a transition between segments of the program, the volume level might equal that of the voices. Listen carefully to the mix and adjust the balance of the various sounds to achieve the desired effect. Remember, though, that the individual sounds will combine into a louder signal.

Some consoles allow you to set the levels of the individual outputs and assign them to a submaster. You can then raise or lower the mixed signal without changing the balance of the mix. With other consoles, you can set the master gain or master volume level and control levels with the individual potentiometers. Although occasional peaking above 0 VU (in the red) is acceptable, the signal should be held below 0 VU (in the black) to prevent distortion.

STORAGE AND RETRIEVAL

The audio signal can be stored on tape or on disc. Since tape recorders are the most commonly used storage devices, we'll begin with them.

Audiotape

Audiotape is made up of a plastic base material that is coated on one side with a layer of ferric oxide particles suspended in a binder and on the other side with a back coating of carbon. The base may be either cellulose acetate or polyester. Polyester tends to be less affected by extremes in temperature and humidity and is stable when stored for long periods of time. Its major disadvantage is that it stretches under tension. Cellulose acetate breaks rather than stretches. Breaks can easily be spliced, but a stretched tape can't be saved; therefore, acetate was once preferred. But acetate-based tapes become brittle when stored. Now, polyester-based tapes can be prestretched, or tensilized, and these tensilized tapes have virtually replaced the acetate-based tapes.

In the manufacturing process, the oxide particles are arranged lengthwise on the tape. In the recording process, the electrical signal creates a magnetic field around the record head. As the tape passes the record head, the oxide particles on the tape are magnetized in proportion to the strength of the magnetic field. The magnetic pattern created corresponds to the original audio signal. The back coating helps reduce slippage as the tape passes the capstan.

Audiotapes vary in thickness from 1½ mils to 1/4 mil (1/1,000 inch). The thicker tape is stronger and less likely to print through. *Print-through* occurs during storage of a recorded tape, when the magnetic field on one layer of tape affects the magnetic field on the layer next to it. This print-through is heard as a slight echo before or after the original audio signal. Storing tapes without rewinding them (tail out) can reduce print-through because the tension on the tape in the play mode is lower than in the rewind mode.

Audiotapes also differ in width. The standard for broadcast use is 1/4 inch for both open-reel and cartridge (cart) tape recorders. Cassette recorders use 1/8-inch tape. Multitrack recorders may use 1/2-, 1-, or 2-inch tapes.

Audiotapes can be referred to as high-output, standard-output, or low-output. These designations reflect the tape's ability to handle loud volumes. Low-output tapes, for example, would be a poor choice for recording a rock band. The output level is determined by the tape's *retentivity* (ability to retain magnetism when the current is turned off) and by the tape's *sensitivity* (maximum output measured in decibels). Another measure of a tape's magnetic properties is *coercivity*, which is the strength of the magnetic field needed to completely erase fully saturated (fully magnetized) tape.

Audiotape Recorders

The two basic parts of the audiotape recorder are the tape transport system and the magnetic heads.

Tape transport system.   The tape transport system is designed to move the tape at a constant speed past the heads. The reel of tape is placed on the supply, or feed, spindle and threaded through the tape guide, past the head assembly, between the capstan and capstan idler, through the take-up idler, to the empty reel on the take-up spindle. When the recorder is activated, the capstan idler pinches the tape against the spinning capstan so that the tape is pulled forward at a constant speed. The supply motor and the take-up motor provide the tension needed to keep the tape feeding smoothly off the supply reel onto the take-up reel. The take-up idler serves as a guide for the tape and as a mechanical on–off switch. If the tape breaks, the take-up idler drops down and shuts off the transport system (Fig. 3-25).

Recorders designed to be used with reels with different hub sizes also have reel-size or tension switches (Fig. 3-26). The tension on the supply and take-up

FIGURE 3-25   Tape transport system.

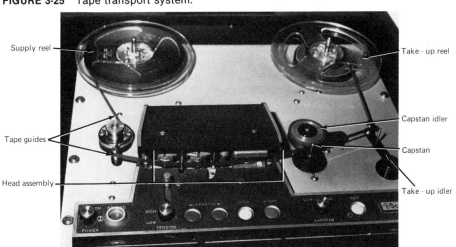

FIGURE 3-26 Reel sizes and hub sizes vary.

reels is set to maintain good tape contact with the heads yet not stretch the tape or affect its speed. This tension is usually adjusted midway between the best tension for a full and an empty reel.

Tape speeds are measured in inches per second (ips). Although 7½ ips is the most commonly used speed, recorders may operate at 15/16, 1⅞, 3¾, 7½, 15, or 30 ips. The faster speeds give better sound quality. In addition, because the magnetic pattern is spread over more tape length, it is easier to locate the slight pause between sounds when editing. Some recorders also have a variable speed control that allows you to raise or lower the pitch as you increase or decrease the playback speed.

Recorders also operate at high speeds in the fast-forward and rewind modes. In each of these modes, the capstan idler releases the tape so that the supply or take-up motor can advance or rewind the tape rapidly. In reverse and fast forward, tape lifters hold the tape away from the heads to protect the tape and the heads (Fig. 3-27).

FIGURE 3-27 Tape lifter holds the tape away from the heads.

Magnetic heads.   Most tape recorders have three heads: erase, record, and playback (Fig. 3-28).

As the tape passes the erase head when the recorder is in the record mode, any recorded information on the tape is removed as the particles on the tape are demagnetized. Remnants of the old audio signal may remain, however, so it's good practice to degauss, or demagnetize, your tapes with a bulk eraser before using them (Fig. 3-29).

The record head acts as a transducer, changing the electrical signal to magnetic flux, which magnetizes the tape. One part of the signal is the original audio signal; the other is a biasing signal. *Bias* is a very high frequency that reduces distortion and increases the accuracy of the recording by changing the transfer characteristics of magnetic information to linear patterns.

Record heads differ in the number of channels and, therefore, in the number of tracks they can lay down on the tape. A one-channel monaural recording head lays down one track, filling almost the entire width of the tape. A two-channel stereo recording head lays down two tracks, each filling about half the width of the tape. Some recording heads are designed to record a monaural or a stereo signal in one direction, then turn the tape over and record a second signal in the opposite direction. Multitrack recorders may have as many as 32 channels (Fig. 3-30).

The playback head also acts as a transducer, changing the magnetic information on the tape into an electrical signal. To play a tape back accurately, the format of the playback head should match the format of the record head that was used to make the recording.

Routine maintenance should include cleaning the heads regularly to prevent a build-up of dust or oxide particles, which can affect the sound quality. Heads and tape guides also need regular demagnetization; with use, they can become magnetized and affect the magnetic patterns on the tape. Check with your technician for the proper procedures to use with your tape recorders.

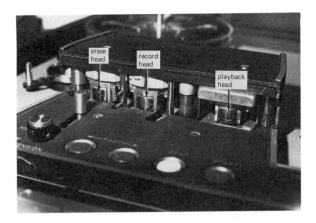

FIGURE 3-28   Tape recorder heads.

FIGURE 3-29 With the degausser on, the tape is lowered into the magnetic field, rotated several times, and lifted out of the magnetic field before the degausser is turned off. The tape is turned over and the process repeated.

Recording and Editing Procedures

After you've set the microphones and taken levels on all the sound sources you'll use in the recording session, be sure to calibrate the readings of the VU meter of the audio console with the VU meter on the tape recorder. Set the tape recorder controls to the record mode. Feed the oscillator's tone through the

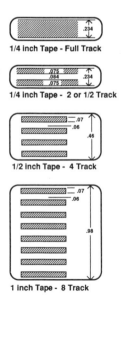

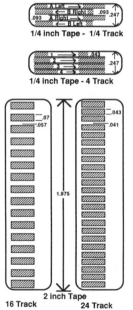

FIGURE 3-30 Recording heads differ in the number of tracks they record onto the tape.

audio console and adjust the volume so that the VU meter is reading 100 percent modulation, or 0 VU (Fig. 3-31). Adjust the recording volume levels on the tape recorder to match.

As we'll discuss in Chapter 4, an important part of shaping most programs is editing. Editing enables you to eliminate unwanted sounds (a speaker's cough or repeated "uh"s) or to combine sound sequences recorded at different times and places into a meaningful whole. Editing can be done manually, by cutting and splicing the tape, or electronically, by dubbing from one tape to another.

Manual editing of a tape requires a few tools. You'll need a cutting block, a marking pen, a razor blade, splicing tape, empty take-up reels, and leader tape (Fig. 3-32). The cutting block for 1/4-inch audio tape has cutting guides to enable you to make precise 90-degree, 45-degree, and 30-degree cuts. Since the 90-degree butt joint is more likely to make an audible sound passing over the playback head, the 45-degree slant joint is better. It also tends to sound smoother because it blends the two sound segments together as the tape is played. On multitrack tapes, the 30-degree joint may be the best choice because there is less time difference between what is cut from the top and bottom tracks.

Splicing tape comes in various widths. For splicing 1/4-inch audiotape, the 7/32-inch width is easier to use because it doesn't require trimming as the wider tapes do. It is available both in a roll and in precut splicing tabs.

Several kinds of leader tape are available, but the most useful is the timing leader tape. Its clear visibility makes cueing easier. And since its plaid markings are exactly 7½ inches apart, it can be used for precise timing between tape segments.

To make an edit, first play the tape to find the edit point. Stop the recorder and, with the volume still up, manually turn the reels back and forth until you locate the exact point between the last sound that you want and the next unwanted sound. That point is now centered over the playback head. Mark the spot with your marking pen (Fig. 3-33).

Continue playing the tape until you come to the end of the section that you want to eliminate. Again, stop the recorder and rock the tape back and forth manually to locate the edit point. Mark it. Now you're ready to make your edit.

FIGURE 3-31 VU meter.

FIGURE 3-32 Editing supplies.

Go back to the first edit point and lay the tape in the channel of the cutting block with the mark on the diagonal cutting groove. Cut the tape with the razor blade. Find the second edit point and make that cut. It's a good idea to devise a system of marking and storing the outtakes so that you'll be able to find discarded sound sequences if you decide you want to use them after all.

To splice the tape, lay the two ends to be joined in the channel of the cutting block. Make sure that the ends just touch but do not overlap. On the back of the tape, apply a piece of splicing tape long enough to cover each side of the splice. Press the splicing tape firmly into place, working out any air bubbles. Then check your edit point by playing that section of the tape.

When you've finished editing, add appropriate leader at the beginning and at the end of the tape. The beginning of your tape should include enough leader tape for threading the recorder, a reference tone to allow anyone playing your tape to calibrate their playback VU meters with the setting you used in recording, and timing leader tape to use in cueing the tape. If there are several sound segments on your tape, separating them with timing leader tape will make each cut easier to locate and cue. At the end of the last segment, splice on another 4 or 5 feet of leader tape.

Manual editing involves physically cutting the tape, discarding unwanted segments, and splicing the wanted segments into the desired order. Electronic editing involves rerecording the sound segments you want in the order you want them. This requires the use of two tape recorders—one to play back on and one to record on. The final tape is compiled by cueing up the first segment on the playback deck (the source deck) and recording it onto the master tape on the record deck. The second segment is then cued up on the source deck. On the record deck, the master tape is cued just past the last sound of the first segment. With the source deck in the playback mode and the record deck in the record mode, both decks are started at the same time and stopped at the end of the second segment. This process is continued until the sound segments have been assembled in the correct order on the master tape.

A

B

C

D

E

FIGURE 3-33   (a) Play the tape until you reach the edit point. (b) Turn the tape slowly back and forth to locate the pause between sounds. (c) Mark that spot over the playback head. (d) Find and mark the second edit point. (e) Lay the tape in the cutting block with the edit point centered over the diagonal groove.

F

G

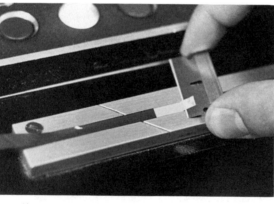

H

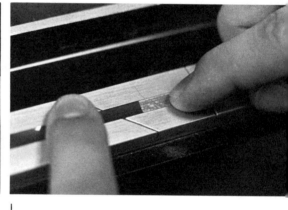

I

J

FIGURE 3-33   (cont.)
(f) Cut the tape. Repeat at the second edit point. (g) Put the two ends to be spliced into the cutting block so they touch. (h) Apply the splicing tape. (i) Smooth. (j) Listen to the edit.

Electronic editing by manually controlling the two recorders can be difficult. It is critical to synchronize the recorders and precisely time the edits. To address these problems, especially in editing videotape, an electronic edit controller was developed to replace the manual operator. Once the proper commands are typed into the controller, a microprocessor takes over and performs the edit automatically. Because this system is used most frequently with videotape, a detailed explanation of it appears in Chapter 13. Videotape editing systems are becoming quite common, and because of the ease of editing these systems provide, using videotape for audio productions is an option to consider. For example, the 1/2-inch video home system (VHS) videotape recorder is often used in recording digital audio.

Cartridge Tape Recorders

Thus far we've been talking about open-reel tape recorders. A more convenient way to store and retrieve short sound segments, such as sound effects, commercials, and news actualities is the cartridge tape recorder. Cartridge tape is a continuous loop of standard ¼-inch audio tape housed in a plastic case (Fig. 3-34). When the cartridge is inserted into the recorder and the play function is activated, the pinch roller presses the tape against the capstan, pulling the tape across the heads. Pressure pads hold the tape firmly against the heads.

Eliminating the need to thread the tape saves time, as does the automatic cueing process. When the tape is recorded, an inaudible cue tone is laid down on the tape. When the tape is played, it continues to play until the loop recycles to the cue tone, where it automatically stops. The tape has, in effect, recued itself.

Some cartridge tape recorders have both record and playback heads. Some have one or the other. None has an erase head, so it's important to bulk erase any cartridge tape before recording on it.

To record on a cartridge tape, set your sound levels and calibrate the VU meters just as you would with a reel-to-reel recorder. Choose a cartridge tape that is just slightly longer than the sound segment you're recording. (If a 10-second

FIGURE 3-34 Cartridge tape.

station promotion were recorded on a 60-second cartridge, the cartridge would continue to cycle for 50 seconds before it was recued and ready to use again.) Insert the cartridge into the recorder and activate the record mode; on some units, this automatically lays the cue tone on the tape. On other units, the cue tone is laid down when you press "play." When you press "play," start your sound immediately; otherwise, there may be a pause, or "dead air," between the cue tone and the beginning of your sound segment.

You may put more than one sound segment on a tape. For example, if an advertiser is running three different commercials in rotation, they could be put in order on the same cartridge. That way, when one commercial is played, the next in the rotation would always be cued and ready to use. To do this, simply record the first commercial, leave a few seconds of silence, and stop the tape. Then, lay down a cue tone, record the second commercial, and so on. In playback, when the unit senses the cue tone, it will stop and the next commercial will be cued up.

Cassette Tape Recorders

Another type of tape recorder that is useful on location is the cassette recorder. The cassette recorder uses a narrow 1/8-inch tape wound in a reel-to-reel format within a plastic case. Almost all cassette recorders run at 1⅞ ips, so it's possible to record as many as 90 minutes per side. In practice, it is better to use tapes that are no longer than 60 minutes (30 minutes per side) because the longer-playing tapes are thinner (1/4 mil rather than 1/2 mil), tend to be more fragile, and may slip, especially in the fast-forward and rewind modes.

Most cassette recorders are portable; they are small and operate on either alternating current (AC) or batteries. This makes them handy for recording interviews or news events on location. Sound quality can be a problem, however. The quality of the built-in microphones is quite poor, and recordings made with them tend to be noisy. You'll get a better recording by using an external microphone plugged into the microphone input jack. The narrow width of the tape and the slower recording speed also contribute to lower sound quality. There simply isn't much tape surface available to lay down the magnetic information.

To improve quality, coatings of chromium dioxide, cobalt-treated oxide, or metal particles have been developed to replace ferric oxide. Of these, the metal-particle tape seems to be most effective in improving sound quality while introducing fewer problems. Cassette recorders are now available with special heads and circuitry to take full advantage of this tape's performance characteristics.

Cassette tapes are difficult to edit. It's best to dub the material from the cassette onto reel-to-reel tape for editing.

Digital Recorders

Although digital audio recorders operate in much the same way as other audio recorders do, the way in which the signal is processed is different. As described in Chapter 2, the analog signal in digital recording is sampled and quantized. The numerical values assigned to the wave form are recorded onto the tape. Digital audio recorders contain special circuitry that performs this conversion, adding in a preamble code that signals the beginning of each digital word, a cyclic redundancy check (CRC) code to detect errors caused by tape defects, and a parity code to correct for these errors.

Many of the problems associated with tape recordings disappear. Tape noise, cross talk, print-through, or wow-and-flutter have no effect on the recorded sound. Multiple generations of a tape can be made without losing quality. Editing becomes more complicated, however. Digital tapes are generally thinner and have thinner oxide coatings, so they must be handled carefully. It is not possible to locate editing points by rocking the tape back and forth across the heads. In addition, cutting the tape with the razor blade can disrupt the sequence of preamble-audio data-CRC code-parity code, creating noise at the splice. Consequently, electronic editing systems are used.

Videotape Recorders

While audio-with-video recording is the most prevalent use of videotape recorders, as mentioned earlier, it is possible to take advantage of the electronic editing capabilities of videotape editing systems and use the videotape recorder as an audio recorder. Videotape provides two audio channels so you can record in stereo. Or, you can record one channel and add a second channel of audio later.

Videotape recorders are also used to record digital audio signals. An analog-to-digital converter samples the waveform to convert it into a series of binary numbers, which are recorded as pulses on the videotape. In playback, a digital-to-analog converter reads the pulses and re-creates the waveform.

Turntables and Discs

Phonograph records and compact discs (CDs) provide another useful way to store audio information. Since the development of magnetic tape, recording directly onto disc has become rare in ordinary production situations. However, prerecorded discs are a rich source of music, sound effects, and historical material, such as speeches.

Turntables.   Like tape recorders, turntables are easy to use to retrieve recorded sounds (Fig. 3-35). When the power is turned on, a drive mechanism rotates the turntable. A gear selector lets you shift speeds from 45 revolutions per minute (rpm) to 33⅓ rpm to 78 rpm. When the tone arm is moved into position above the record and then lowered, the stylus mounted in the cartridge makes contact with the grooves in the record. The cartridge acts as a transducer, converting the vibrations of the stylus into an electrical signal that flows to an input of the audio console.

To cue a record, open the potentiometer on the console to the cue position. Put the gear selector in neutral. Lower the stylus into the groove just before the

on/off switch

tone arm

cartridge

stylus

gear selector

FIGURE 3-35 Turntable.

cut you want. Rotate the turntable clockwise slowly until you hear the first sound, then rotate it counterclockwise about one-eighth of a turn for long-playing (LP) records, about one-quarter turn for 45s. With the power off, put the gear selector into the proper gear. To play the record on cue, turn the power on and simultaneously fade up the volume to the correct level. The back-turn gives the turntable time to get up to speed, and "potting in" the sound lessens the chance of a "wow" if the sound begins before the turntable is at proper speed.

You can achieve a tighter cue by using another method, called "slip cueing." Again, with the gear selector in neutral, find the first sound on the record. Then, holding the edge of the record to keep it from moving, put the turntable into gear and turn the power on. The turntable will be spinning underneath the record. On cue, lift your hand off the record and fade up the volume.

If they are to deliver optimal sound, turntables and records must be treated with care. Protect records from dust, fingerprints, and scratches. Replace the stylus regularly. Treat the tone arm gently; it is carefully balanced to provide just the right amount of pressure to keep the stylus riding in the grooves, and it can be knocked out of adjustment. If your turntable has an idler wheel–type drive mechanism, put it into the neutral gear position when it is not in use. The constant pressure of the metal shaft against the rubber pressure roller can create an indentation that will bump when the turntable is used.

Compact disc. Ordinary phonograph records use analog technology. The variations in air pressure (acoustical energy) are converted to an electrical waveform (an electrical analogy of the variations in air pressure). This electrical signal, in turn, activates the mechanism that etches the groove (a physical analogy of

FIGURE 3-36 Compact disc players can locate and cue cuts of music or sound effects rapidly.

the electrical waveform) in the master wax disc. In the manufacturing process, a die made from the master disc is used to press copies on vinyl discs.

As the turntable stylus "reads" the variations in the shape of the groove, the information is changed back into the electrical waveform. Obviously, dirt, scratches, or wear will change the shape of the groove and, therefore, change the sound reproduced.

With the development of digital and laser technology, CDs have been developed to eliminate these problems. In the recording process, an analog-to-digital converter changes the electrical waveform information into binary numbers. The numbers are stored on the disc as a series of microscopic pits and smooth areas. As the disc is played, a laser beam scans it. The variations in the intensity of the beam reflected back from the disc are read by a detector and translated back into binary numbers, which are converted into the electrical waveform.

CDs have several advantages (Fig. 3-36). As mentioned earlier, digital recordings provide better and more accurate sound reproduction. Unlike the analog discs, in which the audio signal must be compressed to prevent intergroove distortion, the CD can reproduce the entire 100-decibel range. In addition, the aluminized discs used are less likely to warp. Since the actual recorded information is sealed beneath a protective layer, there is no physical contact with the surface of the disc and, therefore, no wear. Distortion from dust or scratches is less likely to occur. And digital information permits closer spacing of the "grooves," so discs can be very compact. A 4¾-inch disc, for example, can hold as much as 73 minutes of sound.

SUMMARY

This chapter has provided an overview of the audio system—the equipment you can use to collect, process, store, and retrieve sounds. The microphone serves as the basic input, collecting sounds and converting them into a form that can be manipulated. The choice of the specific microphone to use should take into consideration the type of generating element the microphone has, its pick-up pattern, its frequency response, and other performance characteristics. Placement of the microphone can be varied to produce the desired effect. Mounting devices, cables, and connectors should be chosen to meet the requirements of the production situation. Electronic synthesizers provide another input, generating a wide spectrum of musical tones and sounds.

The audio console is designed to process the audio input. The input section amplifies the incoming audio signal, controls the volume of the signal, and provides for manipulating the signal with equalizers and echo and reverberation units. Several inputs can be mixed and routed through the output section to recorders or to a transmitter. Volume levels and balance can be checked with various monitoring devices, including VU meters, LED displays, cue speakers, loudspeakers, and earphones.

Audio signals can be stored on tape or disc. Analog tape recorders convert the electrical signal into magnetic information stored on a tape. Digital tape recorders convert the electrical signal into a series of binary numbers, which are translated into magnetic pulses on the tape. Reel-to-reel recorders offer several recording formats, from 1/4-inch single-track monaural to 2-inch multitrack. Editing can be done manually or electronically.

Cartridge tape recorders provide automatic recueing. Cassette recorders are handy for on-location work because they are very portable.

Audio signals can also be stored on records. Turntables in most production facilities can play 78, 45, and 33 ⅓ records. Newer CDs provide more accurate sound reproduction, as well as more durable and more compact records.

The equipment that makes up the audio system provides you with the technical means for creating audio messages. In Chapter 4, we'll consider how to structure the content of those messages.

FOR FURTHER READING

ALTEN, STANLEY R. *Audio in Media* (Belmont, Calif.: Wadsworth, 1981).

WORAM, JOHN M. *The Recording Studio Handbook* (Plainview, N.Y.: ELAR, 1982).

chapter four

Producing the Audio Message

INTRODUCTION

In Chapter 1, we discussed communication as a process that involves a sender encoding an idea so that it can be transmitted to a receiver, who then decodes and reconstructs the idea. In producing audio messages, the sender must take into consideration three basic sets of variables.

First are the requirements of effective communication. As a sender, you must have a clear understanding of what you want to communicate and what effect you want the message to have on the receiver. To increase the probability that your message will be understood, you must consider the receiver's interpretation of the specific verbal and nonverbal elements—the words, the sounds, the music—in the message.

Second are the possibilities and the limitations imposed by the technology used to gather and combine all the components of the audio message and then broadcast or record it for later playback.

Third are the variables related to the organization within which you are working. All organizations—broadcasting stations, cable companies, corporate media departments, advertising agencies, and even classes—impose restrictions. You may have to obtain approval for goals and guidelines, access to production facilities and funding, choice of talent and technical crew, and the initial idea and the final production.

To help you understand how to work your way through all these variables to produce audio messages that communicate clearly and creatively, we will first consider what takes place during preproduction planning, preproduction technical preparation, production, and postproduction.

PREPRODUCTION PLANNING

Preproduction planning encompasses the many steps through which a project proceeds, from formulation of the idea to the final script. It involves (1) indentifying the purpose and intended use of the production, (2) studying the specific audience for which it is intended, (3) researching the subject, (4) deciding upon the overall form of the production, (5) identifying the necessary production facilities, (6) working out a budget, (7) summarizing all this information into a treatment for approval, and then (8) writing the final script.

Purpose

In general, audio messages have one of three general purposes. Some are intended simply to entertain; the typical radio disc-jockey show is an example. Other audio messages are intended to inform the audience; news programs and documentaries are obvious examples. Still other messages are intended to persuade; commercials and public-service announcements fall into this category.

In thinking about the purpose of the audio message you are developing, it helps to consider the specific response you want from the listener. The response most disc jockeys want, for example, is for their listeners to be interested enough in the music and the chatter to stay tuned to the show. Every element that goes into the show is intended to help catch and maintain the audience's interest and to provide them with entertainment.

When the purpose is to inform, you should be very specific about the response you want from your listener. The news reporter, for example, wants the listener to know not only what happened but also who was involved as well as where, when, and why the event happened. The producer of slide-tape presentations for an outpatient healthcare facility may want the viewers or listeners to learn specific facts about their medical condition and the things they should and should not do while they are undergoing treatment.

Audio messages designed to persuade are intended to produce very specific audience responses as well. Commercials are designed to persuade consumers to buy a specific product or use a specific service. Public-service announcements may attempt to persuade listeners to alter their behavior—to stop littering, use more care with firearms, or sign up for water-safety instructions. Other audio messages may try to alter listener attitudes or beliefs. The producers of these messages have specific audience responses in mind when they choose each element that goes into the message.

In identifying the purpose of the audio message you want to produce, you should not only understand your general purpose—to entertain, to inform, or to persuade; you should also decide upon the specific response you want from your listener.

Audience Analysis

In order to achieve your purpose, you need to understand your intended audiences, their needs, and the way in which they will use your message. Advertising agencies carefully research their target audiences before developing an advertising campaign. Broadcast stations pay attention to the demographics of their audiences in planning format changes.

Depending upon the specific message you are producing, you should gather as much information as you can about your target audience. Is it a general audience (anyone who tunes in) or a narrow audience (employees in a particular firm)? What are the demographics and psychographics? *Demographics* include broad categories such as age, sex, education, marital status, economic status, ethnic background, and so forth. *Psychographics* provide more specific information about values and attitudes as well as lifestyle and behaviors, such as buying habits and voting patterns.

You should also assess your listeners' motivations for listening. Perhaps they have tuned in because they are seeking diversion and your program is one of many they are sampling. Perhaps they have been assigned to listen because of the specific information in your message—information their teacher or employer wants them to have. Or they may have personal reasons for wanting the information and so have made an effort to find and listen to your message.

How interested are your listeners in the subject? Your approach will be different if they are already interested or if you need to do something to arouse their interest. Their attitudes about the ideas you'll be presenting are also important. Will you have to counter negative attitudes, or can you count on general acceptance of your ideas? You should also consider how much your listeners know about the subject. Will you have to begin with basic explanations, or can you assume that they know the basics?

Finally, how might your listeners' lives be affected by your message? Most of us are more willing to listen attentively and to accept recommendations if we feel that the ideas will somehow benefit us. Will the information you're providing make your listeners happier, healthier, able to do their jobs more effectively, or will it simply allow them to relax for a while?

The answers to questions such as these will help you to decide the overall approach to your subject matter and to select many of the specific elements you include. Important, too, are questions about how your audio message will reach your listeners.

Distribution

If your production will be broadcast, you will want to understand the station's format and its potential effect on the style and content of your production. You also must know how your production fits into the station's overall programming. Will it be a regular part of an established series or part of a new series? Will the production be broadcast daily, weekly, or is it a one-time special? How long will it be? The content of your production, as well as the overall structure, may differ according to the time of day it is scheduled to be broadcast and according to what precedes and follows it. In addition, there may be specific station policies (as well as federal rules and regulations) that must be considered.

If your production is for nonbroadcast use, you need to know how it will be used. Is it intended to be used, for example, in group training sessions, with discussions before and after it is played? Will it be used in a classroom? Will individuals buy or borrow it for home use? Explanations may differ if printed materials or supplements will accompany your production. Content will certainly be influenced by whether the program is part of a series or must stand alone. Where it is used may also be a factor. Strategies used to gain the attention of shoppers in a mall may differ from those used with listeners in a dealer's showroom. Many of the decisions you make about what to say and how to say it will be determined by the way in which your audio message will be used.

Research

Once you have a clearly defined purpose and an understanding of your audience, it's time to start researching the subject matter. A good place to start is with your own knowledge, but for most productions you will want to go far beyond that. The library is an obvious place to go for all types of print sources, from newspapers, magazines, and books to government documents and files of clippings. Depending on the topic, you might find specialized collections useful. Local historical societies often keep extensive records on important community events and people. Special-interest groups, such as the chamber of commerce or the Audubon Society, or government agencies, such as the county health department or the state tourist bureau, may have the information you need.

Don't overlook people as a source of information. Interviews with experts and ordinary citizens can provide first-hand experiences and personal insights. It may take time and imagination to track down the latest statistic or find an expert willing to record an interview, but such details can make a difference in the effectiveness of your final production.

When doing your research, you should keep comprehensive notes about the source of each piece of information you gather. Accuracy is a major concern. So, too, is crediting your sources. In your production, of course, you will identify the source of any direct quotations. The credibility of your message will be enhanced if you also mention the sources of other information used.

Approach

In the process of defining your goals and researching your subject, you probably started to think about your overall approach to the production. We can classify audio productions in many ways: by genre, by organizational patterns, or by the production elements used.

When we classify productions by genre, we are referring to familiar types such as news stories, features, documentaries, commercials, or dramas. These categories have certain identifying stylistic elements. We expect news stories to be objective, factual accounts of an event. On the other hand, we expect a feature to be entertaining, even as it provides information about an event. Documentaries have a clear point of view. Commercials are intended to be persuasive. Educational materials present new information in a manner that makes it easy for us to understand and remember it. Dramas have plots and characters.

There are also many familiar patterns of organization. A production may start with a standard introduction, followed by the program content, and end with a standard close. The introduction might be preceded by a teaser to catch the attention of the audience. The overall structure of the program might include separate segments linked by various transitional devices. The program content itself may follow a chronological order, a narrative structure, a problem–solution or cause–effect sequence, or a topical order appropriate for the specific subject.

Audio productions can also be classified by the type of production elements used. Broad classifications include live studio broadcasts, live remote broadcasts, taped programs that are recorded in real time without interruptions, and taped programs that are constructed by editing in postproduction. Most radio productions are, in reality, a combination of these. A deejay show, for example, may be live in the studio with prerecorded program elements, such as commercials, or it may be live from a remote location with prerecorded inserts, or it may be a prerecorded syndicated program with live local inserts for station identification and commercials. A news story or feature may be narrated by one reporter, or it may use interviews with several people, or it may use sound bits recorded somewhere on location. A drama almost always involves dialogue, but it may also use narration, sound effects, and music. One production might use one announcer live in the studio. Another might use interviews recorded in the studio or by telephone. Comments or sounds recorded on location might be edited in. Music and sound effects can be added.

The way in which the final production will be used often dictates the form. If you are producing a feature for a radio talk show, for example, the show's format determines the overall style of the feature.

The production facilities available to you also affect your decisions. If you don't have the technical capability to record a telephone interview with the mayor about a proposed city ordinance, you may have to summarize his comments into a script read by an announcer. If your access to a music or sound-effects library is limited, you may have to eliminate music bridges or background sounds that might have added a dimension you wanted.

Time is another factor; both the length of the production and the amount of time you have to spend completing it must be considered. The more complicated the production, the more time it will take to complete.

As you are researching, you will begin to make decisions about the overall form of your production and the various audio elements you want to use. Will you use voice? One or several? What sounds will you use? How will they be integrated into the production—as discrete elements or as background? Will you use music? If so, what type, and how will it fit into the overall message?

Each of these audio elements must be chosen with care. As we mentioned in Chapter 1, the sound of a voice creates an impression of the speaker's gender, age, and personality. Having a particular expert or political candidate explain a process or make a comment may be so important that you will use that person regardless of vocal quality. But when you do have a choice, take advantage of all the mental images your listeners are likely to associate with particular vocal qualities. Listen carefully to individual voices before deciding upon the narrator or actor.

Sound effects, too, should be carefully chosen. Sound-effects libraries (collections of recorded sounds) offer a wide choice of standard sounds with many variations—angry crowds, cheering crowds, restless crowds, and so on. Often the exact sound you want won't be included. It is sometimes possible to mix two recorded sounds to achieve the effect you want. Or you may be able to create your own sound effect live in the studio. The sound of water being poured into a glass or the sound of a page being ripped out of a book may not only sound more authentic but may also be easier to time in production if done live, on-mike. At other times you may want to record the actual sounds on location. Of course, a recording of the "real thing" is sometimes difficult to identify. Often, though, sounds recorded on location, especially when used as background, add an ambiance that suggests the location you want your listeners to imagine.

Music is another element that merits careful consideration. What purpose will the music serve? Will it be a theme to identify the program or character? Will it serve as a transition between various segments? Will it be used to create a mood? How is your intended audience likely to react to it? Will they recognize the individual selection, and, if so, what associations will it evoke? Will their interest in the music, especially if there are lyrics, distract them from more important parts of the message? Properly used, music can enhance your message. Carelessly chosen, it can weaken your message by focusing your listener's attention on the music itself or even altering the intended meaning of your message.

Permissions

Whenever you use prerecorded music or sound effects, direct quotations from printed materials, or recordings of comments, you should make sure that you have the necessary permissions to use the material.

Some standard music and sound-effects libraries grant permission for use at the time you purchase the recordings. However, most recordings are licensed through American Society of Composers, Authors and Publishers (ASCAP), Broadcast Music, Incorporated (BMI), or Society of European Stage Authors and Composers (SESAC), and permission to use must be secured. Broadcast stations and some educational institutions hold blanket contracts with the licensing companies that allow them to pay an annual fee for permission to use any recorded material licensed to those organizations. If you are not covered by such a contract, you should request permission from the person or company holding the copyright to the recording you wish to use. For some uses, the company may set a fee that must be paid before you use the materials; for other uses, it may grant permission without charging a fee.

Print materials, photographs, videos, and films are also covered by copyright laws. Again, if you are going to use copyrighted materials, you may need to obtain permission. In some instances, such as in reviews, paraphrasing material or using short quotations, photographs, or film clips is considered "fair use" and does not require permission. However, you should acknowledge the source of any quotation or information you are using.

Some materials may never have been copyrighted. The copyright on other materials may have expired. These materials would be considered to be in the *public domain,* available for use without fee or permission.

In many situations, when you use a person's recorded comments, you should ask the speaker to sign a standard release form (Fig. 4-1). This form specifies the use for which the recording is intended and states that the person who is signing has agreed to that use.

Production Facilities

Once you have decided on the general form and the various audio elements you would like to use, you can identify the production facilities and equipment you will need. These may range from a portable cassette recorder with an external microphone to an elaborate sound studio with multiple-channel mixing capability.

In some situations, you will be limited to the equipment owned by the station or company for which you work. In other situations, you may be able to augment that with rented equipment or facilities. In virtually all situations, you will be limited by budget and by time constraints.

For all productions, you should carefully think through how to achieve the effects you want. For location recording, what type of audio recorder and microphone best suit the job? For in-studio recording, what inputs will you need? A turntable, cassette recorders, cart recorders, reel-to-reel recorders, multiple-track recorders, microphones? How sophisticated must the audio board be to let you process the signal? Will you need equalization, reverberation, filters, multiple channels delegated to submasters? What type of recording master will you make—monotrack reel-to-reel, cartridge, cassette, stereo, or multitrack? How will you edit the various segments together?

Budget

Budgeting involves estimating how much money will be required to complete the production. Production budgets are usually broken down into two sections. One section contains the above-the-line costs and the other section con-

FIGURE 4-1 Sample release form for recorded interviews. The wording can be modified to fit the needs of various production situations.

RELEASE

I hereby consent to and authorize the audio and video recording of my comments by _____. Further, I authorize the use of those recordings by _____ or others designated by him/her in a program entitled _____. I understand that I will receive no compensation for the use of my comments for that purpose.

Any restrictions to the use of those recordings are specified below:

Signed: _____
Date: _____

tains the below-the-line costs. *Above-the-line costs* include fees paid to the creative personnel—the producer, director, writer, and performers. *Below-the-line costs* include expenses related to the actual production—costs of facilities, equipment, and fees paid to technical personnel.

Preparing a budget estimate will help you determine how much money will be required to complete the production. If funds are limited, it will help you identify areas where reductions can be made. Many of these decisions will influence the final production.

During the production, careful records of expenditures are kept so that the actual cost figures are available and so that the production does not exceed the allotted budget.

Treatment

At this point in your preproduction planning, you are ready to write the treatment. The specific requirements for a treatment may vary, but in general, the *treatment* is a narrative description of the proposed production project. It is designed to give the reader a clear understanding of the purpose of the project, what the final production will be like, and the resources needed to complete the production (Fig. 4-2).

The first section of the treatment should provide clear justification for the project. It should describe (1) the need for the production, (2) the specific audience to be served, (3) the ways in which the audio message will be distributed to the audience, and (4) the specific objectives to be accomplished by the audio message.

The next section should include a narrative description of the actual content of the production. Each scene or segment of the production should be described in terms of (1) the specific point to be made in that scene or segment and (2) how that point will be made. In describing how the point will be made, you should explain how the verbal information will be provided—for example, through interviews or through narration by an expert or announcer—and how sound effects or music will be integrated into the production. When you have finished this section, you have completed a detailed outline for the production.

The final section of the treatment should include information about the personnel, the production facilities and equipment that are needed, and the estimated budget.

Scripting

Once the treatment has been approved, you're ready to prepare the script. As you are writing the script, it may be helpful to think of it as a complete blueprint for the production. By following the script, the technical crew and the talent should be able to produce the audio message exactly as you imagined it.

Almost every production unit uses its own script format. The one described here will be useful to you in your first productions (Fig. 4-3). The script format is designed (1) to allow room for the director and performers to make notes, (2) to permit easy identification of each sound source and each performer, and

PROPOSAL FOR A FEATURE SERIES ON BALLOT ISSUES

In the fall, voters will be asked to decide several complex ballot issues: a statewide system for child care, a hazardous waste site policy, revisions in school funding, and mandatory drug testing for state employees. Outspoken advocates on both sides have tended to sensationalize these issues so that much of the news coverage to date has focused on the controversy rather than on detailed analysis of reasoned arguments. To make an informed choice, voters need to understand the problems these ballot issues address and the implications of a yes or no vote on each of the proposals.

In an effort to provide that information, we propose to produce "Your Choice," a series of 5-minute radio features about these ballot issues. While we hope to reach the entire voting population, our specific target audience is the voter who listens to public radio. The series will be made available to all public radio stations in the state via the state satellite network.

In producing the series, our specific objectives are to provide the listener with information about (1) the nature of the problem addressed by each ballot issue, (2) the effect on the citizens of the state, (3) the various solutions that have been proposed, and (4) the probable effects if the ballot issue is passed or defeated.

The series will use a host to introduce each segment and narrate transitions, interviews with experts, and actualities recorded on location with people affected by the problem.

The format for the series will follow that outlined in the following example.

Proposed Segment on Child Care for "Your Choice"

To capture attention and create interest, this segment opens with an actuality recorded in a home as a single working mother goes through her usual routine of getting her child ready to take to pre-school and herself ready to go to work.

The host then introduces the series and the topic for this discussion: the child care crisis.

Next, interview segments with a member of the governor's task force on child care, a social worker, an elementary school teacher, and a child psychologist explore the growing need for child care, the inadequacies of the present system, and the resulting problems. Narration by the host provides pertinent facts and transitions between interview segments.

The final interview is the conversation between parent, babysitter, and child as the parent arrives at the babysitter's home to pick up the child at the end of the day.

The host closes by referring to the next segment in the series, a discussion about the effects of our current child care system on both children and parents.

Production Needs

We request that a two-person team from the news staff be assigned to write and produce this series and that an intern be assigned to assist with research.

Estimated use of production facilities for the four segments devoted to each ballot issue includes: 3 days portable equipment for on site recording, 1 day editing and studio production. Estimated cost beyond staff salaries and use of in-house production facilities includes $500.00 for travel to interview sites.

FIGURE 4-2 Sample treatment.

CLIENT: Montville Chamber of Commerce
MEDIA: Radio
TIME: 30-second
DATE: begin June 11

MUSIC: SOUSA MARCH UP TO ESTABLISH AND UNDER . . .

ANNCR: Enjoy summer in the park! The Montville Concert
         Band opens the season June 18th with a program of
         rousing music. June 25th jugglers and acrobats
         take over the stage with a comedy routine to lighten
         up your evening.

CART: JOKE FROM SHOW . . . ENDS WITH LAUGHTER . . .

         FADE LAUGHTER UNDER . . .

ANNCR: There's more to come . . . the Chester Community
         Symphony Orchestra, the Downtown Strolling Play-
         ers, Doug Little's Magic Show . . .

MUSIC: "SUMMERTIME" . . . W-C-R JAZZ QUARTET

         INSTRUMENTAL . . . SNEAK IN UNDER . . .

ANNCR: and the W-C-R Jazz Quartet. Enjoy them all . . .
         Thursday evenings, beginning June 18th, at the
         bandshell in Riverside Park.

MUSIC: OUT

FIGURE 4-3   Sample script.

(3) to provide directions for how each sound is to begin, how it is to be played, and how it is to end. Scripts are typed with double or triple spacing between lines. The left margin is 2 inches wide to allow room for notes. The right margin is 1 inch wide. Identifications of each sound and the names of each performer begin at the left margin. Spoken lines of narration or dialogue are indented approximately 1½ inches.

Directions about sound effects, music, or the context in which lines are to be read are typed in upper case so that everyone working on the production can quickly separate technical directions from spoken copy. Lines to be read by the talent are typed in upper and lower case.

Directions to the audio-board operator describe how the sound should begin and how it ends. Typical directions for beginning music might be "sneak in under," "up full," "fade in," "up to establish and fade to background," "cross fade," or "segue." Music might "fade out," "sneak out," or "out." Each of these directions produces a different effect and communicates a different meaning. Fading in a sound is a gradual introduction to that element; beginning the sound at full volume is an abrupt intrusion or arrival of that element. Sneaking music in under the interviewer is often a subtle cue that the interview is ending and the next program segment is about to begin. Establishing a sound calls our attention to it; fading it to the background indicates that although it is still present, something else is more important. A cross fade blends two sounds together by fading in one while the other is fading out, suggesting a close relationship between the two scenes or segments. On the other hand, a segue suggests a more defined separation between the two segments by ending one before beginning the next.

Directions to the talent would include brief comments about how a line should be read or suggestions about what the character is feeling or thinking. Phrases such as "forcefully," "with enthusiasm," "slowly, as he tries to think of a way out," "angrily," or "pause" help the actor or announcer to interpret your intended meaning.

There are several types of scripts with which you should be familiar (Fig. 4-4). One is the *full script.* If you are writing a commercial or public-service announcement, a news story to be read by the anchor, or a radio drama, you would write a full script. The full script includes all the words and all the sound effects that will be heard in the final production.

Another type of script is the *partial script.* If you were writing the script for an interview show or a news feature that included prerecorded segments, you would write a partial script. Since answers to the interviewer's questions or the sound bits recorded on location are almost always spontaneous rather than scripted, the partial script includes the introduction to the program or the feature that will be spoken by the host or reporter. For an interview show, the host's questions might be scripted but the guest's responses would be indicated simply by a mention of the general point covered by the question. Experienced interviewers often prefer to work from a list of topics and ad-lib the questions as the interview progresses. In either case, the partial script allows the interviewer the freedom to follow up on the guest's response. For the feature, the reporter's lead-in to each recorded segment and any transition between segments is scripted, but only the in and out cues—the first and last phrases—of the recorded segments will appear in the script. The close for the program or feature is also scripted.

A third type of script is the *run-down script.* This is the type of script that might be used by the director or board engineer for a show that has a well-established format with standardized recorded elements and ad-lib or scripted segments done live by studio talent. The run-down script consists of a list of the segments that will be included in the show, in the order they will appear, with an indication of the time of each segment, the origin of each, and the in and out cues for each.

PREPRODUCTION TECHNICAL PREPARATION

After the script is written, preproduction moves into the final stage, which involves preparation of all prerecorded elements.

PROGRAM # 13

ZELLERS: In our last two programs we looked at the general character of the American musical stage from 1930 through 1936. In today's program—the last in our series—we're going to finish out the decade.

During the last three years of the 1930's, the depression here at home first deepened, then lifted, while abroad the growing threat of war became an ugly reality. Before the decade was over, Hitler and Mussolini were nibbling away at Europe, Japan was bombing cities in China, Hitler and Stalin had signed a non-aggression pact, and the world was on a roller-coaster ride into World War Two.

How did the American musical stage respond to all of this? Well, for the most part "escape" remained the by-word. But there were exceptions, as there had been earlier in the decade. 1937 was by far the most social-conscious year of the 1930's. Four of the 15 new musicals produced that year took their cue from the headlines of the day. And here's a keynote number from one of those four shows.

MUSIC: "Sing Me a Song of Social Significance"
Album: Pins and Needles   2:47
Side 1, Cut 1

ZELLERS: That was Rose Marie Jun singing the opening number from a 1937 show called *Pins and Needles.* The show was the year's only revue, and it also was the year's biggest success, eventually going through 3 editions and a total run of 1,108 performances. It was a strange animal! A labor show sponsored by the International Ladies Garment Workers' Union and performed by members of that union. Music and lyrics were by outsider Harold Rome, who would later compose scores for shows like *Call Me Mister, Wish You Were Here,* and *Fanny.*

Pins and Needles was a bright and light-hearted show that took pot-shots all over the place—at unemployment, at politics, at events abroad, and even at unionism itself. Have you ever heard a love song expressed through the language of collective bargaining? Well, *Pins and Needles* had one. It was called "One Big Union For Two," and here's Rose Marie Jun again—this time paired up with Jack Carroll—to sing it for us.

MUSIC: Jun & Carroll: "One Big Union for Two"
Album: Pins and Needles   2:53
Side 1, Cut 3

ZELLERS: During much of the 1930s, Labor and Management were at odds, sometimes violently . . . .

A

FIGURE 4-4   (a) A full script sample from one program in a series on the American musical stage with (b) the music play list for that program. (Courtesy of Parker Zellers) (c) Example of a script for a story in a corporate newscast. (Courtesy Domino's Pizza Distribution Corp.) (d) Sample rundown sheet.

PROGRAM # 13
Musical Selections

ITEM	TIME	SOURCE
1. "Sing Me a Song of Social Significance"	2:47	*Pins and Needles* Side 1, Cut 1
2. "One Big Union For Two"	2:53	*Pins and Needles* Side 1, Cut 3
3. Last 2 mins of *Cradle Will Rock*		My Tape (see script for cue) (TAPE REC. STEREO BOTH SIDES)
4. "On the Record"	3:05	*Rodgers & Hart: 1935–1939* Side 2, Cut 1
5. "In the Shade of the New Apple Tree"	4:02	*Harold Sings Arlen* Side 1, Cut 5 (WEMU B-421)
6. "Where or When"	apprx 2:50	Studio Recording
7. "Hail the Political Honeymoon"	1:58	*Stars Over Broadway* Side 2, Cut 3 (see script)
8. "My Heart Belongs to Daddy"	2:34	*Those Wonderful Thirties* Side 4, Cut 3
9. "At the Roxy Music Hall"	2:25	*Rodgers & Hart Revisited* Side 2, Cut 1 (WEMU B-2367)
10. "Falling in Love with Love"	2:35	*Boys from Syracuse* Side 1, Cut 5 (OMITTING VERSE) WEMU #30
11. "Are You Having Any Fun?"	2:30	*Scandals, Follies, etc* EMU Library NW 215 (WEMU also has album)
12. "All the Things You Are"	apprx 2:30	Studio Recording
13. "I Like to Recognize the Tune"	2:40	*Rodgers & Hart: 1935–1939* Side 2, Cut 6
14. "Friendship"	2:32	*Stars Over Broadway* Side 1, Cut 1 (OMITTING OPENING DIALOGUE)

x x x x

B

FIGURE 4-4   (cont.)

Recording on Location

You will often want to use sounds recorded outside the studio. In a news story, for example, you might want to use portions of the actual proceedings of the city council meeting as well as statements from leaders of the citizens' group that is protesting the council's action. For a feature about the new tigers at the

---

WDPD Vol 2 No 7   Cross/Minnesota Anniversary

Being in business for ten years is a great accomplishment. D-N-C Cross/
Minnesota recently held their tenth anniversary. As manager Gregg Cross
told W-D-P-D reporter Kristina Peterson, the day was filled with the Domino's
spirit and a look from the past to the future.

INTERVIEW CROSS #9   In: First, when was the anniversary . . .
                      Out: . . . economically justifiable to do.

Congratulations D-N-C Cross/Minnesota! Here's to ten more years and
ten more, and ten more. . . .

END

C

FIGURE 4-4   (cont.)

---

zoo, you may want to include background sounds of the animals and the spectators. On-the-spot recordings can add authenticity as well as excitement to your
productions; however, they do require careful planning to achieve good technical
quality.

Although it is not always possible, scouting the location is an important first
step. Are there distracting noises that will interfere with your recording? Noisy
fans in ventilating systems, clattering typewriters, machinery, traffic, even hums
from fluorescent lights can overpower the sounds you are trying to record. How
will the acoustics of the room affect microphone placement? Are there enough
electrical outlets? If speakers will be using a public-address system, are there provisions for tapping directly into the auditorium's sound system? Will you need
to use more than one microphone to cover all the sounds you want to record?

Careful evaluation of the location, in addition to careful review of the overall concept for the production, will help you choose the appropriate equipment
for on-location recording. What performance characteristics should the microphone have? A moving-coil dynamic microphone picks up the frequency range
of the human voice quite effectively and is generally more rugged and less apt
to suffer damage. A condenser microphone might need more careful handling
but would give better pick-up on music because of a wider frequency response.
An omnidirectional microphone on a desk stand might work best for a conversation among three people seated around a table. A directional microphone
mounted on the speaker's podium would help isolate the speaker's voice and
eliminate some of the background noise from the audience. A shotgun microphone mounted on a fish-pole could be used to follow a moving speaker and
keep the voice on beam.

What type of tape recorder would be best? A small battery-operated cassette
recorder with a hand-held microphone would allow you to move around quickly.

RUN-DOWN SHEET

Show: Sunrise
Air Time: 5:30–5:44 am
Date: September 16

SEGMENT		SOURCE	TIME
Theme		cart # 27	00:05
Opening	In: This is Sunrise . . . . Out: . . . but first the news.	studio A	00:15
News	In: This is Farm Net News. Out: _____ reporting.	network	02:00
Local news	In: I'm _____ . Out: . . . and now the weather.	studio A	02:00
Weather	In: Good morning . . . . Out: . . . of the U.S. Weather Bureau.	tape #5 (weather net)	02:00
Commodities	In: On the commodities market . . . . Out: . . . reporting for Sunrise.	tape #7	02:00
Interview	In: This morning _____ joins us . . . Out: Thank you for joining us on Sunrise.	cart #10	05:00
Closing	In: Tomorrow we'll be talking with . . . Out: . . . for another edition of Sunrise.	studio A	00:35
Theme		cart #27	00:05

D

FIGURE 4-4 (cont.)

A multitrack reel-to-reel recorder might produce better recording quality but would give you no mobility. Using a digital recorder adds even more equipment.

Can you achieve the effect you want by running the microphone directly into the tape recorder, or do you need to be able to mix the inputs from two or more microphones? If you will need to mix inputs, you'll need a good headset for monitoring the sound mix, along with a portable mixing console.

In addition to microphones, mounting devices, and tape recorders, you will also need batteries or electrical cords and extension cords, plus the cables needed to connect all the pieces of equipment.

A good habit to develop is to test every piece of equipment as you're packing to go out, and to retest every piece as soon as you are set up on location. Equipment does fail, but if you discover it early, you can save yourself the frustration of coming back with tapes that can't be used.

Preparing Sound Bits

In most cases, the recordings you make on location must be edited before they are ready to use in a production. The editing may involve rerecording sound bits you intend to use onto cartridges or splicing them onto a reel of tape with timing leader separating the segments. In many cases, sound effects from records and short music bridges can also be transferred to the cartridge or tape.

It is important to think through the production and organize the prerecorded elements so that they can be cued quickly and accurately in the order in which they will be used. Records may be convenient for playing long passages of music, but trying to cue up a sound effect on a record with many cuts per side is difficult. Cartridges cue automatically. Several cuts can be recorded in sequence with cue tones so that the next cut will be cued automatically. One disadvantage of putting several cuts on one cartridge is that the entire cartridge has to cycle through to replay a cut. Segments on reel-to-reel tape marked with leader tape can be located quickly and cued by sight. Cassette tapes, like records, are more difficult to cue.

As you prepare the audio bits, label each one clearly and then time them. Include this information on the script used in production.

REHEARSAL AND PRODUCTION

Production Team

In audio production, a production team can consist of one person or many. At a small radio station, for example, the deejay may be a one-person production team responsible for everything from planning the show and writing copy to engineering the show and being the on-air talent. At a large advertising agency, many people are involved in the completion of a radio commercial. Whether the production team is small or large, there are certain jobs that must be done. Understanding each team member's responsibilities will help you function more effectively, whether you are filling one role or many.

The *producer* is responsible for overseeing the entire project. This includes controlling the creative process, organizing the people and facilities needed to complete the production, and making sure that the production costs stay within the budget.

The *director* is responsible for turning the producer's concept into a finished production. While the producer may make the final decision on casting, script, and overall production values, it is the director who is in charge of the cast and crew during rehearsal, production, and postproduction.

The *assistant director* may be assigned many duties by a director. A major responsibility during some productions is the timing of the production. During complicated productions, the assistant director may be asked to give some cues or may even be put in charge of some rehearsals.

The *audio engineer* is responsible for everything related to the technical process of recording the production. Such tasks include setting up microphones, checking the sound levels for the performers and all music and sound effects, and following the director's instructions during the production so that each sound begins and ends at the proper time and the mix creates the effect called for in the script.

Production assistants may be assigned any number of jobs. Some may assist the producer in lining up talent, reserving facilities, making arrangements for on-location recordings, and other detail work. Some may assist the director in rehearsals or during production. Some may assist the engineer by setting up microphones, cueing records and tapes, or operating the recorder being used to record the production.

The responsibility of the *talent* is to give the director the performance needed to create the character and mood or meaning required by the script.

In any given production situation, one person may perform more than one job. For example, the producer may also be the director. The talent may also be the audio board operator. But production work is team work; whether the production team is small or large, every member of the team must be cooperative and willing to contribute to make the final production work.

Production Language

In communicating with one another, the members of the production team use both verbal commands and hand signals. Although the specific commands may vary from one production team to another, all try to keep commands short, simple, and clear (Fig. 4-5).

In many audio production facilities, the talent in the studio will be separated from the audio engineer and the director in the control room. Microphones are positioned so that the talent can see the production crew through a glass window. Hand signals are used to communicate from control room to studio (Fig. 4-6). At times, the talent may also wear headphones so that the director or engineer can talk to them or so that they can hear the program audio and take their cue from that. See Fig. 4-7 for an example of a script with commands penciled in the margin.

Command	Meaning
"roll tape"	Start the record tape.
"stop tape"	Stop the record tape.
"open mic"	Bring the fader for the microphone up to the pre-set level.
"close mic"	Bring the fader for the microphone all the way down.
"_____ up"	Quickly bring the volume for that source (music or sound effect on cartridge, cassette, turntable, tape recorder) up to the desired level.
"fade in _____"	Gradually bring the volume for that source up to the desired level.
"sneak in _____"	Very slowly bring the volume for that source up to a background level.
"_____ under"	Bring the volume for that source down to a background level.
"crossfade _____"	Bring the volume for one source all the way down while bringing the volume for the second source up.
"segue _____"	As one sound ends, bring up the volume for the second source with no pause between the two.
"_____ out"	Quickly bring the volume for that source all the way down.
"fade out _____"	Gradually bring the volume for that source all the way down.
"sneak out _____"	Very slowly bring the volume for that source all the way down.
"start ___ dead pot"	Start the source (cartridge, cassette, turntable, tape recorder) with the fader down.
"ready _____"	Get ready to carry out that command.

FIGURE 4-5   Verbal commands.

Back-timing

Most productions are back-timed. That is, the time cues given indicate the time remaining until the end of the production or the end of the particular segment. The frequency of time cues depends upon the length of the production and the preference of the director or talent. During a network program, the director or talent at the local affiliate may want a time cue to alert them to an upcoming cut-away for the local news insert and, depending upon the length of the local newscast, other time cues with a countdown to help them end the local segment and rejoin the network on time. Other directors or talent may prefer to watch the clock themselves and want few, if any, time cues. If prerecorded segments are used during the show, the directors or talent may want time cues while

A

B

C

D

E

FIGURE 4-6 Hand signals are used to communicate with talent. (a) Talk so the audio board operator can take a level. (b) Move away from the microphone. (c) Move toward the microphone. (d) Standby. (e) Cue. Start talking. You're on the air.

F

G

H

I

J

FIGURE 4-6   (cont.)
(f) Speed up. (g) Slow down. (h) 30 seconds left. (i) Wrap it up. 15 seconds left. (j) Cut.

roll tape
open mic

	CLIENT:	Montville Chamber of Commerce
	MEDIA:	Radio
	TIME:	30-second
	DATE:	begin June 11

music up
and under
| | MUSIC: | SOUSA MARCH UP TO ESTABLISH AND UNDER . . . |

cue | | ANNCR: | Enjoy summer in the park! The Montville Concert Band opens the season June 18th with a program of rousing music. June 25th jugglers and acrobats take over the stage with a comedy routine to lighten up your evening. |

cart up
cart under | CART: | JOKE FROM SHOW . . . ENDS WITH LAUGHTER . . . |
| | | FADE LAUGHTER UNDER . . . |

cue | | ANNCR: | There's more to come . . . the Chester Community Symphony Orchestra, the Downtown Strolling Players, Doug Little's Magic Show . . . |

sneak music in | MUSIC: | "SUMMERTIME" . . . W-C-R JAZZ QUARTET |
| | | INSTRUMENTAL . . . SNEAK IN UNDER . . . |

| | ANNCR: | and the W-C-R Jazz Quartet. Enjoy them all . . . Thursday evenings, beginning June 18th, at the bandshell in Riverside Park. |

music out
close mic
stop tape | MUSIC: | OUT |

FIGURE 4-7 An example of the director's commands used in producing this script.

the prerecorded segments are playing in order to be ready for the end of the recording.

The audio engineer may also back-time some recorded elements. If, for example, the theme music is 60 seconds long and the last note should end the program, the record must be started 60 seconds before the program is to end. You would not usually want the audience to hear the theme for that long a period, so the audio engineer would begin the record with the potentiometer or fader down ("dead pot") and bring the volume up when the director called for theme (Fig. 4-8).

Rehearsal

Before calling the talent and crew together for a rehearsal, the director should have a clear idea of how all the production elements fit together to create meaning and mood. Developing this idea may involve conferences with the producer and writer. It involves careful study of the script.

TIMING RUNDOWN

Show: Midday
Air time: 12:00:00–12:28:30 pm

Segment	Segment Time	Elapsed Time (end of segment)	Back Time (end of segment)
Start		12:00:00	00:28:30
Opening	00:00:30	12:00:30	00:28:00
News	00:10:00	12:10:30	00:18:00
Commercial	00:01:00	12:11:30	00:17:00
Weather	00:01:00	12:12:30	00:16:00
Consumer Corner Interview	00:04:00	12:16:30	00:12:00
Commercial	00:01:00	12:17:30	00:11:00
Listener call-in	00:06:30	12:24:00	00:04:30
What's New Feature	00:02:00	12:26:00	00:02:30
Commercial	00:01:00	12:27:00	00:01:30
Consumer Calendar	00:01:00	12:28:00	00:00:30
Closing	00:00:30	12:28:30	00:00:00

FIGURE 4-8   Back time indicates time remaining to the end of the show.

At the first rehearsal, it is helpful if the director discusses the script with the cast and crew and explains the overall effect they are being asked to achieve. A first run-through should help establish the style of the vocal delivery, ensure proper microphone placement, and familiarize everyone with how the live and prerecorded elements fit together. A second run-through can concentrate on timing. The number of additional rehearsals needed depends on the complexity of the production and the experience of the cast and crew.

PRODUCTION

The actual production proceeds much as a rehearsal does, with a few exceptions. If the program is being aired live, it continues uninterrupted even if mistakes are made. If the program is being taped for later use, one or more takes may be recorded. If errors are made, the tape can be stopped while the director decides on a good place in the script to start again so that, in postproduction, the two partial takes can be edited together. If the director has allowed the recording to

continue but decides that a particular line could be more effective with a different reading, that line can be recorded and edited into the program later.

POSTPRODUCTION

As indicated, postproduction may involve editing segments together or correcting mistakes by replacing one section of the tape with another. Postproduction
may also involve adding additional sound tracks to the mix. For example, ambient sound from location can be mixed with the voice segments recorded in the
studio, or a music bed can be added under the voice. It would also include adding
the proper leader to the tape and labeling the tape for identification.

SUMMARY

To produce an effective audio message, you must consider the requirements for good
communication, the possibilities and limitations of the technology, and the needs of the
organization within which you are working. These factors affect decisions made during
preproduction planning, preproduction technical preparation, production, and postproduction.

Preproduction planning encompasses all the steps leading up to the preparation of
the actual script for the production. It begins with decisions about the purpose of the
message and an analysis of the intended audience and the circumstances in which they
will hear the message. The information about the subject needed for the script is gathered
through research. In choosing the approach that will be used, decisions are made about
the overall style, patterns of organization, and production elements that will be included.
Permissions to use copyrighted materials are secured. A detailed list of the production
facilities that will be needed is made. A budget is written. All of this information is then
written into the treatment, which describes the purpose of the project, the actual content
of the production, and the resources needed to complete the production.

Writing the script is the final step of preproduction planning. For some productions, you will write a full script. For others, a partial script or a run-down script is more
appropriate.

Preproduction technical preparation involves preparing all the sound bits that will
be used in the final production. This may require recording on location. Scouting the
location will help you decide what microphones, audio mixers, cables, and other accessories will be needed. Most on-location recordings require editing. Other sound effects and
music inserts can be transferred to a cartridge for easier cueing.

During rehearsal and production, the members of the production team perform
specialized functions. The producer is responsible for overseeing the entire project. The
director translates the producer's ideas into the finished production. An assistant director
may be assigned various responsibilities, including timing the production. The audio engineer coordinates the technical process of recording the production. One or more production assistants may perform a variety of tasks. Talent follows the director's signals in
performing the script. In communicating with one another, the members of the production team use both verbal and hand cues.

The production itself may be live, or it may be recorded.

In postproduction, segments are edited together, errors are corrected, and the sound track is "sweetened" by mixing in other sound effects and music.

For Further Reading

JOSEPHSON, LARRY, ed. *Telling the Story: The National Public Radio Guide to Radio Journalism.* (Dubuque, Iowa: Kendall/Hunt, 1983).

ORLIK, PETER B. *Broadcast Copywriting.* (Boston: Allyn & Bacon, 1986).

chapter five _____

Applications: Audio Production _____

INTRODUCTION

Thus far we've attempted to help you appreciate the unique potential of audio messages to communicate with many different audiences. We've described commonly used production equipment, and we've suggested an approach that will help you create effective audio productions.

In this chapter, we'd like to introduce you to professionals working in a variety of production situations and share with you their comments about how they approach specific assignments. As you'll note, several common concerns exist, despite the differences in audience, purpose, and production situation. One of these is the need for planning and thorough preparation. Whether they were describing the process of reserving telephone lines for a remote broadcast or lining up guests for a show, all stressed the importance of work done before the actual production begins.

Another common theme is the importance of team work. The creative ideas that come from brainstorming or the ease with which the production itself is carried out all stem from the interaction between members of the production team. In comments that were made about specific situations, it was clear that these professionals not only respect but also enjoy working with people who think of themselves as members of a team working to accomplish a common goal.

In addition, most of the people to whom we talked mentioned the need to respond quickly and creatively to production problems. Many were working on limited budgets and had to find alternate solutions to technical needs. Some have faced last-minute failure of equipment or changes in program content. All are committed to high technical quality in the work they do.

PRODUCING RADIO COMMERCIALS

One of the challenges for both writers and production personnel at radio stations is to create commercials that keep listeners tuned in while selling the product or service. At radio station WIQB-FM, continuity director Tony McReynolds and production director Rob Reinhart have developed an approach that works well for local clients. As an example of that approach, they described how one commercial was produced.

The process typically begins when the radio sales person brings in an order from the client. In this case, the order was from Kitchen Port, a store specializing in items needed to prepare and serve anything from a snack to a gourmet meal. Kitchen Port wanted to let the public know about its new bridal registry service. Specific information to be included was a listing of the types of merchandise available, a free-gift offer for brides who registered, a mystery gift, and a tie-in with a free wedding-planning booklet that was being published in the community. The client wanted a commercial that would be funny and creative, but they had no preconceived ideas about it.

As the writer, McReynolds approached the assignment by thinking about the client. Kitchen Port was an unusual place to register for gifts, so the ad would have to make Kitchen Port memorable. In addition, the spot was a product ad, but unlike most products, the features of the bridal registry could not be neatly summarized in one line. They had to include a long list of items to sell, specific information about the service, and the client's address. Holding a listener's attention through all of that would be a problem.

In working together as a creative team, McReynolds and Reinhart have developed a personal approach to copywriting. They try to make each spot "listenable," with at least one funny line, effect, character, or style of delivery to create repeat interest. As they point out, the same commercial will be played many times; humor that relies on a punch line or a pun wears out rapidly, so such a spot loses its entertainment value. Instead, they try to build humor into the characters' personalities. The fun comes from absurd comments their characters make about absurd situations. As he is writing, McReynolds knows how the lines will sound when delivered because he and Reinhart are also the talent for their commercials.

The basic structure for the commercials they develop is humor-announcer-humor. The first line is written to give the listener time to adjust to the fact that a new announcement has started and to establish the scenario in which the characters are involved. The first gag is planned to get the listeners' attention. The second gag is set up before the announcer comes in to provide factual information, such as the client's address and hours of operation. The end of the spot provides a resolution for the second gag so that the listener has a reason to keep listening through the announcer's message. Rather than ending with a punch line, the commercials often end with the dialogue fading out as the characters are still talking.

For Kitchen Port, the ad was to be directed to women, who traditionally register for bridal registries. From their experience, McReynolds and Reinhart believe that in radio both men and women will listen more to a man's voice. A radio ad directed to women could be performed by a man. This became the basis for the first gag in the spot. A man would register for the Kitchen Port bridal registry. McReynolds was counting on people's reaction of surprise to break through the clutter that surrounds any radio commercial. The second gag was planned to help sell the service. A man was going to get married in order to get all those great gifts from Kitchen Port. The dialogue exchange is funny, but it never loses sight of Kitchen Port or the idea that Kitchen Port is a good place to register for wedding gifts. Instead, the second gag is used as a way to break up the long list of items to be sold. (Figure 5-1 is a copy of the Kitchen Port commercial script.)

After the spot was written, it was submitted to the client for approval. Then production began. The usual procedure for McReynolds and Reinhart is to read through a script once to familiarize themselves with the copy. A second reading is done to time the spot. A third is done for timing the jokes and to smooth out any rough spots. The tape is running on this third reading because what happens spontaneously in this take is often funny and can't be recaptured in later takes. By this time the copy is memorized, so the talent can work on refining the delivery and the overlapping dialogue.

At this stage, the Kitchen Port ad started changing. The original characters just weren't working. The script was good, but the characters were too exaggerated. The idea of a yuppie lunch came up. In that context, the characters evolved into two rather matter-of-fact characters. That low-key delivery fit right into McReynolds and Reinhart's style of saying things in a funny way rather than saying funny things.

Because of the fast pace of the dialogue and the overlapping lines, the spot had to be recorded in one take. Stopping to pick up from a mistake and rerecord lines didn't work. After the dialogue was completed, background sound effects were added to create a piano-bar atmosphere. Then the spot was mixed down to a cartridge for use on the air.

In producing commercials, Reinhart insists on crisp, clear technical quality. He uses a four-track recorder, and the dialogue for each character is put on a separate track so that the volume levels and equalization can be adjusted separately in mixdown. The announcer is put on a third track, and sound effects are added to the fourth track.

In talking about local radio production, McReynolds and Reinhart identified some of the problems and some of the advantages they experience. Radio commercials tend to be clustered, so in any given commercial break, two or three of the spots that they have created may be aired. Thus they are constantly competing with themselves to win the listeners' attention. They also have a high volume of commercials to write and produce. As a result, they are always working under pressure to get spots produced and on the air rapidly. After the copy is written, the usual production time for a commercial is 10 minutes. By contrast, production time for the Kitchen Port spot ran close to 3 hours. That was possible because of the creative freedom that working at a local station provides. As both

SFX: PIANO BAR MUSIC AND CROWD IN BACKGROUND

FRIEND:	Bob, I just got your wedding invitation and . . .
BOB:	I'm in the Kitchen Port bridal registry, too. So you'll have no problem finding me just the right gift.
FRIEND:	Right. But this says, announcing the marriage of Bob and TBA. Who's TBA?
BOB:	To be announced.
FRIEND:	To be announced?
BOB:	At a later date.
FRIEND:	Bob . . .
BOB:	See, I haven't actually proposed to anyone yet.
FRIEND:	You need a bride, Bob.
BOB:	Oh, I know. But weddings take such a long time to organize. That's why the first thing I did was register with Kitchen Port's bridal registry. No one can stock a newlywed's kitchen like Kitchen Port.
FRIEND:	They do have great wedding gifts.
BOB:	Fine glassware, cutlery, china, linens . . .
FRIEND:	You do need a bride, Bob.
BOB:	Really nifty appliances.
FRIEND:	I don't think you can cut this corner, Bob.
BOB:	See, this way I know I'll get wedding gifts I can really use. Neat things you can't find in most stores.
FRIEND:	Bob . . .
BOB:	They even gave me a free gift just for registering.
FRIEND:	Cart before the horse, Bob.
BOB:	And Kitchen Port offers those little extra services to make wedding plans easier. Expert advice, free gift wrapping with delivery available. Even a free copy of the Ann Arbor Wedding Consultant, a really helpful booklet on planning a wedding.
FRIEND:	That's good, Bob, because I'm sure it'll tell you that when you're planning a wedding you need a bride first.
BOB:	Well, I'll just use the bridal registry to register for a bride.
FRIEND:	You can't do that, Bob.
BOB:	Really?
FRIEND:	Really.
BOB:	Well, I think the name's a little misleading.
FRIEND:	Not for most people.
BOB:	Really? I would have thought . . .
SFX:	OUT
ANNCR:	The Kitchen Port bridal registry for the wedding gift you'll love to use. In Kerrytown, 415 North Fifth Avenue, in Ann Arbor.

FIGURE 5-1 Script for Kitchen Port ad. (Courtesy of Reinhart, McReynolds & Magnus Audio Advertising)

writer and one of the voices for the commercial, McReynolds had the freedom to change the copy when it did not seem to be working during production. By contrast, ads created by an advertising agency go through many approval stages and must be recorded as written with no changes.

MUSIC RECORDING

Interlochen Arts Academy, located in northern Michigan, is internationally recognized for the excellence of the training its young students receive in music, theatre, dance, and the visual arts. As manager of recording services, David Greenspan is responsible for recording many of the musical performances. These recordings have several purposes. Stored in the archives, they serve as a document of the various concerts presented by the students. As coproducer for the nationally syndicated radio program "Music from Interlochen," Greenspan selects the best for use on that program. Some of the recordings are used as study tapes for faculty and students. Other sessions are edited into audition tapes for the students.

All recording is done on 1/4-inch, two-track stereo recorders at 15 inches per second. A dbx noise-reduction system is used to permit a greater dynamic range, more clarity during soft passages, and no distortion of loud passages. Because most concerts are longer than the recording time on one reel of tape, two machines are used so that the second can be started before the first has run out. If one reel ends in the middle of a selection, the two reels can be edited together in postproduction. Condenser microphones are used because they have a better frequency response.

In setting up for the recording session, the heads and the tape-transport system on the recorders are cleaned. Each machine is checked visually for overall working condition and signs of wear. The tapes are then threaded, and the levels on the audio console and the recorders are calibrated by recording a 1-kHz tone at 0 dB with the dbx system off. (The dbx system can give misleading levels.) A 10-kHz tone is then recorded. (-10 kHz is used if the recording speed is 7½.) This is followed by a section of blank tape or leader tape. The dbx unit is turned on and the recorders are ready.

Ideally, when recording a live session, all microphones and mix levels are set in rehearsal. At times, a test recording is made and played for the conductor, who can then request changes in the mix. In reality, it is not always possible to set levels in rehearsal. In such a case, experience and expertise are invaluable in finding the correct levels quickly during the first number. Under such conditions, that first selection is often considered lost.

The number and placement of microphones varies according to where the recording is to be made and which group is being recorded. Two concerts recorded in Corson Auditorium in May 1987 provide examples of the difference.

The first was a concert by the 69-member Interlochen Arts Academy Band. For this event, a stereo microphone was suspended from the ceiling of the audito-

FIGURE 5-2   From the audio booth at Corson Auditorium, the recording engineer has a clear view of the stage. (Courtesy of Wayne Brill, Interlochen Center for the Arts)

rium. This microphone contained a Blumlein pair that feeds into a pattern-control box, allowing the pattern to be adjusted for more or less left–right separation. Except for adding a bit of reverberation, the signal was not processed.

The second was a jazz concert by the studio orchestra. For this concert, in addition to the Blumlein left–right pair, 14 microphones were added for the instruments and six for the drum kit. The Blumlein pair provided the overall pickup of the orchestra. The individual microphones served as accents for particular sections or solo instruments. This mix, too, was fed through a reverberation unit for added brightness.

To make setup easier and faster, microphone cables were grouped by the section of the orchestra to which they ran, and each group was fastened together in a snake. Microphone stands were designated for specific instruments. Connectors were labeled to indicate instrument and connector-box channel. Monitors for the musicians were set up on stage left and stage right, one near the drums and one near the french horns.

During setup, each instrument does a sound check to set levels. The house and monitor mix is then checked with the full orchestra. The audio console allows the sound engineer to feed three separate mixes: one to the speakers in the auditorium, one to the monitors on stage, and one to the tape recorders. The mixes will be different because the audience is hearing the actual orchestra enhanced by the loudspeaker mix. If the tape recorder were to receive only the loudspeaker mix, the balance between the various instruments would not duplicate what the audience hears, so a separate record mix is needed.

In describing the effect he is trying to create in the recording, Greenspan explains that what he hears when sitting in the audience is what he tries to make happen on the tape. His objective is to record the event as accurately as possible. A good stereo mix should enable the listener to point to where each instrument is located.

Working in an educational setting such as this requires both good technical skills and good human relations skills. As Greenspan points out, in order to produce high-quality recordings, one needs to understand not only the equipment but also how to trouble-shoot and solve technical problems. In addition to understanding the operation of the technical system used for recording, one must also understand the organizational system of the institution. Successful recording sessions often require working with a variety of people, convincing them of your technical needs, and obtaining cooperation from several departments.

NETWORK BROADCAST OF A LIVE EVENT

The Montreux Jazz Festival is a summer tradition in Detroit, Michigan (Fig. 5-3). For several years, the concerts staged in Hart Plaza were carried by area public radio station WEMU. In 1984, they were carried live by the National Public Radio (NPR) network. In all, WEMU was feeding the network six hours of live programming each night for four days. Harold Beer, currently studio engineer at WKAR, was then the chief engineer for the network feed. He described the process of organizing the broadcast.

Planning started about two months before the broadcast. Festival organizers had hired a sound reinforcement contractor to provide the microphone setup and sound mix for the public-address (PA) system and for the on-stage monitors

FIGURE 5-3 Montreux Jazz Festival. (Courtesy of WEMU)

for the musicians. Arrangements were made with that contractor to provide a split to feed the output of the microphones to WEMU.

NPR was contacted to arrange for the necessary time on the satellite for the broadcast. Provisions were then made for a transportable satellite uplink to be moved to the festival site in Hart Plaza.

The budget was limited. The largest expenditure was for satellite time for the broadcast. Next were the fees paid to the musicians. The remaining costs were for personnel and equipment. It was necessary to borrow and rent equipment other than that owned by the station. For example, a 24-channel audio board was rented for the music mix, which was to be done by a free-lancer who specialized in live music mixes.

Personnel were located at three sites: the stage itself, the remote truck, and the satellite uplink location. The director had overall responsibility for getting the broadcast on and off the air on time. A schedule of events had been sent to each station that was going to carry the broadcast. With all the potential delays and changes inherent in live events, a major concern for the director was keeping the broadcast as close to the schedule as possible. The director controlled the timing of breaks for network identification or local announcements. In addition, to fill the time between sets, the director was responsible for scheduling guests for interviews. A production assistant and a stage director worked with the director. The stage director served as the link between the director and the performers, the PA technicians, and others backstage.

The engineering staff included a recording engineer, a broadcast mix engineer, an uplink engineer, and a chief engineer, who coordinated the technical operations. In addition, a production assistant was assigned to the recording truck to relay information from the stage to the recording engineer, to load tape machines and label tapes, to time the performance, and to perform other tasks as needed. Two local announcers served as on-air talent.

On the day before the broadcast, all the gear was assembled and checked. Cables were then run from the on-stage microphones to the recording truck, where the mix for the broadcast and the music recording was to be done. Two Ampex 440 recorders were used so that the recording could be lapped by starting a second reel as the first was running out. Lines were run from the remote truck to the broadcast location, where the local announcers and taped features were to be mixed with the music feed from the recording truck. Other lines relayed this broadcast mix to the satellite uplink.

A video camera set up on stage fed a monitor in the recording truck so that the engineer could watch the stage to anticipate solos by the various musicians and introductions by the stage announcer. Voice communication links between truck and stage helped in solving problems such as microphone placement. Telephones were installed at both the broadcast and uplink sites.

The festival's program schedule called for each group to play for 60 or 90 minutes, with 30 minutes between groups for the stage change. The PA feed provided 24 channels, with no fewer than 8 channels being used for any act. To simplify the change between bands, some instruments were assigned particular channels. For example, the microphones for the drums would be in the same channels for all groups. In addition, the recording engineer added equalization, reverberation, and a compressor to the feed from the stage. For the broadcast mix, two ambience microphones were added—one for left and one for right channels—as well as announcer microphones.

In choosing and placing microphones, the PA system operators were concerned about feedback, so they chose rugged microphones with tight pickup patterns. For music recording and broadcast, the WEMU engineers were more concerned about using microphones that would provide high-quality sound and placing them to minimize leakage from one instrument into another instrument's microphone. To resolve differences, extra microphones were added where needed for the broadcast signal.

In evaluating the broadcast, Beer emphasized the importance of comprehensive planning, good communication, and being prepared to deal with problems as they occur. A misunderstanding with the festival planners led to an uncertain source of power for the uplink. That created delays in setup. Another problem stemmed from the fact that the stage lighting was not available until the night of the first broadcast. The electrical noise created by the light dimmers and some bad connections radiated into the audio cables, creating buzzes and hums. Locating and eliminating all of these wasn't finished until the second night of the broadcast.

For a live broadcast of this duration to go smoothly, good communication between all units is essential. Although communication links had been planned, it quickly became apparent that the chief engineer, who was moving from site to site, needed a walkie-talkie or pager so that he would be contacted quickly as problems arose. The director also needed better communication links with the broadcast engineer. They had visual contact, but hand signals were sometimes confusing and, at night, weren't always visible. In general, better communication between locations was needed to enable staff to respond to problems quickly.

Important, too, was the ability to anticipate and repair breakdowns. Working with such a variety of equipment, much of it unfamiliar, meant having a dozen of every type of connector that might be needed as well as extra cable and a hot soldering iron to make up cables or repair broken ones. Since audiotape equipment goes out of alignment easily when moved—and on a remote everything was being moved—routine checks were done on the tape recorders.

Although the entire production might have been easier if the budget had been larger, one of the greatest challenges for the crew was to produce a network-quality remote live music broadcast with limited resources.

LOCAL SPORTS REMOTE

Another example of remote radio production is the sports broadcast. As production manager at WUOM-FM, Peggy J Watson's responsibilities have included engineering the broadcasts of the University of Michigan football games carried by

WUOM. For these broadcasts, her job is to make sure all the pregame technical arrangements are made, to set up the equipment at the remote site, to serve as engineer at the remote location, and to coordinate the broadcast with the board operator on duty at the WUOM studios.

For the home games, pregame planning involves checking the remote equipment and packing it for the trip to the stadium. The press box at the stadium has existing phone lines running directly to the board at WUOM, so the mixing board can be connected to those lines. Phone lines must be ordered for away games, and Watson arrives at the location several hours early to make sure that the lines have been installed and are working properly. Then a phone coupler is used to enable the remote engineer to dial the studio to establish an open line for the broadcast.

Other equipment used for the typical broadcast includes a receiver used to monitor the air signal, headsets, and microphones. To allow members of the remote crew to communicate with one another, headsets are worn by the engineer, the play-by-play announcer, the color announcer, the statistician, and the spotter. Each headset is connected to the talkback system via a separate box equipped with a cough switch to let each person control when his microphone is feeding the system. The headsets allow the crew to monitor two feeds: the program out from the mixing board at the stadium and the air signal being broadcast by the station. Only the two announcers' microphones are connected to the mixing board. The announcers use high-quality condenser microphones fitted with windscreens. A parabolic microphone mounted on the roof of the stadium is used to

FIGURE 5-4   In the University of Michigan press box, radio announcers use a video monitor for a closeup view and replays. (Courtesy of University of Michigan Photo Services)

pick up ambient sound. Wind sometimes moves this microphone out of alignment, so the engineer is always prepared to drop an omnidirectional microphone out of the press-box window to pick up the crowd noise and music at halftime.

Once the equipment is in place, the loose cables are taped down so people won't trip over them. The remote engineer then uses a regular telephone to call from the press box to the studio. This line is left open during the broadcast to allow direct communication between press box and studio.

As part of the setup procedure, the engineer at the stadium feeds a tone back to the studio. The board operator at the studio matches levels with the mixing console there.

During the broadcast itself, it is difficult to predict which announcer will talk and when. So the announcers use the talkback switches to control when their microphones are actually open. Although the remote engineer doesn't open and close those microphones, she does ride gain on all of the microphones and on the mix that is fed back to the studio.

At the studio, the board operator inserts the open and closing themes, the station identifications, and other breaks. Because this team has worked together for so many years, a script or rundown sheet isn't needed. The remote announcer simply uses standard cues whenever the studio operator is to take over for an insert from the studio.

In talking about the problems she encounters in covering the games, Watson listed wear and tear on the equipment first. One of the most common problems is static or shorts caused by broken wires. To be prepared for this, she always takes along extra microphones and cables. Other problems occur during the game when the announcers forget to close the talkback switch and thus inadvertently find themselves on the air. Watson also mentioned the importance of watching levels during the game, especially when the announcers are excited.

On the road, a major concern is whether the phone company will have the lines ready to relay the broadcast back to the WUOM studios. The quality of these remote feeds may differ because some phone lines sound better than others. The satellite, when it is available, provides consistently clear sound quality.

These remote broadcasts are recorded at the studio. The tapes are saved by the announcer to be used for highlights and features in future broadcasts. Watson listens to them to check the overall technical quality of the broadcast and to find ways to improve the next broadcast.

RADIO TALK SHOW

When radio listeners in southeast Michigan and northwest Ohio tune in to the J. P. McCarthy morning show, they hear a fast-paced mix of news, sports, commercials, music, and interviews on a wide range of subjects. It's a mix delivered with a flair that has made McCarthy a Detroit favorite and radio station WJR a consistent leader in a highly competitive market.

What those listeners don't hear is what happens off the air, behind the scenes, as the bits and pieces of the program are being pulled together. Bill Plegue, the show's producer, describes his position as being at the heart of the show.

Plegue's day starts at 4:15 AM, when he arrives at the station and makes the coffee. Until the show goes on the air at 6:00 AM, he collects dates and historical facts that might be interesting sidelights for the listeners. He scans the computer news feed for features and light stories. He prepares the sports copy and the sports cuts to be used on the air. Then he lines up the guests that were booked the day before to be interviewed by telephone.

The show follows a clock-hour format (Fig. 5-5). The news segments are prepared and reported by the WJR news department. The music is programmed by the computer on a random-selection basis from the play lists compiled by the music director. For his program, McCarthy has the right to make changes in that preprogrammed list and to request other selections from the music library.

Plegue thinks in terms of two audiences: one that listens from 6:00 to

---

CLOCK HOUR FORMAT

00:00–12:30	news
12:30–15:30	music
15:30–16:30	spot
16:30–25:00	interview
25:00–27:00	traffic/weather
28:00–30:00	spot
30:00–33:00	news
33:00–34:00	spot
34:00–35:00	traffic
35:00–36:00	spot
36:00–44:00	sports
44:00–45:00	spot
45:00–48:00	weather
48:00–50:00	spot/interview cut
53:00–55:00	traffic
55:00–57:00	spot
57:00–58:30	instrumental music
59:00–00:00	spot

EXCEPTIONS TO CLOCK HOUR

8:30:00–8:35:00	Paul Harvey
8:35:00–8:36:00	spot
8:36:00–8:37:30	traffic
8:37:30–8:38:30	spot
8:38:30–8:44:00	sports

FIGURE 5-5   Clock hour format for the J. P. McCarthy morning show. (Courtesy of Bill Plegue.)

8:00 AM and a second that listens from 8:00 to 10:00 AM. Thus, highlights from some guest interviews can be repeated later. Since a tape is always running on the show, Plegue can work with Cliff Coleman, the director, to cue up specific segments or comments from the interviews that McCarthy may want to use again.

Another of the producer's responsibilities during the show is to screen the listeners' calls. In response to questions, listeners can call in to offer their comments. Plegue answers the phone and decides whether to put the caller on the air. This responsibility obviously requires sound judgment about which callers to put on the air and a great deal of tact in handling those who are not chosen.

Once the show is off the air, Plegue takes a short break and then returns to his office to prepare for the next day. The show is built on the assumption that people want information, so much of Plegue's time is spent reading, listening, and watching for interesting material. Once an idea suggests itself, research must be done, background information collected, and guests located for the interviews. Four to six guests are usually booked for each show.

In discussing his job, Plegue stressed the importance of good public relations skills. He is constantly dealing with people, often asking them to be awake and available for interviews at times that are not convenient for them because of their own schedules or time zone differences. Team spirit, too, is important to the success of the show. He and Coleman work as a team to make sure that each show goes smoothly, and he relies on Coleman's opinions when checking out new ideas for the show.

For anyone who wants to become a producer, Plegue recommends getting as much experience as possible, being willing to start out in a small market, working hard, being versatile, and learning to deal with the pressures that go with broadcasting.

RADIO NEWS

Clark Smith is news director at WEMU-FM, a public radio affiliate. Among the beat reporters he supervises are college students working on a part-time basis to gain experience in broadcast journalism. In addition to maintaining high standards in writing and reporting, these students are expected to produce good technical quality in the recordings they prepare for the newscasts.

A reporter assigned to cover a local story, such as a meeting of the city council, usually takes along a cassette tape recorder, a dynamic microphone, and a good-quality tape. The tape recorder must be capable of producing a broadcast-quality recording and must have both microphone-level and line-level inputs as well as an output jack.

Before the meeting, the reporter scans the agenda and makes judgments about which items are likely to produce stories with news value. Then, during appropriate breaks in the meeting or after it, the reporter interviews participants and records their comments.

Back at the studio, the story is written and the audio segments to be used on air as actualities are transferred from cassette to cartridge. The audio bites usually are not edited. If editing is needed, care is taken to avoid changing the meaning of the interviewee's comments. For ease of editing, the cassette is dubbed to reel, then edited and transferred to cartridge. In the on-air reporter's script, the sound bite is identified by name of speaker, cartridge number, and out cue.

If the beat reporter is to record the entire story, the sound bite is transferred to cartridge; the reporter then records the story onto reel, inserting the sound bite. The recording is done on reel because it is much easier to edit to correct errors. When complete, the recorded story is transferred to cartridge for use in the newscast (Fig. 5-6).

At times, interviews are done by telephone. For these, the telephone voicer can be recorded directly onto cartridge.

Another source of voicers are news feeds from Michigan Public Radio. These feeds are received via satellite and recorded onto reel-to-reel tape. The stories selected for use are then transferred to cartridge.

A major concern is maintaining good quality in the recordings. FM listeners are accustomed to high fidelity and expect it not only in music, but also in voice. Another concern is sensitivity to the difference between the VU meter level and the apparent volume level created by presence in the voice recording. Ideally, this sense of presence must be consistent from live voice to recorded voice. This is accomplished by careful placement of the microphone when recording in the field.

FIGURE 5-6   WEMU newscast. (Courtesy of WEMU)

CORPORATE NEWS

Corporations have traditionally used newsletters, memoranda, and other print materials to communicate with employees. These materials are intended to keep employees informed about company policies and activities, to create a corporate identity, and to provide instructions about how to carry out specific tasks. Many companies are turning to video productions to accomplish these goals. While less common, some are making use of audio recordings. Domino's Pizza Distribution Corp. is one such company. This company acts as a supplier for local franchisees and, like its parent company, recognizes the importance of providing information and training to employees to increase their motivation and productivity.

As director of audiovisual communications for Domino's Pizza Distribution Corp., Jeff Smith had been involved in using audio tapes as training and motivational materials targeted for the very narrow audience of the company's certified dough makers. When he realized that the company's drivers were not being reached by existing information networks, he turned to audio. The drivers making cross-country deliveries were, with their partners, on the road for 24 hours at a time and were isolated from much corporate activity. An audio cassette that they could take along in the truck seemed to be the answer. WDPD was created.

At first the WDPD tapes were limited to information useful specifically to the drivers, but as the drivers began to carry the tapes around, other employees wanted a similar service. Thus the content of the tapes was expanded to include critical issues that affect the entire company.

As executive producer and cohost, Smith is responsible for the content of the show. One of his goals is to reinforce the company's philosophy, values, and attitudes. In each show, he tries to include information about all segments of the corporation. News stories are designed to provide information about where the company stands and where it is going. Ideas for the show come from many sources. Each operational unit of the company is polled for information, the staff watches various publications for stories, and activities of all executive groups are monitored via their newsletters and updates.

A new WDPD tape is produced each month. Each is approximately 90 minutes long. Recording and duplication is planned so that the tapes can be distributed at the beginning of the month.

The WDPD staff includes Smith, cohost Elaine Cockerham, a reporter, and a free-lance director. The staff meets twice a month to critique the last show and discuss ideas for the next. As ideas are generated, specific assignments are made. Gathering information for the show continues right up to air time.

The format for WDPD is similar to that of a radio talk show. Each show contains a mixture of straight news stories read by the cohosts, voicers from pre-recorded telephone interviews, and music. Most stories emphasize the activities and accomplishments of specific employees. To further personalize the show, the cohosts often provide informal ad-libs or comments on the news stories.

Rather than make an investment to equip and maintain an audio production facility, Smith finds it more cost-effective to do the actual production in an outside sound-recording studio. Taping and postproduction usually takes a full day. The session begins as the director distributes copies of the script to the co-hosts and provides the recording engineer with the voicers that have been edited onto reel-to-reel tape. The script includes a run-down page with each segment and its time length listed in order. The talent script includes the in and out cues for each tape bite. The engineer has a second run-down sheet, which includes the location of each voicer on the tapes, the in and out cues, and the running time. Music selections are on cassette. Sound effects are occasionally added from the studio's CD library.

During the session, the cohosts work in a sound booth on separate micro-phones. Headsets allow them to monitor the program audio. The director, work-ing with the recording engineer in the control room, can communicate with them through a talkback system. Since the show is being recorded rather than broad-cast "live," any one of the team can ask to stop the recording to make changes in the script, correct mistakes, or add elements that would make the tape more interesting.

Recording is done on a four-track recorder. Each microphone is assigned to a separate track, voicers are put on another, and music is put on the fourth. This method allows the engineer the flexibility of rewinding and correcting one track without touching the other tracks during the recording session. During mix-down, the ability to control the separate tracks individually gives the engineer more precise control of the final mix.

WDPD was created to fill a specific need. In talking about its success with its intended audience and with others who have become regular listeners, Smith emphasized the usefulness of this type of communication in helping to reinforce corporate philosophy, values, and attitudes (PVAs). To him, these PVAs are essen-tial in establishing the way in which the corporation functions, so they need to be understood by every employee.

In addition, Smith is aware of the number of otherwise valuable employees who, because of a learning disability, have difficulty getting information through printed materials. He sees audiotapes as a practical and useful way to provide training and information for these employees.

AUDIO FOR VIDEO

As in radio, audio for video productions may be done in the studio or on loca-tion, using the techniques of live production or editing in postproduction. The specific needs of video productions are discussed in detail in the chapters that follow, but some of the important differences are worth mentioning here.

Television studio production presents several challenges to the audio engi-neer. First, acoustics in television studios are often far from ideal. In the typical television studio, hard, smooth floor surfaces for easy camera movement and space for sets and lighting grids take precedence over good acoustical design.

Second, there is noise created by camera movement and crew activity. Third, in many productions, talent does not remain in one position but moves around the set.

To adapt to these conditions, two basic approaches to miking talent have developed in studio production. One is to mount a directional microphone on a boom, which can be rotated or moved to keep the performer within the pickup pattern of the microphone. Because the microphone is directional, off-camera noises are minimized. However, the distance between talent and microphone required to keep the microphone out of the shot makes it more difficult to maintain good presence.

The other approach is to assign a separate microphone to each performer. Lavaliers or clip-on microphones are often used. Properly positioned, these give good presence and little pickup of off-camera noise. Depending upon the requirements of the particular production, mounting directional microphones on stands in front of each performer or using hand-held microphones are other options. If the talent will be moving around the set or into the studio audience, wireless microphones might be used.

Location production presents many of the same problems as remote production for radio. Specific techniques for recording audio for video on location are discussed in Chapter 13.

In addition to all the aesthetic issues involved in audio production, video production presents additional considerations. One is the decision about whether the microphone can be seen. The presence of a microphone makes a clear statement to the viewers that they are watching a video production. The illusion that what is happening is an actual (or fictional) event that we are watching unobserved is broken by the constant reminder that a video crew is on the job choosing this view for us.

Another issue involves the way in which the audio and video interact. In creating meaning for us, the sounds and words may support what we are seeing or they may contradict it. An actor's smile and hearty handshake may turn sinister when the background music is heavy and ominous. Our interpretation of an image and our emotional response to it are influenced by what we hear. A close-up of an object may seem to be an abstract pattern until the narrator explains that this is the nucleus of a cell. The audio track can also control the way in which we look at the image. A narrator's words, or sounds created by objects within the frame, direct our attention to specific details. The unique requirements of video production are explored in the following section.

SUMMARY

As the examples in this chapter illustrate, professionals working in audio production today are creating a wide variety of materials. Despite this diversity, these professionals approach their assignments in similar ways. They begin with a well-defined purpose and a specific audience in mind. They devote ample time to preproduction planning. They try to anticipate problems and, if problems occur, to develop creative solutions. And, they strive for excellent technical quality in their productions.

In Chapters 1 to 5 of this book, we have provided you with basic information about audio equipment. We have suggested ways you can use it to produce effective audio messages. Through practice, you can become technically proficient. By using your imagination, you can explore the creative potentials of the medium.

FOR FURTHER READING

O'DONNELL, LEWIS B., PHILIP BENOIT, and CARL HAUSMAN. *Modern Radio Production* (Belmont, Calif.: Wadsworth, 1986).

STEPHENS, MITCHELL. *Broadcast News* 2d (New York: Holt, Rinehart and Winston, 1986).

chapter six ⎯⎯⎯⎯⎯⎯⎯⎯⎯⎯⎯⎯⎯⎯⎯⎯

Video Communication ⎯⎯⎯⎯⎯⎯

INTRODUCTION

Video is a process of communication that uses electronically reproduced moving images, speech, sound effects, and music. It is also an industry that uses complicated equipment, expensive facilities, and vast amounts of human effort to produce and distribute programs. Video takes many forms, ranging from expensive network productions to simple consumer recordings of a child's birthday party. Its purposes include documentation of important events, instruction, persuasion, and artistic expression. In carrying out these functions, video communicates according to a set of understood aesthetic conventions and operates under a number of economic, social, and technological constraints.

We have two aims in this section of the book. First, we will discuss how video works, the characteristics of the equipment used, writing, picture composition, editing, and various production approaches. Video production is more than mastering a series of techniques, however. It also involves understanding the medium's strengths and weaknesses. Therefore, our second aim in this section is to make you aware of the general nature of the medium so that you can use it to maximum effectiveness.

THE SCOPE OF VIDEO PRODUCTION

Video production can be described in two broad categories: telecast and nontelecast. The *telecast* category includes programs by networks, independent production companies, and local stations. *Nontelecast* includes corporate, medical, legal, instructional, and personal applications. Cable television is technically nontele-cast, but many of its programs are similar in quality, purpose, and style to telecast programs.

Telecast Applications

Networks.   Both the commercial networks and the noncommercial net-works have access to elaborate production facilities, vast amounts of money, and highly qualified production personnel. The three commercial networks produce their own news and public affairs programs, soap operas, and some other enter-tainment programs. They can do almost any kind of production that creativity, equipment, money, time, and talent will allow. From a technical standpoint, net-work productions reach a high level of quality.

While it does no production of its own, the Public Broadcasting Service (PBS) acquires high-quality programs from independent production companies, local stations, and foreign broadcast services. The British Broadcasting Corpora-tion (BBC) and other European production centers have provided many out-standing programs to PBS during the past several years.

At the network level, a video production can become an expensive and com-plicated process. Producers, directors, writers, performers, and crew members can spend millions of dollars and hundreds of hours creating miniseries, docu-mentaries, and other types of programs for distribution to millions of people. A network production facility is a complex machine with miles of wire, cameras, monitors, tape recorders, lights, sets, and props. In addition, the networks have extensive mobile production facilities and employ satellite links.

Independent production companies.   Many of the programs aired by the networks are produced by independent production companies such as MCA-TV, Twentieth-Century Fox Television, and Lorimar Telepictures. They also make many of the commercials that the networks air. The amount of equipment, per-sonnel, and production dollars available for the production of situation come-dies, police dramas, and assorted commercials rivals what the networks can do themselves.

Local stations.   Traditionally, local stations try to limit their involvement in production, except for news, talk shows, and occasional documentaries. This policy is maintained because productions are very expensive and time-consuming. Most local stations fill their broadcast day with programs provided by the networks and syndicated programming services. Feature films also fill large blocks of airtime. Some very large television stations in major markets do maintain extensive production facilities and generate many local programs. These stations are often owned and operated by one of the commercial networks. The majority of local television stations cannot sustain anything close to the level of local production possible at these large stations.

Local stations do expend a considerable amount of money and effort in the production of newscasts, however. These programs are not only important to local audiences, but they also represent one of the few ways in which individual stations can clearly differentiate themselves from other stations in the area. Newscasts are also an important source of revenue for stations because they attract large audiences, and the stations can charge top dollar for commercials run during them.

The production facilities at most local stations are modest. Most local stations have a studio with a permanent set for all newscasts and perhaps another one for interview shows. They maintain a mobile unit and a few remote cameras. Productions are kept simple and straightforward so that they can be carried out with a minimum expenditure of money and rehearsal time. A local station will very seldom undertake the production of a complicated program such as a drama. This kind of production would be just too expensive and time-consuming.

Nontelecast Applications

During the past few years, the use of video in many kinds of nontelecast applications has dramatically increased. As we have noted, the widespread availability of less expensive, more reliable, and more portable equipment, plus easy-to-use editors and video cassette recorders (VCRs), has encouraged these nontelecast uses of video.

Corporate. The business community has been quick to embrace video for many different purposes. Some large corporations maintain high-quality production facilities that are capable of producing training videos and recording presentations, meetings, and conferences (Fig. 6-1). Videotapes can be sent by mail to branch offices or distributed by satellite. Corporations use video to demonstrate new products to salespeople and update employees on issues of importance to the company. Live video conferences are sometimes set up so that executives from around the country can meet to discuss current problems. Some companies

FIGURE 6-1 Domino's Pizza Satellite Network broadcasts a corporate meeting from Drummond Island, Michigan. (Courtesy of Domino's Pizza Satellite Network)

maintain large videotape duplicating facilities and their own satellite intercon-
nections.

Health services. The medical and dental professions have used video for
many years to record surgical procedures (Fig. 6-2), but this use has expanded
rapidly in recent years. It is now possible to diagnose illnesses by video and to
bring the latest medical techniques from around the world to any location by
satellite transmission. Medical and dental schools often use high-resolution
equipment fitted with special close-up lenses to record operations and then play
them back for students. As an instructional tool, video has largely replaced the
old surgical amphitheatre.

In other applications, psychiatrists, psychologists, and social workers often
videotape interviews with patients and record psychological tests. Marriage coun-
selors sometimes record sessions and then play them back to couples to reveal
the subtleties of their interactions.

Education. Schools, colleges, and universities have always been interested
in using video for instructional purposes and have operated production facilities
since the early 1950s. Some educational institutions produce instructional videos
which are played to large groups of students. For a time, it was hoped that teaching by television would solve the problems caused by teacher shortages, but it
was discovered that this method has some drawbacks. Today, video is usually used
to supplement, rather than replace, the instructor.

Public school systems often operate a media center to produce video materials for classroom use. These materials are sometimes transmitted to individual
schools by the local cable system or fed by a microwave distribution system.

Many colleges and universities have a campus video distribution network
which can feed programs to classrooms. The system might have studios at the
headend where programs can be produced. In addition, a large number of col-

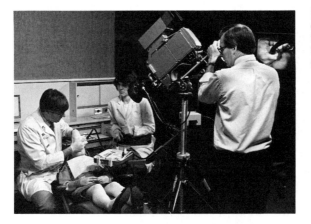

FIGURE 6-2 A dental procedure is recorded on videotape
for students to study at a later
time. (Courtesy of University of Michigan School of Dentistry)

leges and universities maintain video facilities that are used to teach television production in conjunction with degree programs in radio, television, and film.

Government. The federal government is one of the world's largest producers of videotapes and motion pictures. They are distributed around the world through the U.S. Information Agency and the Armed Forces Radio and Television Network. State and local government agencies are also involved in many different kinds of video projects, ranging from police training to surveying road conditions.

Religious organizations. Religious groups have always used radio and television to disseminate inspirational messages. For many years, churches have depended upon local radio and television stations to carry Sunday services, and this is still the case in most communities.

Networks occasionally broadcast Christmas and Easter celebrations. The Christmas Day service from the Washington Cathedral has been a holiday tradition for many years (Fig. 6-3). Recently, services from other countries have been made available through satellite transmission. The annual Service of Lessons and Carols from King's College Chapel, Cambridge, and the Christmas Eve mass from St. Peter's in Rome are now available in the United States.

These traditional uses of video have been supplemented by evangelical groups, who often maintain their own studios and prepare programs for distribution by satellite to cable systems or to local stations by mailing of videotapes. Some of these programs include healing services for shut-ins and requests for

FIGURE 6-3 Video cameras cover a 1988 service from Washington's National Cathedral. (Photo © Morton Broffman)

donations. Video has become an indispensable part of many evangelical organizations, and they employ many production personnel on a permanent basis.

Consumer applications.   There has been an explosive growth of consumer uses for video. The small, portable video camera has largely replaced the film camera because it can provide instant playback. People record weddings, graduations, parties, and vacation trips. Many small companies specialize in producing these kinds of recordings for individuals. Some of these companies make "day-in-the-life" tapes, which record an individual's typical activities throughout an entire day.

Creative applications.   Small-format (that is, ½-inch tape or smaller) consumer video has also become an expressive tool for video artists. Using a wide variety of special-effects devices, imaginative camera work and editing, artists can employ video for purely aesthetic purposes. Rather than using video to record reality, these artists are often interested in abstract uses of color, line, and composition. Video art has become an exciting new way for creative minds to communicate.

Cable.   Programs ranging from broadcast quality to small-format video are carried on cable. Many cable channels are reserved for existing broadcast stations, and others are set aside for superstations and special cable program services such as Home Box Office, Showtime, and the Disney Channel. The programs carried on these channels are of broadcast quality.

Cable systems usually maintain a small studio in which relatively simple local programs can be produced. In addition, they might carry local sports and other community activities (Fig. 6-4). Some cable systems make equipment available to the general public and transmit video productions made by individuals so long as they meet accepted standards of good taste. Locally produced cable productions vary considerably in quality depending upon the size of the operation and the emphasis placed on local production. Some cable companies strive for broadcast quality and maintain expensive equipment to achieve it, while other cable companies support only modest production efforts.

APPROACHES TO VIDEO PRODUCTION

Video productions can be made in two basic ways: the multiple-camera and the single-camera approaches.

Multiple-Camera Production

For many years, all television programs were produced "live" in a studio using a multiple-camera approach. Newscasts, dramas, and variety shows were staged in front of three or more cameras, and the director selected shots from among those fed by the separate cameras. All editing was done in "real time,"

FIGURE 6-4 (top) Exterior of remote production van used by a cable company. (bottom) Interior of remote van, showing production facilities used for local productions. (Both photos courtesy of Maclean Hunter Cable TV, Taylor, Michigan)

and the program was sent out to audiences instantaneously. The only way to delay a program was to make a film record from a monitor. This "kinescope" could then be broadcast later or sent to individual stations.

In the 1950s, the introduction of videotape made it possible to produce entire programs "live on tape" and then edit out mistakes. It was also possible to tape individual segments and edit them together later. The advantage of the multiple-camera approach, either live or live on tape, is that it is relatively fast, and editing decisions are made on the spot. However, such an approach requires considerable rehearsal time and some aesthetic compromises. For example, lighting cannot be adjusted for individual camera positions but must be kept generally adequate for all possible camera locations. This results in a rather flat look which is characteristic of many television programs. Individual scenes cannot be polished to perfection, and very little creative editing can be done.

A recent development has been the introduction of the multiple-camera, multiple-tape approach. In this method, each studio camera feeds its signal into a separate VTR. At the same time, the cameras also send a signal to a switcher. The program is directed and switched in real time in the conventional way, and a "live-on-tape" reference tape is prepared. In postproduction, the editors go back to the isolated videotapes from each separate camera and prepare a final version of the production. They can choose different angles, remove mistakes, employ different transitional devices, and generally clean up the tape. This multiple camera–multiple videotape approach is often called the ISO (isolated camera) method.

Single-Camera Approach

The introduction of high-quality portable equipment and the need for greater control over the production have led to the single-camera approach. This method is similar to film production in that each shot is lit and blocked separately. Many different "takes" are made, and the best one is selected later, during postproduction editing. This approach gives the director maximum control because each setup is carefully planned and adjusted until it is perfect. The approach also results in better performances and a better-quality image because lights have been individually set for each camera position. More sophisticated editing is also possible since considerably more time is spent on this phase of the production than is the case in the multiple-camera approach. The disadvantage of the single-camera technique is that it is time-consuming and costly. When quality is more important than time or money, the single-camera approach might be the best method.

THE PRODUCTION CREW

Most video productions require the close cooperation of many individuals who work together on a production team. The team can be divided roughly into two groups. In the first group are the creative personnel, including writers, performers, producers, and directors. The second group consists of the production crew of camera operators, editors, lighting technicians, and engineers. For budgetary purposes, expenses for the creative personnel are considered "above-the-line" costs, and those for the production crew are "below-the-line" costs.

The Creative Team

The creative team for any production is responsible for coming up with ideas, writing scripts, selecting talent, rehearsing, and guiding the production of the program. The producer is usually responsible for developing ideas, acquiring financial backing, collecting talent, selecting studios or locations, and putting the entire package together prior to production. However, the producer's responsibilities vary considerably depending upon the situation.

The director is responsible for carrying out the producer's ideas during production. The director selects camera shots, supervises lighting, rehearses actors, and oversees editing in postproduction. In some situations, the producer also functions as the director. The producer and director work closely with writers, art directors, set designers, and other creative personnel prior to actual production. The technical crew is responsible for following the instructions of the director during actual production. We will discuss the production team in greater detail in Chapter 12.

Needless to say, the successful functioning of any production team requires not only that individual members be proficient in their specific tasks, but also that they be able to work with others. There is little room for individual eccentricities in many production situations, and one of the important rules of television production is learning how to cooperate with other members of the team.

This dependence on a production crew inevitably leads to a certain impersonality in programs and a standardization of style from one production to another. There is little opportunity for a director to experiment with a production or to make a personal statement.

THE LANGUAGE OF VIDEO

From the moment we awaken in the morning until we go to bed at night, we perceive the sights and sounds of the world around us. Communication is a process of selecting and ordering our experiences and thoughts and transmitting them to others. Writers use an arbitrary system of symbols called words, which represent objects, emotions, and thoughts. The words are arranged into sentences, and if we are literate in that particular language, we can understand what the writer is trying to communicate.

Video is a more direct means of communication. It does not use arbitrary symbols of things, but rather electronically produced images of the things themselves. The producer of a video message must select which things are to be shown, decide how they are to be presented, and arrange them in a particular order by means of editing. Video also uses speech, sound effects, and music, but its primary means of communication is visual.

The word is the smallest unit of meaning in language, and there is no exact video equivalent for it. The closest thing to it is the individual moving image recorded in a single run of the camera. This is called a *shot*. Individual shots are arranged in a particular order to make up larger units of meaning. Shots are gathered into scenes, and the scenes are combined into sequences. The way in which shots are arranged is an important part of the meaning communicated by a video message.

Finally, the visual component of the video message is supported by speech, sound effects, and sometimes music. Speech can be in the form of dialogue spoken by persons on the screen or as a narration which explains or comments on the visual action. Sound effects can result from activity on the screen, or they can be added later in postproduction. Music, too, can be provided by an on-screen source or can be added later.

Because video looks so much like reality, it is easy to forget that video production involves carefully selecting images, arranging them in a particular way, and combining them with speech, sound effects, and music.

When the purpose of the video message is merely to record or document reality, there is very little selection and manipulation. The director of a presidential news conference or a space-shuttle launch wishes to convey accurately what is happening in the real world. Most video productions do involve considerable manipulation of images and sounds, however. A television drama might look like reality, but in fact it is performed by actors and shot on a set under carefully aimed artificial lights. On the other hand, video art makes no pretense of adhering to reality. Here, the visual and aural elements are manipulated freely to suit the artist's creative purposes.

Reading the Video Message

It is often assumed that anyone can understand a video message without prior training, but this is not the case. Just as people learn to comprehend a language in its spoken and written forms, so too do people learn to read video and film messages.

Experiments have shown that people who have had no previous exposure to video and film have a difficult time making sense of it. In the 1920s, anthropologist William Hudson discovered that members of certain African tribes could not read three-dimensional depth cues from a two-dimensional film image.[1] Similarly, moving-camera shots, closeups, rapid editing, dissolves, and many other common film techniques can potentially confuse a naive viewer. It is easy to imagine that a person who had never seen a film before might misinterpret a closeup of an actor's head to mean that the individual had suffered decapitation! Fortunately, most of us understand these conventions of video language because experience has taught us what they mean.

Physiological factors.   Our ability to read a video image relies on two physiological factors called the phi phenomenon and the persistence of vision. Together, they produce the illusion of movement upon which video and film rely.

The *phi phenomenon* can be demonstrated in a laboratory by placing two lights near each other (Fig. 6-5). One is turned on just after the other has been turned off. If the timing is within certain parameters and the distance between the lights is just right, the viewer will see a single light moving across from one position to the other. The viewer sees an apparent movement when in fact the lights are stationary. In the motion picture and in video, each frame presents the moving object in a slightly different position. The viewer perceives an apparent movement of the object between these two points.

Persistence of vision refers to the eye's inability to follow rapid changes in brightness (Fig. 6-6). If a single light is turned on and off slowly, and then at an increasing rate, the eye will eventually perceive the flashing light as a steadily shining one.

In the motion picture, the eye sees a series of rapidly projected still photo-

---

[1]See James Monaco, *How to Read a Film: The Art, Technology, Language, History, and Theory of Film and Media.* (New York: Oxford University Press, 1981), p. 121.

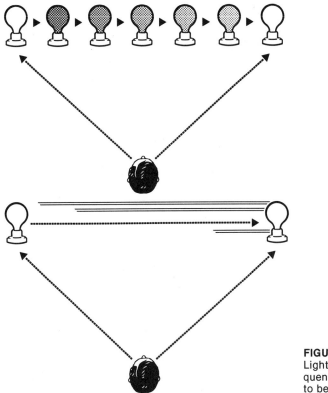

FIGURE 6-5 Phi phenomenon. Lights flashing rapidly in sequence from left to right appear to be a single moving light.

graphs. While the image of one is retained by the retina, another takes its place. The viewer perceives the rapidly flashing individual images as a continous one.

In video, persistence of vision not only helps us to retain a previous frame until another takes its place, but also allows us to see frames as a whole as the scanning beam traces across them. We retain an image of the scanning spot long after it has moved to another point. (See the discussion of scanning in Chapter 7.) The persistence of vision blends the separate frames, and the phi phenom-

FIGURE 6-6 Persistence of vision. Image on left is retained briefly until image on right takes its place. Phi-phenomenon gives apparent motion to the two separate images.

enon allows us to see apparent movement between the slight displacement of objects from one frame to another.

Learned factors.   Beyond these physiological factors, much of our ability to read video and film images depends upon learning. Our individual abilities and cultural experiences might cause our readings to be slightly different, but most of us are able to get the general idea.

Most of us learn that an image that grows larger on the screen is an indication that the camera is getting closer or that the focal length of the lens is changing. We don't interpret it to mean that the object is getting physically larger. We apply our knowledge of size consistency from the real world to what we see on the screen. Similarly, we interpret the standard editing sequence of long shot, medium shot, closeup to mean that we are moving closer to the object on the screen and not that it has gotten bigger and has simultaneously been chopped up into pieces. In viewing a conversation between two people that is shown by a series of alternating closeups, we assume that the person not shown at a particular moment is still present. Our sense of consistency of size and space based upon our real world experience helps us to recognize these video conventions for what they are.

We also learn to recognize three-dimensional cues from the two-dimensional screen. If we see two people on the screen and one is considerably smaller than the other, we interpret this to mean that the smaller person is some distance away. Similarly, we use gradations in color and texture as well as partial obscuration and convergence lines to suggest a sense of depth. (See Chapter 10 for a more detailed discussion of depth cues.)

Film and video rely heavily upon editing, and viewers need to learn what it means. If one shot follows another, we assume that the second bears some relationship to the first. We tend to connect them in our minds. Soviet filmmaker Sergei Eisenstein relied on the viewer's tendency to do this to create between-shot connections that were not actually there. He sometimes juxtaposed unlike objects by editing so that viewers would make a metaphorical connection between the two. In his film *Strike* (1924), Eisenstein cut from people being attacked by soldiers to a view of animals being slaughtered. Most viewers saw the connection.

Film and video makers eliminate unnecessary action by means of editing, and we learn how to interpret this. We can see a person entering a building in one shot and see her walking into her room in the next shot. We do not need to see her get into the elevator, ride to the tenth floor, get out her key, and unlock the door to correctly interpret what is happening. From our experience in viewing films and videos, we are able to fill in the missing parts of the edited sequence.

We also learn to assign meaning to other video and film conventions such as camera angles, dissolves, superimpositions, and split screens. We learn, for example, that a character shot from a low angle is supposed to be powerful or threatening, that a dissolve can imply a lapse of time, and that a superimposition signals a close connection between the objects simultaneously on the screen.

Although we can usually agree on the meaning of many video and film conventions, some of them remain an individual matter. In his book *Signs and Meaning in the Cinema*, Peter Wollen states that the visual image communicates on at least three different levels: the iconic, the indexical, and symbolic.[2] An image of locomotive wheels turning is first of all an icon, or visual model, of the real thing. Most of us would interpret it in that way. The same image also functions as an index or reference to a larger set of images of transportation and mechanization. Finally, the locomotive wheels can be a symbol—that is, a reference to a thing or idea to which it bears no physical resemblance. In this case, the wheels could symbolize power. Although we all might be able to agree upon the iconic function of an image, we might have some disagreement about its indexical or symbolic functions. Beyond a certain point, our readings of visual images become a highly personal matter.

Conventions of the Video Language

For several paragraphs, we have been talking about conventions which apply both to film and video. Yet there are some noticeable stylistic differences between the two media which are worth noting. These exist in part because of the different technologies which film and video employ.

Video technology. Regardless of the production circumstances and purposes of their creators, all video messages are made with basically the same equipment. Although there is quite a bit of difference in cost and sophistication between a professional television camera and a small-format home unit, both operate in essentially the same way.

The scanning process used in video cameras produces an image which is relatively low in resolution compared to that of 35-mm film. This means that the video camera cannot reproduce the range of detail possible in a motion picture. Video cameras are also more limited in their ability to render a wide range of contrasts and subtle differences in color values.

The low resolution of the video image is particularly noticeable when it is projected on a large screen. The video screen is kept rather small so that the loss of detail is less apparent. Video screens have a shape that is close to the older film aspect ratio of 3 units high to 4 units wide. This means that feature films shot in wide screen cannot be shown on video formats without cropping the right and left sides of the screen.

The resolution of the video image can be improved by increasing the number of scan lines, and the present high-definition television (HDTV) system developed by the Japan Broadcasting Corporation (NHK) uses 1,125 lines of resolution. The resulting image is virtually indistinguishable from 35-mm theatrical film. It is possible that HDTV will be introduced as an alternative to theatrical film before it is widely available to consumers. For the time being, technology limits video to a low-resolution image that is rather small in size.

---

[2]See Peter Wollen, *Signs and Meaning in the Cinema*, 2d ed. (New York: Viking, 1972). Also summarized in Monaco, p. 133.

The results of these technological features are important. They demand an extensive use of closeups, and this is one of the major differences between video and motion pictures. A film director might comfortably shoot a magnificent desert panorama, knowing that its details will show up clearly on the big screen. The video director runs the risk of having the detail lost in the poor resolution of the video image and the expansiveness of the scene diminished by its reduction to a small screen.

The human face is the most common subject for video closeups. It can be rendered on the screen in a size that equals or comes close to its size in real life. Also, video tends to use many closeups of objects and other details of a scene.

Another consequence of video's small screen size is that there is very little latitude for vertical or horizontal composition. You cannot comfortably show three people in closeup standing side by side. The only relatively unrestricted direction is from front to back, so the tendency is to place objects slightly in front of one another. In addition to allowing more objects to be placed within the frame, such composition in depth also helps to suggest a third dimension and helps to relieve the screen's flatness.

In his essay "Cinemascope: Before and After," film scholar Charles Barr suggests that editing was adopted by filmmakers in part to compensate for the small size of early screens.[3] It would seem that the same is true for video. Because only a small field of view can be shown on the video screen, directors tend to break down the larger scene into small components and move from one to another of them by means of editing. While a film director working with a large screen might show several people engaged in a conversation by means of a single unedited take (such compositions were fairly common in wide-screen films), the video director would probably cut back and forth among a series of separate closeups showing each individual. We often see this strategy during interview shows where several guests are present. After a quick establishing shot, the director proceeds to closeups edited to follow the conversation.

In addition to editing, video directors also use a great deal of camera movement and zooming to create a sense of space and to overcome the limitations of the small screen. This dependence on closeups, editing, composition in depth, and movement within the frame are basic conventions of video language made necessary in part by the technology that it uses.

Video Style

In addition to the stylistic conventions dictated by technology, there are others that arise out of the purposes, circumstances of production, and conditions of reception of different video messages.

Purposes.   A video message often adopts a visual style that best suits the communication purposes for which it is designed. Commercial television pro-

---

[3]See Charles Barr, "Cinemascope: Before and After," *Film Quarterly* 16, No. 4, 1963. Reprinted in Gerald Mast and Marshall Cohen, *Film Theory and Criticism*, 3d ed. (New York: Oxford University Press, 1985), p. 159.

grams, for example, are mainly intended to attract and hold an audience's attention so that they will watch the commercials. The programs use a style based on repetition, elaborate computer graphics, rapid editing, and constant zooming or camera movement or both. The screen image is kept in constant motion to hold the viewer's attention. The commercials themselves use bright colors, unusual perspectives, loud music, insistent narrations, and creative visuals to urge audiences to buy a particular product or service.

On the other hand, corporate, medical, and instructional video often adopts a much less complicated style designed to communicate information clearly. Business meetings, surgical procedures, and history lessons are usually presented in a straightforward manner with minimal use of stylistic devices. In these situations, the subject matter is more important than the style of presentation. This is not to say that style is ignored, but rather that it cannot take precedence over content. There is a trend in nonbroadcast applications of video to adopt styles that resemble commercial television to the extent that finances and equipment permit.

Public (noncommercial) television uses many different visual styles, depending upon the purposes of the program. Instructional materials can be presented in a direct style, while other productions might use a more elaborate, stylistic approach. Sometimes there is an unusual match between purpose and style, as in the case of *Sesame Street*. In this program, the techniques of commercial television were used to present instructional materials to preschoolers. Perhaps the producers of the program felt that children would be more likely to pay attention to a commercial style since this was the one with which they were most familiar.

In recent years, public television has adopted a more commercial style of presentation because audiences seem to prefer it. Indeed, the influence of commercial television is so great that audiences tend to measure all video productions against it. If a program does not have the high technical quality, rapidly moving visual image, and elaborate graphics, viewers think of it as inferior regardless of its content.

Production circumstances.   Another determinant of style is the production situation in which a particular video message is made. We would expect a studio production to look different from one shot on location, and an expensive program to look different from a less expensive one.

In the 1950s, "live" television dramas had a distinctive look because they were shot in a studio without a break. They contained a great deal of camera movement to overcome the studio's cramped look, a straightforward, uncomplicated editing style, and the use of long closeups of photographs, letters, murder weapons, and so on to give the cast and crew time to set up for the next scene.

Production circumstances are partially responsible for the constant repetition of program ideas, sets, and characters on commercial television. The networks and stations have a voracious appetite for program materials, and there is not enough time or money to fill each hour with something original. Newscasts, game shows, and dramas use the same sets and narrative devices over and over.

A movie director can spend five years and several million dollars making a feature film, but video directors do not have this luxury. The serious constraints of time and money inevitably result in easily repeated formulas.

Conditions of reception.   Most video messages are received under unfavorable conditions for maximum attention and retention. They must compete with the stereo, the telephone, and neighbors ringing the doorbell. Audiences do not—indeed, cannot—pay as much attention to a video program as they can to a feature film shown in the isolation of a theatre. To compensate for this, most video productions strive for simplicity, clarity, and repetition in their structure, use of graphics, and overall design.

Another problem faced by broadcast television is that audiences have unpredictable tuning habits. A network television program must grab and hold the viewers' attention as they flip the dial or press the buttons on a remote tuning control. This is why so many broadcast television programs rely on elaborate opening graphics and music.

Viewers often do not tune in at the beginning of a program. If they are to remain with a show, they must be able to determine quickly what has already happened and what is likely to follow. In short, they must be able to recognize their chronological position in the program. The use of familiar structures facilitates this. For example, newscasts are ordered in a very predictable fashion, and frequent announcements are made during the program to inform viewers about what is coming next. Viewers who tune in during the sports can assume with some accuracy that the international news is over and that the weather will probably follow. Similarly, a drama with a familiar cast of characters and regularly repeated narrative strategies can be tuned in at midpoint without too much difficulty in determining what has probably happened so far.

Applications for Production

A complete discussion of the language and stylistic conventions of video is beyond the scope of this book. It is sufficient to say here that production students should be aware of the stylistic conventions of video and attempt to use them to best advantage.

Also, you should be sensitive to the fact that a wide variety of video styles are available. Even though the style of commercial broadcasting is the most familiar, it is not always the most appropriate. Many production students try to imitate the elaborate visual effects of commercial television with equipment that is inadequate to the task. Every effort should be made to match the style to the subject, the intended audience, and the realistic limitations imposed by equipment, time, and money.

SUMMARY

Video is a process of communication that uses electronically reproduced moving images, speech, sound effects, and music. The term *video* once referred only to broadcast television, but today it includes corporate, medical, legal, personal, and other applications.

Many video messages are intended for broadcast over networks, stations, and cable systems. Most of these are produced using expensive equipment and experienced person-nel. Networks, independent program producers, and local stations provide the bulk of broadcast video productions.

There has been a rapid expansion of nonbroadcast video applications. Corpora-tions and businesses use video for instructional purposes, conferences, and promotion. The medical, dental, and legal professions also use video for many different purposes. Schools, the federal government, religious organizations, and cable systems use video in many ways. Today almost anyone can use small-format, personal video for artistic or docu-mentary purposes.

There are two basic approaches to video production. Multiple-camera production involves the use of several cameras in a studio and simultaneous editing through the switcher. Single-camera production is similar to film practice in that each shot is carefully composed, rehearsed, and recorded many times until a satisfactory result is obtained. In the single-camera approach, editing is done in postproduction. The ISO approach in-volves multiple-camera shooting, but each camera feeds a separate videotape recorder.

Video productions usually require the close cooperation of many people. Pro-ducers, directors, writers, and performers make up the creative team, and their costs are considered to be "above the line." The production crew of camerapersons, switchers, audio and lighting technicians, and assistants follow the instructions of the creative per-sonnel. Crew costs are considered to be "below the line." Working on a production team requires individual expertise as well as the ability to cooperate with others. The depen-dence on production crews encourages a certain uniformity in style among programs.

Video language is made up of individual shots arranged by means of editing. Speech, sound effects, and music are also important elements of the video language. Our ability to read this language is based upon the physiological factors of the phi phenom-enon and the persistence of vision. Beyond these, much of our ability to read video is learned.

Some conventions of the video language are the result of the technology that it uses. Video's poor resolution and small screen encourage the use of closeups, composition in depth, camera movement, zooming, and rapid editing. Other conventions are the result of the particular video's purpose, circumstances of production, and intended audience. Differences in these factors lead to a variety of video styles.

Production students should be aware of the stylistic conventions of video and learn to use them to best advantage. They should strive to choose stylistic approaches that are appropriate to the production's purpose, production situation, and intended audience.

FOR FURTHER READING

KAUFMAN, LLOYD. *Sight and Mind: An Introduction to Visual Perception* (New York: Oxford University Press, 1974).

KINDEM, GORHAM. *The Moving Image: Production Principles and Practices* (Glenview, Ill.: Scott, Foresman, 1987).

MADSEN, ROY PAUL. *The Impact of Film: How Ideas Are Communicated Through Cinema and Television* (New York: Macmillan, 1973).

MONACO, JAMES. *How to Read a Film: The Art, Technology, Language, History and Theory of Film and Media* (New York: Oxford University Press, 1984).

chapter seven _____

The Physics of Video _____

INTRODUCTION

As we've seen, many factors influence video productions as we know them. Some of these factors arise from the nature of the specific production situation, some from the nature of the industry, some from aesthetic considerations, some from conventions that have evolved over time, and some from the technology used.

In this chapter, we'll begin an exploration of the possibilities and the limitations presented by technology. To understand them, we must understand the physical properties of light, the optical systems that collect the light to produce the visual images we want to record or transmit, and the electronic systems that allow us to change the light into electrical signals that can be manipulated and then transmitted or recorded. Chapter 8 will discuss how specific pieces of equipment use those properties and principles.

THE PHYSICAL PROPERTIES OF LIGHT

Light is a form of electromagnetic energy generated when the atoms in a substance are excited and the electrons in the atoms begin to reorient themselves in relationship to the nuclei. Two different models have been used to try to explain the specific properties of light. In one, light is described as individual quanta, or particles of energy, radiating from the light-emitting body. These quanta are called *photons*. In the other model, which is similar to the sine-wave model used to depict acoustical energy, light is described as waves of energy.

Visible light has a relatively narrow frequency range most commonly described by wave length. The human eye can detect light waves ranging from 400 to 700 nanometers (nm) in length. (A nanometer is one-billionth of a meter in length.) An electromagnetic wave longer than 700 nm does not stimulate the photoreceptors in the eye. Electromagnetic waves shorter than 400 nm are absorbed mostly by the lens of the eye and don't reach the photoreceptors.

Visible light, then, is made up of a range of frequencies. Each of these frequencies has a specific wave length. As you'll recall, frequency refers to the number of cycles or waves passing a given point in a given time interval. Thus, the shorter the wave length, the higher the frequency.

The photoreceptors in our eyes respond differently to these variations in wave length. We interpret these variations as different colors. When light that seems to us to be white passes through a prism, it is separated into a rainbow of colors. Each of these colors represents a different frequency (Fig. 7-1). The longer waves in the spectrum of visible light are red. The waves in the middle range are green. The shorter waves are blue.

These differences in wave length are also referred to as differences in color temperature. Blackbody radiation provides a means of comparing the color temperature of various light sources. (A blackbody is an object that, theoretically, absorbs all light waves reaching its surface.) When material is heated, it will either be destroyed or begin to emit light. A blackbody thermal radiator emits light the intensity and wave length of which depends solely on the temperature of the body. As the heat is increased, the wave lengths reach the threshold of visible light. As the heat continues to increase, the wave lengths become correspondingly shorter. Thus, at a temperature above 1,000 degrees Kelvin, a weak red color will be visible. At 2,000 degrees Kelvin, the intensity of the red has increased. At 3,000 degrees Kelvin, the light is a bright orange-yellow. At 4,000 degrees Kelvin, it is

FIGURE 7-1 On the electromagnetic spectrum, visible light occupies a narrow band of wavelengths. Each of these wavelengths is perceived as a particular color.

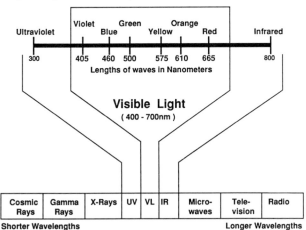

yellow. At 5,000 degrees Kelvin, the body is radiating a mixture of all the wave lengths in the visible spectrum and the light appears white. As temperatures continue to increase, the light becomes blue.

When we say that a light source is 5,000 degrees Kelvin, we mean that the proportion of wave lengths given off by that source is equivalent to the combination of wave lengths emitted by a blackbody at that temperature. The light source itself is not physically that hot. In fact, the physical temperature of some lights, such as fluorescent lamps, may be quite cool while their color temperature is relatively high.

Rating light sources by their color temperature expressed in degrees Kelvin allows us to compare the properties of those light sources. For example, direct sunlight has a color temperature of about 5,000 degrees Kelvin and contains a well-balanced mixture of red, green, and blue light waves. This combination produces a white light. The color temperature of an ordinary household lamp (an incandescent lamp) is about 2,700 degrees Kelvin. The filament is giving off a higher proportion of red light waves. Ordinary fluorescent lamps are about 4,800 degrees Kelvin and have a higher proportion of blue light waves.

All light, then, is not the same. It varies according to the relative proportions of the various frequencies it contains. A room lighted with ordinary incandescent lamps has a warm look because of the higher proportion of frequencies toward the red end of the spectrum. A room lighted with ordinary fluorescent lamps appears cool because of the higher proportion of frequencies in the green and blue parts of the spectrum. At about noon on a clear day, the sun gives off white light containing a balance of all the frequencies. With video cameras, the relationship between the color temperature of the light in which you are shooting and the accuracy with which colors are reproduced is important (Fig. 7-2).

Most of the light in our surroundings is reflected light. As the electromag-

FIGURE 7-2   Color temperature of light sources commonly found in location shooting.

Source of Light	Color Temperature in Degrees Kelvin
Household lamps	2650°K to 2980°K
Tungsten-halogen lamps (television studio standard)	3200°K
Photoflood	3800°K
Blue photoflood	4800°K
Fluorescent lamps	4500°K to 6500°K
Sunlight (noon)	5400°K
Daylight fluorescent lamps	5500°K
Overcast day	6500°K
Blue sky	8000°K

netic waves travel from the source of the light, they encounter all kinds of objects in their path. Some waves are absorbed by the surface of the object they strike. Some pass through the object. Some of the light waves are reflected from the surface of the object. These reflected light waves are diffused, or reflected in various directions. The smoother the surface, the less the amount of diffusion. Thus, a highly polished surface reflects the light at almost the same angle at which the light hits the surface. Light reflecting from a matte surface is diffused, or scattered, in many directions.

The color of the object is determined by the particular light waves being reflected off its surface. If white light (which is a balanced combination of red, green, and blue) strikes the surface of a white table, all three colors are reflected. If the white light falls on a blue chair sitting near the table, the red and green light waves will be absorbed and the blue light waves will be reflected. Likewise, a yellow flower on the table is reflecting back both red and green light waves, while the blue light waves are absorbed. The proportions of red, green, and blue light waves reaching our eyes determines the color we see.

This additive principle is important in working with color in video. As we combine (or add) light waves of the red, green, and blue primary colors, we can create a wide range of colors. This additive principle can be illustrated by directing three separate light beams—one red, one green, and one blue—at a white surface. If the three beams overlap, we see only white. If we separate the three beams so that they don't overlap, we see the three distinct colors. If we move the beams so that they overlap slightly, we see white where all three intersect, yellow where the red and green overlap, cyan where the blue and green overlap, and magenta where the blue and red overlap. By changing the proportion of red, green, and blue light waves, we can produce the full range of colors.

The color we see, then, depends upon both the *incident light* (the wave lengths falling on the object) and the *reflected light* (the wave lengths not absorbed by the object). Sunlight at about noon on a clear day produces the full range of visible light waves. Thus, colors are determined by which light waves are absorbed by the object. For example, in sunlight, a red book appears red because it is absorbing the blue and green light waves and reflecting the red light waves. But if the light falling on that book is fluorescent light, which has a higher proportion of green and blue light waves, there are fewer red light waves to be reflected back, and the book will tend toward black.

Several terms are used to express the various qualities of light and color. *Luminance* refers to brightness, or the intensity of the light reflecting from the surface. Luminance values might in theory range from 0, representing perfect black, which reflects no light, to 100 representing perfect white, which reflects all light. *Hue* refers to that quality by which we distinguish one color from another. Thus hue is what we mean when we say that a color is red or yellow or green or blue or purple. *Chroma* refers to the saturation, or purity, of the color. A saturated color has no white diluting it and has a high chroma. As white dilutes the color, it becomes pale; as it moves closer and closer to white or a neutral gray, it has a lower chroma. (See Fig 7-3.)

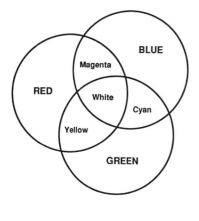

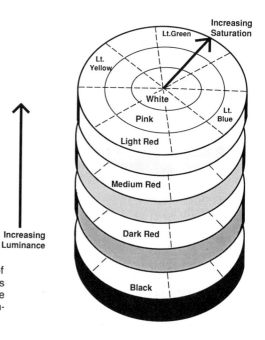

FIGURE 7-3 (above) Adding the three primary colors of light (red, blue, green) produces the secondary colors and white. (right) Increasing luminance increases the brightness of the color. Increasing saturation increases the chroma.

OPTICS

Some objects, rather than absorbing or reflecting light waves, allow them to pass through. As light waves travel through the object, their speed changes. Because the object has a greater density than the air through which the light waves were passing, they will slow down when they enter the object. Then, as they leave the object on the other side and reenter the air, the light waves will increase their speed. As the light waves slow down, they are refracted, or bent. Then, as they resume speed, they are again refracted.

The degree of refraction depends upon the density of the material and the angle at which the light enters it. Thus, ordinary window glass refracts light as it enters and again as it leaves the glass. Since the two surfaces are parallel to each other, the angle of refraction on entering is, in a sense, corrected by the angle of refraction created as the light exits so that the path of the light is displaced rather than altered in direction. Prisms, on the other hand, because of the angles of their surfaces, change the direction of the light (Fig. 7-4). The ability to change the direction in which light travels is important in the development of lenses.

Video cameras, like cameras used in still photography or motion pictures, need some means of gathering the light waves being reflected from the scene and concentrating them onto a photosensitive surface. The camera lens makes this possible. As the light waves pass through the lens of the camera, they are refracted so that they are directed toward a single point of focus. In the video camera, the light is focused on the face of the pickup tube.

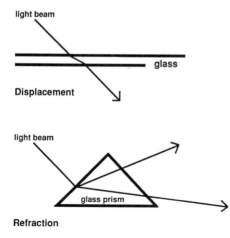

light beam

glass

Displacement

light beam

glass prism

Refraction

FIGURE 7-4 Light displacement and refraction.

Lenses have different optical properties that become important when you are composing shots or trying to achieve particular aesthetic effects. One characteristic is *focal length*. The focal length of a lens is measured from the optical center of the lens to the plane on which the image is in focus.

The focal length of the lens determines the *angle of view* (Fig. 7-5). Angle of view is often referred to as *field of view* because the angle of view determines how

FIGURE 7-5 The shorter the focal length of the lens, the wider the field of view and the more of the object we see. The longer the focal length, the narrower the field of view and the less of the object we see.

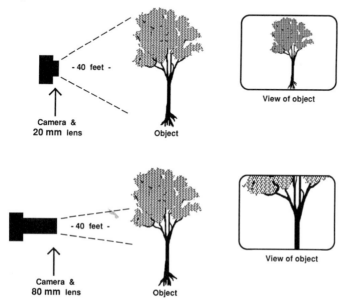

- 40 feet -

View of object

Camera &
20 mm lens

Object

- 40 feet -

View of object

Camera &
80 mm lens

Object

much of the scene will be seen by the camera. A lens with a short focal length, for example, has a wide angle, or wide field of view. A lens with a long focal length has a narrow angle, or narrow field of view.

Another property of lenses that is important in video production is depth of field. When the camera is focused on a subject, there is a limited area in front of and behind that subject that appears to be in focus. This distance from the farthest to the nearest point that is in acceptable focus is called *depth of field.* Depth of field is affected by several factors. One of these is the focal length of the lens. A lens with a short focal length produces a great depth of field. A lens with a long focal length produces a shallow depth of field.

Depth of field is also affected by the distance of the subject from the lens. Moving the subject closer to the lens and focusing creates a shorter depth of field. Moving the subject farther away from the lens and focusing creates a greater depth of field.

A third factor influencing depth of field is the *f-stop,* or the size of the aperture or iris opening. The aperture, or iris, is a diaphragm made up of moveable, overlapping leaves that can be opened or closed to control the amount of light falling on the face of the pickup tube. The f-stop indicates the size of the opening. The f-stop number represents the ratio between the focal length of the lens and the diameter of the aperture opening (f-stop = F/D); thus, the smaller the f-stop, the larger the iris opening (Fig. 7-6). The larger the f-stop, the smaller the opening. Depth of field increases as the f-stop increases (or as the size of the aperture decreases).

In Chapter 9, we'll discuss how focal length, subject–camera distance, f-stop, and depth of field can be used to create specific aesthetic effects. Just one of these is the way in which the focal length of the lens is related to the perspective of the scene. The depth of a scene videotaped with a lens with a long focal length, or a telephoto lens, appears to be compressed. Objects that are separated by considerable foreground-to-background distance appear as if they are very near to each other. On the other hand, a scene videotaped with a lens with a short focal length appears to have much more depth than it really has. Relative distance from the camera is exaggerated so that objects that are close appear to be farther apart. A lens with a normal focal length creates a perspective similar to the perspective we see with our eyes. In photography, the focal length that is normal is close to the diagonal measurement of the film stock being used. In video, the focal length that is normal is close to the measurement of the diameter of the target area of the pickup tube.

Your choice of a lens depends on the specific effect you wish to achieve. Virtually all video cameras in use today have zoom-lens systems. A zoom lens is a lens with a variable focal length. Within the zoom-lens housing is not one lens, but a series of lenses. When you zoom, the lenses move back and forth in relationship to one another. These various distances create the optical characteristics of a range of focal lengths. Thus, within one lens system, you have the equivalent of a selection of lenses. Choosing the lens that will give you the aesthetic and

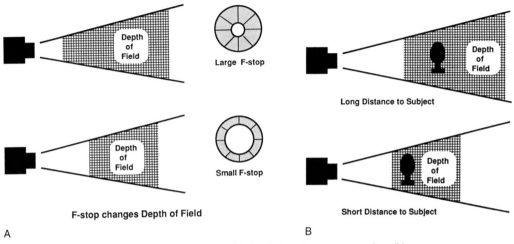

A

B

FIGURE 7-6   The depth of field decreases as (a) the f-stop decreases, and as (b) the distance between the camera and subject decreases.

communicative effects needed in a given situation will be discussed later, in Chapter 9.

Another optical system that is important in color-television cameras is the beam-splitting system. In order to reproduce color, the light reflecting from the scene must be separated into the three primary colors—red, blue, and green.

There are three different methods of separating light into the red, blue, and green wave lengths (Fig. 7-7). One is a prism system. Light coming through the lens passes through a series of prisms cemented together. The rear surface of the prisms have dichroic coatings that reflect particular wave lengths. As the light enters the lens and passes through the first prism, the blue light waves are refracted and directed into the blue pickup tube. The second prism refracts the red light waves and directs them into the red pickup tube. The green light passes through a third prism into the green pickup tube.

A second method of separating red, blue, and green light waves uses a series of dichroic mirrors. As light passes through the lens, it strikes the surface of a mirror that acts as a yellow pass filter. It reflects the blue light waves, but allows the red and green light waves (which combine to make yellow) to pass through. Another mirror directs the blue light waves into the blue pickup tube. The red and green light waves are then divided by a second dichroic mirror, this one acting as a green pass filter. The red light waves are reflected so that they strike a mirror that directs them into the red pickup tube. The green light waves pass through the mirror into the green pickup tube.

The third method for separating colors is used in the single-tube color camera. In this method, color separation is accomplished by mounting filter stripes

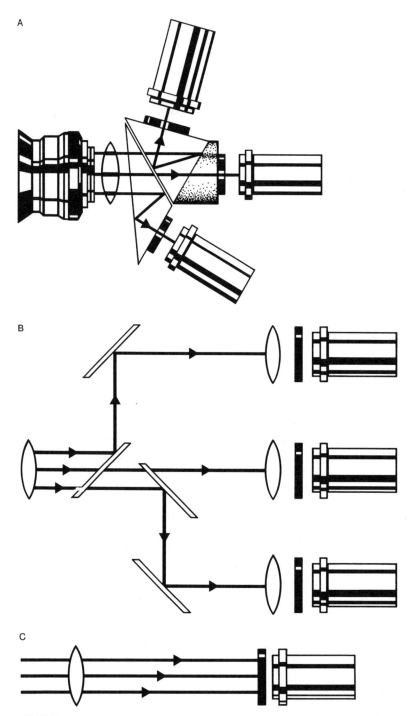

FIGURE 7-7 In a tube camera, light may be separated into red, blue, and green with (a) a prism system or (b) a series of dichroic mirrors. In single tube cameras (c), a filter with alternating stripes of red, blue, and green is mounted on the face of the pickup tube.

on the face of the pickup tube. As light falls on the tube, the red, green, and blue filter stripes allow only a single color to pass through each stripe. The resolution of the color image is limited by how fine these stripes are.

In general, the single-tube color camera using the filter stripes to separate red, green, and blue light waves is smaller than cameras using beam-splitting optical systems. While improvements continue to be made in the design of single-tube cameras, the three-tube camera usually produces better color reproduction and resolution. To ensure that the three images overlap precisely, the three-tube camera must be aligned or registered during set-up. With the development of microprocessors, this registration process can be done automatically.

ELECTRONICS

Video cameras are electronic cameras. The light waves entering the camera through the lens and being focused on the face of the pickup tube must be converted into an electrical signal. To do this, the pickup tube acts as a transducer.

The light entering the camera is focused onto the surface of the pickup tube, which contains the photoconductive layer. As light strikes this photoconductive layer, it changes the electrical charge of the photosensitive material. An electron gun within the pickup tube scans the surface of the photoconductor, restoring the original charge and, in the process, releasing the electrical signal created by the reaction of the light and the photosensitive material. This electrical signal is the video signal. Its strength varies with the differences in the intensity of the light. Thus, bright spots of light produce a stronger signal, and darker areas produce a weaker signal.

Because the system can handle only one bit of information at a time, the electron gun scans the image bit by bit, line by line. Beginning in the upper left of the image, it scans each line from left to right, moving from the top to the bottom of the image. It then moves back to the upper left to begin again.

To reproduce the image as this electrical information reaches the picture tube in the television receiver, another electron gun scans the surface of the picture tube, which is coated with dots of materials that glow when excited by a stream of electrons. The intensity of each glowing dot depends upon the strength of the electrical charge reaching it. The stronger the charge, the brighter the dots will be.

In developing the NTSC (National Television Systems Committee) standard, the system used in the United States, several technical problems had to be addressed. In addition to such matters as cost and bandwidth, major considerations were resolution of the image and the elimination of flicker. As in motion pictures, in order to create the illusion of movement, one image must be replaced by another rapidly enough so that we are not aware of the separation between the two images. In video, because the image is built line by line, there is the additional problem of the first line beginning to fade as the next lines are appearing.

The standard that was developed was an interlace scanning system based on 525 lines, 30 frames per second. In interlace scanning, the electron gun in the pickup tube scans the odd-numbered lines first, then scans the even-numbered lines. Each of these scans makes up one field. The two fields together make up one frame. And, because electrical current in the United States operates at 60 cycles per second, the scanning rate for video cameras is 60 fields per second, or 30 frames per second. See Fig. 7-8.

The picture tube in the receiver operates in the same way. The image is reproduced by scanning every other line, 60 fields per second, 30 frames per second. Displaying the image in this way takes advantage of the way in which the human eye works. As light enters the eye through the lens, it is focused on the retina. There the photoreceptors—the rods and cones—produce a photochemical reaction to the light reaching them. This photochemical reaction activates the nerve cells in the optic nerve, which carries the signal to the brain. The brain then processes this information, attaches meaning to it so that perception takes place, and we "see" the image.

In this neurological process, the image is retained for a split second. This

FIGURE 7-8 (a) An electron gun scans the photoconductive surface at the face of the pickup tube, releasing the electrical charge. (b) The image is recreated as an electron gun scans the surface of the picture tube, causing it to glow. (c) The electron beam is turned off as the gun returns to the beginning of each line.

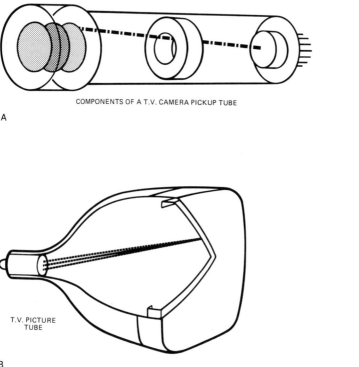

COMPONENTS OF A T.V. CAMERA PICKUP TUBE

A

T.V. PICTURE TUBE

B

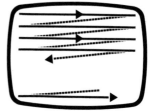

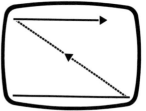

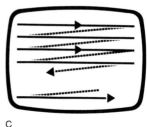

C

is often referred to as *persistence of vision*. We continue to "see" an image for a fraction of a second after it disappears. By changing images quickly enough, we can make them seem continuous. Since our eye retains each image for a fraction of a second, the images blend together and seem to be one continuous action. With fewer images per second, we might well perceive the changing of the images as flicker. The rate of change at which we no longer perceive the change is the *critical flicker frequency* and is related to the intensity of light. Depending on the brightness of the image, this critical flicker frequency may range from 30 to 60 images per second. In motion pictures, for example, each frame is a still photograph. But when the film is projected, each frame is flashed on the screen twice so that 48 images (24 frames, each shown twice) appear and disappear in a second.

In the same way, as the electron gun scans the surface of the pickup tube, it creates 60 separate fields, or 30 frames per second. The television image is actually a series of appearing and disappearing dots. But persistence of vision allows us to "see" what appears to be a continuous image. And because of the phi phenomenon, we connect the slight changes in the images and see the changes as movement across the screen.

In order to reproduce the image exactly as it appeared on the surface of the camera's pickup tube, the scanning of the pickup tube and the picture tube must match up dot for dot and line for line. To keep all of this working in unison, a sync generator produces a series of timing pulses that are sent along with the video signal. These sync pulses are read by the various units in the video system and are used as instructions for timing the scanning of each line.

At the time the technology for transmitting a color signal was becoming practical in the United States, many homes were already using black-and-white receivers. Those receivers would have been useless if they could not receive the color signal. So making color television transmission compatible with the existing black-and-white system was a major consideration.

A second major concern was the bandwidth assigned for each television channel. In allocating channels for television broadcasting, the Federal Communication Commission (FCC) has assigned a bandwidth of 6 MHz for each television channel. This was quite adequate for the monochrome video signal. But, as we've just mentioned, the image in color television is divided into three separate color signals. To transmit each of these separately would require a bandwidth of 18 MHz. Obviously, using an 18-MHz bandwidth rather than the existing 6-MHz bandwidth would drastically reduce the number of possible television channels.

To resolve these two problems, the NTSC recommended a system that uses a luminance signal to carry the brightness information and a chrominance signal to carry the color information. The two signals and the synchronizing signals are combined or encoded to form a composite video signal that is used to modulate the carrier wave. The black-and-white receiver uses the luminance signal to produce a monochrome picture while ignoring the chrominance signal. A color receiver uses both signals. The luminance signal supplies brightness, while the chrominance signal supplies information about the hue and saturation.

A waveform monitor provides a visual display of the video signal. Some portions of the display represent the image being scanned; some portions represent other parts of the video signal. Figure 7-9 is a waveform display of two fields, or one frame, of the video signal being generated by a camera with its lens capped. The portion of the signal at zero is the *blanking level,* the level to which the signal falls when the beam is turned off at the end of each line to allow the electron gun to retrace its path to begin scanning the next line without creating a visible line as it moves back across the image. The portion of the signal at −40 is the sync pulse. The portion between −20 and +20 is the *color burst.* As we've mentioned, sync pulses act as timing signals to synchronize the scanning of the image by the camera with the scanning that re-creates that image on the monitor. The color burst serves as a reference signal for interpreting the color information that was combined with the luminance information.

The image being scanned is uniformly dark because the camera's lens is capped. The image is represented by the portion of the display falling at 7.5 IRE (Institute of Radio Engineers). This level is the usual level for reference black or the pedestal. This is the darkest level in the image.

Figure 7-10 is a waveform display of the signal being generated as the camera is shooting a white surface that is uniformly lighted to produce a peak white signal level. As you'll note, the portion of the display representing the image being scanned is now at 100 IRE. In order to prevent interference with the audio track and to prevent overloading the recorder's inputs, the clipping level is usually set at 100 IRE. This means that highlights in the scene that might peak above 100 IRE will be clipped off.

Figure 7-11 includes a studio scene and the waveform display it produces. By comparing the scene with its waveform display, you can see how the peaks and valleys in the waveform correspond to the bright and dark areas of the scene.

The video system is limited in its ability to reproduce accurately the entire range of brightness that the human eye can discern. Most video cameras are capable of reproducing a contrast range of approximately 30:1. *Contrast range* refers to the degrees of brightness, from darkest to lightest, in a given scene. A contrast

FIGURE 7-9 Waveform produced by a camera with the lens capped.

FIGURE 7-10 Waveform produced by a camera focused on a white surface lighted to produce a peak white signal.

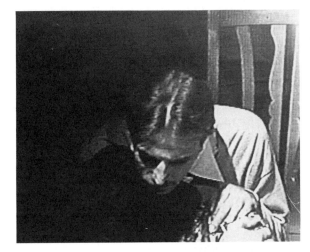

FIGURE 7-11 The peaks in the waveform correspond to the brightness levels in the scene.

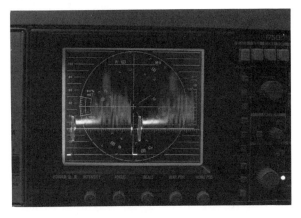

range of 30:1 means that the brightest area in the scene is 30 times brighter than the darkest area in the scene. If the contrast range in the scene exceeds the range that the camera can reproduce, detail will be lost. If the darker areas are compressed, details in the shadow areas that we can see with our eye will appear uniformly black on the video screen. If the lighter areas are compressed, the whites will be clipped and details in the bright areas will be lost.

As a general guide, it is best to avoid having pure white and pure black in the same scene. The contrast range is greater than 30:1, and detail will be lost in the shadow areas or in the highlight areas. This does not mean that you should never use pure white or pure black. It simply means that if you do introduce white, the darkest areas should be in the mid-grey range. If you introduce black, the lightest areas should be in the mid-grey range.

To avoid losing details, it is customary to use television white and television black instead of pure white and pure black. Television white is a shade of grey that has a 60-percent reflectance. Television black is a shade of grey that has a 3-percent reflectance.

A standard nine-step grey scale used in setting up video cameras uses television white with a reflectance of 60 percent and television black with a reflectance of 3 percent, producing a contrast range of 20:1. The progression is logarithmic, so that each shade is about 1.45 times darker (or lighter) than the preceding shade (Fig. 7-12). This grey scale also provides a reference for choosing shades of brightness that are well-defined from one another in the video image. Remember, though, that most cameras today are capable of reproducing at least a 30:1 contrast range, so you should not be too concerned if your lightest or darkest area exceeds that of the nine-step grey scale.

Color bars are a standard reference by which to set chrominance levels (Fig. 7-13). They are generated electronically by the camera or by a color-bar generator. Because they are generated electronically, they have no relationship to the scene that the camera may be used to shoot, but they do provide a reference by which different cameras can be matched. And when they are recorded at the beginning of the videotape, they can be used during postproduction to adjust playback units to avoid errors in reproducing the colors in the original recording.

The pickup tube transduces light energy into electrical energy to create the video image; thus, all video cameras need a minimum light level to operate. The operating light level varies from camera to camera, but each camera's requirements are listed in the specifications for that camera. The minimum light level needed to produce an image will not necessarily give you an optimum image, however. Inherent in every electrical signal is noise. In the video image, noise shows up as a flickering grainy texture in the image. To produce a clean, sharp image, the light levels must be high enough to override this noise. The signal-to-noise ratio must be high enough to produce an acceptable image.

You must be concerned about having enough light for a video camera to produce clean pictures, but you must also be careful about light levels that are too high. Extremely bright lights shining directly onto the pickup tube produce such an intense charge that it cannot be released by the scanning of the electron

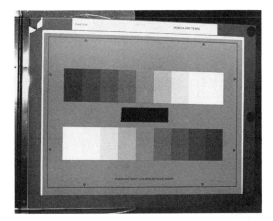

FIGURE 7-12 Nine-step grey scale and its waveform.

FIGURE 7-13 Waveform produced by color bars.

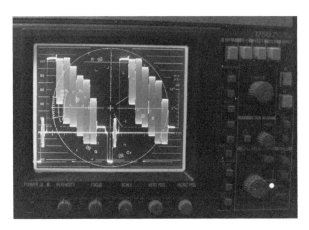

gun. The bright spot will be burned in so that that area of the pickup tube will no longer respond to changes in the light levels falling on it. The burn-in will show up as a spot in all other images produced by the camera.

Noise in the image and lag are two problems that you may encounter related to low lighting. *Lag* is the retention of the image after the camera has moved to another shot. Problems related to intense lighting include burn-in and comet tailing. *Comet-tailing* is the stream of light following the image as the camera moves across the scene.

NEW TECHNOLOGIES

Several interesting new technologies are emerging in video production. Some of these are now in use in production facilities. Others are entering the home video market while research continues to make them acceptable for professional applications.

High-definition television (HDTV) attempts to do what its name implies: to improve the definition, or resolution, of the image. This is accomplished by increasing the number of scan lines. To further enhance the viewing experience, HDTV systems usually include a modified wide-screen aspect ratio (ratio of height to width) and a larger screen size. These changes mean that HDTV is not compatible with the existing video system. Cameras, recorders, monitors, time-base correctors, and the like must be designed for processing the image. In addition, HDTV requires a much greater bandwidth for broadcasting. Thus, to use HDTV in normal television broadcasting, frequencies would have to be reassigned and, since the bandwidth would be greater, fewer frequencies would be available for broadcast use. Home receivers, too, would have to be replaced with receivers capable of displaying the HDTV image. The most immediate application of HDTV in the United States is likely to be in the motion picture industry, in direct-broadcast satellite transmissions, and in cable systems using fiber optic cables to carry the signal.

Another technological advance that is finding application in postproduction facilites is component video. Whenever the chrominance information and the luminance information are encoded into a composite signal, as they are for broadcasting, there is a problem with image defects. A common one is *chroma crawl,* which appears as a barber pole–like effect on edges of color areas. Another is *cross-luminance,* which shows up in a wavy pattern in areas of fine detail, such as a checked or tweed pattern in clothing. Component recording eliminates these problems by keeping the chrominance and the luminance information separate and recording them on separate channels. Component recording also makes it possible to manipulate the signal in postproduction without introducing the noise that occurs when a composite signal is decoded first. Matting, color correction, and so forth can be done without loss of image quality.

In video, digital recording helps to preserve the quality of the original signal. By sampling the video waveform and converting the height of the wave to a numerical value, the signal can be recorded, transmitted, manipulated, or duplicated without being affected by noise. In digital form, the video image can be manipulated in many ways to produce any number of special effects. In playback, the numerical values in the digital signal are used to reconstruct the analog waveform.

In cameras, solid-state sensors are being developed to replace the pickup tubes currently in use. The solid-state sensor is, in essence, a chip onto which the image is focused. As light strikes the pixels (picture elements) in the chip, an electrical charge is built up. The strength of the charge varies with the intensity of the light striking the pixel. Rather than scanning the charged surface with an electron beam, other methods are used. If the sensor is a metal oxide semiconductor, each of the pixels is, in fact, a separate capacitor that can be read just as bits of information stored in a computer memory are read. If the sensor is a charge-coupled device (CCD), the charges from the pixels in each row will be transferred down the line and read out at the end of the line. Solid-state sensors offer advantages over the pickup tube. They are much less susceptible to damage from intense light, so burn-in and comet-tailing are not a concern. There is less geometric distortion in the image. And registration, set in the factory, does not have to be set again. Problems related to manufacturing defect-free sensors, to image distortions such as blooming and vertical smear, and to the need for higher light levels are being addressed. Solid-state sensors are now common in consumer-quality video cameras. Some television news departments are adopting CCD cameras for location shooting. Work continues to make them economically feasible in cameras that must deliver the higher-quality signal needed for other broadcast applications.

SUMMARY

Light is a form of electromagnetic energy made up of a range of frequencies. We interpret the differences in wave lengths as differences in color. These differences in wave lengths are also referred to as differences in color temperature, measured in degrees Kelvin. Light varies according to the relative proportions of the various frequencies it contains. These variations affect the way in which the video camera reproduces the colors in the scene it is recording.

Video cameras use two optical systems. One is a lens that gathers light waves being reflected from the scene and focuses them on the face of the pickup tube. These lenses have different optical properties—different focal lengths, fields of view, and depths of field—that become important in achieving specific aesthetic effects. Most video cameras are equipped with a zoom lens that provides a choice of lenses within the same lens housing.

The other optical system is a beam-splitting system. This may be a prism system, a series of dichroic mirrors, or a stripe filter. All separate the light entering through the lens of the camera into the three primary colors: red, blue, and green.

The pickup tube in the camera acts as a transducer, converting the light energy into electrical energy. An electron beam scans the surface of the pickup tube line by line, releasing the electrical charge. In the NTSC interlace scanning system, the odd-numbered lines are scanned for one field, the even-numbered lines for a second field. The two fields make up one frame. The resulting video information is encoded into a composite signal including a luminance signal (which a black-and-white receiver uses to produce a monochrome picture and a color receiver uses to produce brightness), a chrominance signal (which a color receiver uses for color information), and sync pulses (which keep all the various components working in unison).

A waveform monitor provides a visual display of the video signal. The grey scale and color bars are standard references by which cameras and playback equipment are set.

The video system is limited in its ability to reproduce a scene. The contrast range that most cameras can handle is about 30:1. In addition, operating light levels must be high enough to override the noise in the system. But highlights must not be so intense that they cause burn-in.

New technologies that are overcoming some of the problems experienced with present equipment include HDTV, component video, digital recording, and solid-state sensors.

FOR FURTHER READING

INGRAM, DAVE. *Video Electronics Technology* (Blue Ridge Summit, Penn.: Tab Books, 1983).

MATHIAS, HARRY, and RICHARD PATTERSON. *Electronic Cinematography* (Belmont, Calif.: Wadsworth, 1985).

NOLL, EDWARD M. *Broadcast Radio and Television Handbook,* 6th ed. (Indianapolis: Howard W. Sams & Co., Inc., 1983).

chapter eight ⸻⸻⸻⸻⸻⸻

The Video System ⸻⸻⸻⸻⸻

INTRODUCTION

In Chapters 6 and 7, we talked about some general characteristics of video and discussed the technical aspects of its functioning. In this chapter, we will consider the pieces of equipment that are used to make video productions. Because the technology is changing so rapidly, any detailed descriptions of specific items of equipment are likely to be out of date within a few months. Therefore, we will limit our discussion to general characteristics of various kinds of equipment and stress how individual pieces fit into a larger production system (see Fig. 8-1).

COMPONENTS OF THE VIDEO SYSTEM

The video system has three major functions. The first is *transduction,* or the conversion of energy from one form to another. In this case, light is transformed into electricity. The second is *processing,* in which electrical signals from different inputs are combined and possibly altered. The third function is *storage and retrieval,* in which the processed signals are converted into a form that allows them to be retrieved at a later date. In the case of live broadcast transmission, this step is bypassed as the processed signals are sent directly to a receiver.

The video system also has several secondary functions, including monitoring, amplification, and synchronization. Along the way through the system, signals are displayed on camera, studio, and control-room monitors so that production personnel can view them. Preamplifiers and amplifiers boost signal strength periodically, and sync generators provide a sync pulse to keep scanning functions

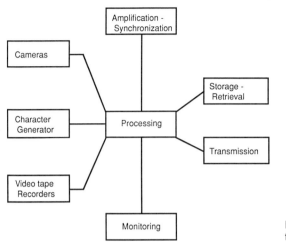

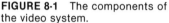

FIGURE 8-1   The components of the video system.

in step with one another. The video system also has correction functions that alter and adjust the signal to keep colors properly balanced and to maintain contrast within certain parameters. Other auxiliary pieces of equipment include time-base correctors, waveform monitors, and color-bar generators. However, our main concern here is with the equipment that is used in the transducing, processing, and storage and retrieval phases of the video system.

INPUTS

The input portion of the video system consists of equipment that generates a video signal that is fed into the rest of the system. This equipment typically includes cameras (studio, remote, film islands), character generators, frame storers, and videotape recorders. Although videotape recorders can function as inputs, they also serve as signal-storage devices, so we will discuss them later.

Cameras

The camera gathers light by means of its lens system, converts that light into electrical energy, and amplifies that energy before it is sent into the rest of the system. There are many different kinds of video cameras available, and they vary considerably in purpose, price, and performance characteristics.

Performance characteristics.   No video camera can produce an image that is as clear and detailed as that which is seen by the human eye. All video cameras operate within certain limitations, although some overcome these better than others. Some cameras meet the technical standards for broadcast purposes in studios or on location. They produce a high-quality picture but are very expensive. Another group of cameras produce an image that does not meet broadcast standards, but is nonetheless of very high quality. These cameras are used in industrial, corporate, and educational settings. A final group of cameras is designed for nonbroadcast use, and their quality is often lower than that of the cameras in the other two groups.

Resolution.   An important measure of a camera's performance capability is its resolution—that is, how much detail of the original image it is able to reproduce. A camera's vertical resolution is determined in part by the number of horizontal scan lines it uses. Cameras operating according to NTSC standards must provide 525 horizontal scan lines. Cameras used in the Phase Alternate Line (PAL) and Sequential Couleur a Memorie (SECAM) systems found in Europe must provide 625 horizontal scan lines. HDTV cameras employ more scan lines. Even though not all of the scan lines are used for the picture, the potential for high resolution is greater as the available number of scan lines increases.

Horizontal resolution is determined by the number of picture elements (pixels) displayed along the horizontal line. This is influenced by the size of the pickup tube, the optics, and the electronics of the camera.

Operating Light Levels.   Another important performance characteristic is the camera's ability to produce a satisfactory image under low lighting conditions. In the 1940s and 1950s, the black-and-white Image-Orthicon cameras required hundreds of footcandles of light to produce a good image. Modern cameras are much more sensitive to light, and many can produce an image with as little as 3 to 5 footcandles of illumination. This is not to say that the image produced by such a low light level is of good quality, but merely that the camera can produce an image of some sort. Generally speaking, low light levels produce a low signal-to-noise ratio, which can lead to annoying grain on a video image. This happens when the signal coming from the camera is not much stronger than the electronic noise within the system. Higher light levels result in a greater signal-to-noise ratio, which raises the video signal well above the system's noise. Many cameras produce a good image at about 125 to 150 footcandles. Some cameras can compensate for low light levels by means of a video gain function, but this only makes the image brighter; it does not compensate for inadequate lighting.

Contrast Range/Ratio.   Cameras also differ in their ability to handle great contrasts between light and dark. The human eye can manage a contrast range of 100 to 1. That is, the brightest portion of an image can be 100 times brighter than the darkest portion. However, video cameras must operate within a much more restricted range of 30 to 1, or even 20 to 1. If the range exceeds these limits, the camera must be adjusted accordingly. This could mean reducing overall brightness to accommodate a very bright portion of the scene, or increasing the camera's sensitivity to accommodate darker portions. An adjustment in either direction will cause picture detail to be lost. To avoid this, the elements of the scene should be kept within the contrast range for which the camera is designed to operate.

Fall-off.   An associated measure of camera performance is *fall-off*. This term describes the speed at which a bright portion of a scene blends into a darker portion. In cameras with fast fall-off, this demarcation is rather abrupt, and subtleties of shading are lost. A camera with a slow fall-off renders a more gradual transition from bright to dark and shows more gradations in contrast.

Picture Distortion.   Video cameras are subject to varying kinds of picture distortion such as lag, comet-tailing, blooming, and burn-in. *Lag* is the persistence of an after-image, or ghost, on the face of the picture tube, and it usually occurs at low light levels. A similar effect is *comet-tailing,* which is a streak that lingers on the picture tube after a bright object has moved across it. *Blooming* can occur around bright objects as a multicolored smear on the screen.

Burn-in is the result of focusing the camera on a highly contrasting image for too long. An after-image will be retained on the face of the picture tube and may not disappear for several seconds. A severe burn-in sometimes results in permanent damage to a picture tube. Modern cameras are much less susceptible to these defects than older models, but it is still advisable to avoid highly contrasting scenes. An operator should not point the camera at an extremely bright light source, such as the sun or a studio light.

White Balance.   Ideally, color cameras should reproduce the color values of the original scene without distortion, but to do this, they must be given a reference. This is done by placing a white card in front of the camera and adjusting it so that the reproduced image is also white. If this is done correctly, all other colors will be reproduced at their proper value. However, this balance will remain constant only for a given color temperature. If the studio lights are dimmed or the camera is moved to a different location, it will have to be white-balanced again. Some cameras provide an automatic white-balancing control, while others must be balanced by an engineer.

Parts of the Camera

Video cameras consist of two main parts: (1) the camera head and (2) a control unit variously called the camera control unit (CCU) or camera processing unit (CPU). The *camera head* consists of the pickup tubes, the internal optical system, preamplification equipment, an external optical system (lenses), a monitor, tally lights, focus knobs, monitor shading controls, cable connections, and an intercom jack. The *control unit* is usually separated from the camera head. It permits alignment, white balance, color registration, and contrast controls. In addition, the camera head and control unit are connected to a power supply and a sync generator.

Pickup tubes.   The most important element in the camera head is the pickup tube. Its job is to convert the optical image focused on its face by the lens into an electrical equivalent. In color cameras, an internal optical system consisting of dichroic mirrors or prisms breaks down the colors of the original scene into the additive primary colors of red, green, and blue and directs each one to its own pickup tube. Some cameras use a slightly different method, with only one pickup tube. (See Chapter 7 for a more detailed explanation.)

Pickup tubes have undergone an evolution since television began, and this has brought about changes in production techniques. Over the past 30 years, pickup tubes have become more rugged, reliable, and smaller. They now offer better resolution, greater picture stability, and less susceptibility to burn-in and other types of image distortion. As a result, video cameras have become smaller and less delicate. They can now operate on batteries and can produce images under low light conditions. These improvements have brought about a dramatic increase in location shooting. Video cameras now have a portability formerly reserved for film cameras, and they have largely replaced motion-picture cameras for newsgathering and other types of location work.

Pickup tubes differ in size and in the composition of the photoconductive materials used. Some studio cameras use pickup tubes with a diameter of 1¼ inch. Other common sizes are 1 inch and 2/3 inch. The 2/3-inch pickup tube is standard for field cameras and is capable of producing a broadcast-quality image.

It was once common to compare large-diameter pickup tubes to the 35-mm film format and the smaller 2/3-inch diameter tubes to 16-mm film. However, recent improvements in the manufacture of smaller-diameter pickup tubes has invalidated the old correlation between smaller diameter and poor image quality. Today, the difference in image quality is more a function of the type of videotape recorder (VTR) used with the camera than the diameter of the pickup tube.

Image-Orthicon tubes are no longer being manufactured, so technically, all pickup tubes are of the vidicon type. They are marketed under trade names such as Plumbicon, Saticon, and Newvicon. The names indicate the various types of photoconductive materials used by manufacturers. However, the term *vidicon* is still used to refer to lower-quality pickup tubes used in nonbroadcast equipment.

The charge-coupled device.   The charge-coupled device (CCD) is an alternative to the camera pickup tube. It is a small silicon chip approximately 1 centimeter (cm) square (Fig. 8-2). Its surface is covered with tiny pixels (sensor elements) which become electrically charged when struck by light. Rather than having this information read off by a scanning gun, as is the case in the traditional pickup tube, timing mechanisms within the CCD shift each horizontal line of information to the top of the chip, where it is passed one charge at a time through a gate and out of the chip. Internal timing clocks shift first the odd lines and then the even ones to accomplish a pattern of interlace scanning that is like a standard pickup tube's. The CCD offers a durability and dependability that surpasses the traditional pickup tube, but its image quality is not as good. That problem will undoubtedly be solved in the near future. Because it is small and flat, the CCD will enable cameras to become even smaller.

Lenses.   The video camera's external optical system consists of lenses which gather light and focus it on the pickup tube. Lenses vary in type and quality

FIGURE 8-2   A charge-coupled-device (left) replaces vidicon tubes (right) in a color camera. (Courtesy of Sony Corporation of America)

and have an important effect on the quality of the image produced by the camera. A low-quality lens will produce a poor image from an otherwise good camera.

Older video cameras were equipped with a set of fixed-focal-length lenses attached to a turret which could be rotated by the operator (Fig. 8-3). The usual configuration was a wide angle, a normal, and a telephoto lens. Some turrets contained a fourth lens, and this could be either an extreme wide-angle or an extreme telephoto lens. Directors often included instructions to the camera oper-

FIGURE 8-3   In the early 1970s, students at The University of North Carolina televised a production of *A Lion in Winter* using cameras with turret lenses. (Courtesy of The University of North Carolina at Chapel Hill)

ator to "flip" or "rack" to a particular lens while off the air. Production students once practiced diligently to make these "flips" silent.

Since the 1960s, lens turrets have largely been replaced by variable-focal-length zoom lenses. These lenses contain several elements that can be moved back and forth to produce the same effect as several lenses of different focal lengths, of which there is an infinite number within the limits of the zoom range. The zoom lens was widely adopted by the television industry because it made camera work so much easier. Rather than pushing the camera back and forth and flipping to different lenses, the operator could easily go from a wide angle to a closeup by means of the zoom lens.

The zoom was originally intended to facilitate changes in focal length between shots, but now it is commonly used to do so within the shot on-the-air. This has radically altered the visual appearance of television productions. Long static shots and moving-camera shots have been replaced by rapid on-the-air zooms.

Zoom lenses are usually designated by two numbers. The first gives the ratio between the shortest and longest focal lengths. The second gives the focal length of the widest angle setting. The designation 10 × 12.5 means that the longest focal length is ten times greater than the shortest and that the shortest would be 12.5 mm. Such a lens could zoom from 12.5 mm to 125 mm.

The video industry employs three different types of zoom lenses. The studio zoom is designed for studio cameras. This lens can zoom from a fairly wide shot to a reasonably close shot with no difficulty. A range of 10 or 15 times would be the norm for a studio zoom.

A field zoom employs a much greater zoom range so that closeup shots of distant action can be achieved without physically moving the cameras close to the event. Field zooms do not have as wide an angle setting as a studio zoom and sometimes have a range of 40 times.

Electronic news-gathering (ENG) and electronic field production (EFP) cameras employ a smaller, lighter zoom lens system with a range of 10, 15, or sometimes 20 to 1.

Range extenders.   It is possible to attach range extenders to zoom lenses. These multiply the focal length through the entire range. An extender with a factor of 2 would change the zoom range of a 10 × 12.5 lens from 12.5/125 to 25/250.

Some cameras have variable-power range extenders, and these allow the operator to vary the multiplication factor of the zoom range as necessary. One drawback of range extenders is that they eliminate the widest angle position. Another is that they cause some deterioration of the image because the light has to pass through additional lens elements. It is also possible to set some zoom lenses in a macro mode. This allows the operator to come quite close to an object and fill the screen with an extreme closeup of something as small as a postage stamp.

Although most cameras today have zoom lenses, there are situations in which lenses with a fixed focal length are preferred. Such situations include productions for HDTV and other applications in which a very high-quality image is desired. Because lenses with a fixed focal length have fewer lens elements through which the light must pass, they will generally produce a somewhat sharper image.

Zoom and focus controls.   The focus and focal length of a zoom lens can be controlled either manually or electrically. On some cameras, the zoom and focus control is a rod that extends from the lens system through the body of the camera. The rod terminates in a knob at the back of the camera. By pushing the rod toward the body of the camera, the operator zooms in. By pulling it out, the operator zooms out. The lens can be focused by twisting the knob at the end of the rod to the right or to the left. Other cameras accomplish these adjustments by means of small servo motors located in the lens system. The operator can press a small lever located on the pan/tilt handle back and forth, and the lens zooms in and out. Many controls permit the operator to vary the speed of the zoom by the distance to the right or left that the lever is moved. Focus is accomplished in a similar fashion by the operator's turning a handle attached to the second pan/tilt control. Some zoom controls are fitted with shot boxes, which allow the operator to preselect different zoom speeds and several zoom positions at the touch of a button (Fig. 8-4).

Presetting the zoom focus.   The zoom and focus control must be "preset" for each position of the camera. If this is not done, the lens will go out of focus at some point during the zoom range. Presetting is accomplished by zooming in on the tightest shot and focusing the image. It should then stay in focus for the entire range. If the camera's position is changed relative to the objects in front of it, however, the preset process will have to be repeated for the new position. It is virtually impossible to preset the focus on ENG and EFP cameras because their operators are constantly moving about. In the field, it is customary for the operator to "follow focus," or continuously adjust it as necessary.

FIGURE 8-4   Camera focus and zoom controls.

Other camera controls.   Video cameras have a number of other controls which vary depending upon the type of camera, its cost, and the degree to which its functions are automated (Fig. 8-5). On the front of a typical studio camera, the operator will find a tally light, which shows when the camera is "hot" or "on-line." There will also be a plug and volume control for the headset, which connects the operator to the studio communication system, and shading controls for the monitor. These controls affect only the quality of the monitor's image; they do not influence the picture being sent out by the camera.

Types of Cameras

We have already described how video cameras can be classified according to broadcast, industrial, and consumer categories. They can also be classified according to use. Some cameras are intended only for studio application, others primarily for remote work, and some can be converted to use in either application.

Studio cameras.   A wide range of studio cameras is available, and like other cameras, they vary considerably in quality and price. A "top-of-the-line" studio camera with lenses and attachments can cost as much as $100,000. Such cameras generate a high-resolution, broadcast-quality image and offer a variety of special features. Purchasers can often specify the kinds of pickup tubes, lenses, and other features. These cameras usually weigh somewhat more than their portable counterparts and can be serviced more easily. They usually have separate CCUs which contain computers that can perform a variety of setup, monitoring, and troubleshooting functions. The computers can also store information about gain, iris, and other settings.

There are also studio cameras available for under $50,000, and some for

FIGURE 8-5 Controls, cable attachment, and monitor on studio camera.

less than $20,000. As the price drops, so does the quality. Usually, less expensive cameras require higher light levels, but when used properly, their picture quality can be quite acceptable for nonbroadcast applications.

Convertibles.   Minaturization of parts, lower power requirements, and automation of setup and control functions have made it possible for cameras to function in the studio and on location. Several manufacturers make cameras that can be converted easily from one function to another (Fig. 8-6). Such cameras can be made "field ready" by removing the studio monitor, changing cable connections, and switching to 12-volt direct current (DC) battery operation. Convertibles can produce a broadcast-quality image in either the studio or on location.

ENG and EFP cameras.   ENG and EFP cameras are another group of cameras designed exclusively for field operations. The terms *ENG* and *EFP* refer more to the uses to which the cameras are put rather than to differences in design. Because ENG and EFP cameras are subject to so much abuse in the field, some stations find it economical to buy several less expensive "disposable" ENG and EFP units for $20,000 each rather than one high-quality ENG and EFP camera at $50,000. The less expensive units produce a broadcast-quality image, but do not have as long an operating life as the more expensive units. ENG and EFP cameras usually employ computerized setup boxes which perform critical air-ready adjustments in a few moments. The camera will then remember the settings during actual operation. ENG and EFP cameras supply a signal to an attached

FIGURE 8-6   A broadcast quality camera that can be converted from studio to remote use. (Courtesy of Ikegami Electronics (U.S.A.), Inc.)

VTR carried by an assistant or send it via cable or microwave to a nearby production truck (Fig. 8-7).

Recording cameras.   Carrying around a separate VTR has always been a problem in location shooting, but until recently, self-contained "camcorders" did not produce a broadcast-quality signal. Some manufacturers have designed broadcast-quality cameras which contain a built-in VTR. This eliminates the need to have a second operator or to relay the camera's signal to a distant point where VTRs are located. Broadcast quality is achieved by special circuitry and with the use of a much faster tape speed. These units use either 1/2-inch or 1/4-inch videotape.

Consumer units.   A large number of inexpensive video cameras are available for the consumer market. These generally cost less than $3,000 and have many automated features. They are designed for use with 1/4-inch or 1/2-inch videotape formats, and they do not produce a broadcast-quality image. Some of these cameras employ separate VTRs, and others have the tape unit built in.

These consumer units usually employ a single pickup tube and are quite lightweight and reliable. They can produce an image under low light conditions, and they frequently have automatic white balance, color balance, ultrasonic automatic focus, in-camera tilting capability, and other features designed to make them easy to use and attractive to the general public.

"Cinematography" cameras.   Many film-camera operators have been reluctant to use video cameras because they function differently from traditional motion-picture cameras. Yet there is an increasing demand for "film-style" shooting using cameras with fixed-focal-length lenses. Some manufacturers have introduced video cameras that are purposely designed to imitate the operating characteristics of motion-picture cameras. These "cinematography" cameras look very much like their film counterparts, and accept standard motion-picture camera lenses (Fig. 8-8). They employ "through-the-lens" reflex viewfinders and accept

FIGURE 8-7   A broadcast quality camera designed for ENG/EFP use. (Courtesy of Ikegami Electronics (U.S.A.), Inc.)

FIGURE 8-8 A "cinematography" video camera that produces a high-definition image. (Courtesy of Ikegami Electronics (U.S.A.), Inc.)

film-camera filters. These cameras are also designed to fit on standard film-camera mounting devices.

The Camera Control Unit

A video camera must be adjusted or set up for each operating situation, and its output must be monitored continuously. Adjustments include setting contrast ratios (by setting master black or pedestal and white levels or iris), white balance, and color registration. In a multiple-camera operation, it is important that all cameras be matched so that settings remain the same from one camera to another.

The CCU performs two important functions. First, it enables the engineer to make the initial setup adjustments. Second, it permits a continuous monitoring of the camera's output during a production. Digitally operated cameras often have two or more separate CCUs. A setup box performs initial adjustments, and a base station or CPU monitors a camera's performance during actual operation. A single setup box can be used for several different cameras and can then be unplugged once initial adjustments have been made. Cameras used for location shooting can be made air ready by a setup box, and then the camera itself will automatically remember the initial settings.

Camera Mounting Devices

Although new technologies have significantly reduced the weight of video cameras, all except the lightest home units are too heavy to hold steady for long periods of time. In the studio, it is customary to mount the camera on some kind of mobile base which allows smooth movement in many directions. In the field, the camera is either held with a grip or attached to a counterweighted body mount.

Head assemblies.   Studio cameras can be attached to their bases in several ways. The wedge mount, which is very popular, consists of a metal plate firmly attached to the bottom of the camera head. It fits into a matching plate on the top of the mounting device. The wedge mount is particularly useful when cameras must be removed for ENG and EFP work because it allows them to be detached quickly.

The device that holds the camera in place must allow horizontal and vertical movement of the camera itself and should provide counterbalancing so that regardless of the position of the camera, it will remain in place if the operator releases her grasp. Several different devices accomplish this by means of arrangements of cams, fluid-filled cylinders, gears, and friction mounts. A popular mount is the cradle head, which permits the camera to be counterbalanced even when tilted to extreme angles. All of these devices have controls by which the operator can regulate the amount of horizontal or vertical drag. (See Fig. 8-9.)

Camera bases.   Studio cameras can be placed on several kinds of bases which provide stability and smoothness of operation (Fig. 8-10). The simplest is the tripod. It is inexpensive and easy to set up, but it does not permit the location or height of the camera to be changed during a shot. Some tripods are fitted with wheels and pedestals which do allow some on-air movement.

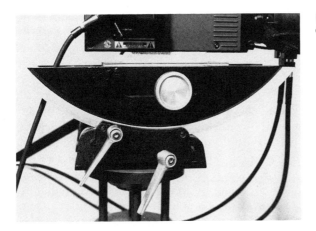

FIGURE 8-9 A video camera's cradle head mount.

FIGURE 8-10   A studio pedestal.

Studio pedestals come in several different configurations and permit the camera to be wheeled about and its height to be changed on the air. The counterweight pedestal is a popular device of this type. The camera sits on top of a column attached to counterweights. The operator moves the camera up or down by exerting pressure on a pedestal ring. As the column moves up or down, the counterweights move in the opposite direction. When properly balanced, the camera remains at any desired height without the aid of the operator.

Pedestals are mounted on three wheels which can be directed by turning the pedestal ring to the right or left. Usually, the operator can select a "crab," or parallel steering, and a "tracking," or tricycle configuration. The selection is made by means of a foot pedal. In the "crab" position, all wheels are arranged parallel to one another. In the tracking position, only the lead wheel is steerable, while the back two remain in a fixed position, just like on a child's tricycle.

Pedestals can raise or lower a camera's height approximately three feet. When greater height is required, cameras can be mounted on large dollies and cranes. These usually require two or more operators and are found only in large studios.

Body mounts.   A great deal of camera work is done outside the studio, and even the best camera operators need help in holding a heavy camera steady over a long period of time. Several different kinds of body mounts have been developed for this purpose. The simplest merely distribute the camera's weight to the back and torso by means of a brace. The more complicated Steadicam counteracts the operator's movement by means of weights and springs so that the camera itself remains steady. Because of the combined weight of the camera and the supporting devices, body mounts can be used only for short periods of time without tiring the operator.

The Film Chain, or Telecine

Another important input into the video system is the telecine, or film chain (Fig. 8-11). It allows the conversion of film or slide images into a video signal. The unit is often located in a room adjacent to the studio or in a corner of the control room. It consists of a special video camera, a 16-mm film projector, and two or more 35-mm slide projectors. The entire apparatus is firmly bolted to the floor to guarantee complete stability.

Images from the film and slide projectors are directed to a multiplexer, which consists of a combination of mirrors and prisms. The multiplexer sends the images to the face of the camera pickup tube. The film chain usually has a device that permits optical dissolving from one projector to another. This is particularly helpful when a series of slides are changed on the air.

The film-chain operator threads up the film and arranges slides in their correct sequence in the trays. If the director intends to dissolve from one slide to another, they must be alternated between trays. The film chain/telecine appears as a separate input on the video switcher and can be "put on line" like any other video source.

While still a valuable component of the video production system, the film chain/telecine is gradually being replaced by frame-store devices. Many films have already been transferred to videotape, so there is less need for 16-mm facilities than there was in the past.

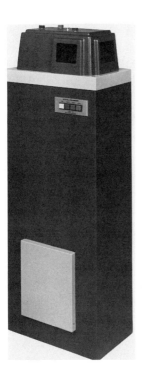

FIGURE 8-11   A telecine/film chain. (Courtesy of The Zei-Mark Corporation)

Character Generation, Animation, and Frame-Store Systems

The introduction of computers and digital technologies has provided the makers of video productions with an almost limitless capability to generate graphics, artwork, and animated sequences, and to store and manipulate camera-produced video images.

In its basic form, a character generator consists of a computer keyboard, a software package, and a memory system (Fig. 8-12). The operator can type in graphics and select from a variety of typefaces, backgrounds, and colors. The graphics can be made to crawl horizontally off the screen or roll off vertically. Entire sequences of graphics can be stored in the generator's memory system.

Animation units allow the operator to generate original drawings, color them, select hard or soft edges, rotate them in space, and create moving, three-dimensional effects. Original art can be combined with real images in a wide variety of ways. Local stations are using such animation systems extensively to produce exciting graphics for newscasts and station breaks. Once composed, animation sequences can be stored in the system's memory for later recall.

Frame grabbers and frame storers have virtually replaced the slide component of the film chain/telecine system. A frame grabber can capture an individual frame from a camera or VTR and store it on disc for later access. Some systems permit the storage of up to 100,000 individual frames. Several thousand of these can be recalled in a split second and shown in any sequence.

SIGNAL PROCESSING

Video production requires a means by which signals generated by different inputs can be selected, manipulated, and mixed together. Transitions between different inputs must also be provided. These functions are carried out by the video production switcher (Fig. 8-13). This device is used to select images during a live

FIGURE 8-12 A character generator with keyboard and display.

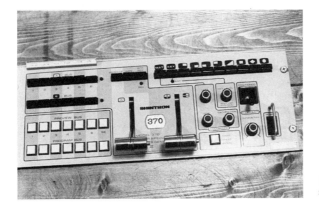

FIGURE 8-13 A production switcher.

broadcast or live-on-tape production. It can also be used to mix inputs from several different VTRs during postproduction editing if it is connected to an A/B roll editing system.

The production switcher is located in the control room of a production facility and is often placed next to the director's station. In some situations, the director does the switching, but it is usually carried out by the technical director (TD) or switcher, who follows the director's commands. (Note that the term *switcher* refers both to the piece of equipment and to its operator.)

On a wall in front of the switcher is a bank of video monitors that show the video inputs from cameras, VTRs, film chain/telecine, character generator, frame storer, and other video inputs. There will also be a monitor marked "line" or "program" and another marked "preview" or "preset." The line monitor shows the signal that is going to the transmitter or to the master VTR. The "preview" monitor allows the director to look at special effects or upcoming shots before they are put on the line.

Functions of the Switcher

Switchers are available in many different configurations and degrees of complexity, but basically they all perform three functions: (1) select from a variety of video inputs which image will go on line, (2) provide transitions between images, and (3) generate special effects. Rather than attempt to explain step by step how a switcher works (because the one you use might be quite different from the one in an example), we will describe the general principles behind how the three functions of any switcher are carried out.

Selection of line image. All switchers have a "program" or "line" buss which consists of individual pushbuttons for each video input. To place a desired video input on line, the operator presses the desired button. The appropriate source then appears on line. The program buss also includes a button that puts up a black signal and perhaps another that places color bars on the line.

Transitions.   This simple configuration permits only straight cut transitions, and most production situations require a method for executing other types of transitions, such as dissolves, fades, superimpositions, and wipes.

To make these transitions possible, the switcher must have additional control busses. These include two identical busses connected by a fader bar, which constitute the mix, or fade unit. In addition, there is a preview buss, which allows the operator to preview a particular transition before it actually goes on line. Fades, dissolves, and superimpositions are performed by selecting the desired sources on the two mix busses and moving the fader bar from one buss to the other. Dissolves and fades from one picture source to another can be executed in this way. A superimposition is accomplished by stopping the fader bar at a midposition between the two busses.

Special-effects unit.   Many switchers have an additional special-effects unit, which permits keys and other effects as well as more elaborate transitions than the mix unit does. A special-effects unit consists of additional busses, selector buttons for wipe transitions, a joystick positioner, and keying controls.

Wipe transitions.   The special-effects unit allows the operator to carry out transitions from one video source to another in the form of many kinds of wipes (Fig. 8-14). These include horizontal and vertical wipes, corner wipes, and spotlight effects. The operator selects the kind of wipe desired, punches up the two video sources on the special effects busses, and moves the fader bar between the two. The joystick allows some of the wipes to be positioned (an oval wipe can be moved about like a spotlight), and other controls permit the selection of hard or

FIGURE 8-14   Four different wipe transitions. (a) Corner wipe. (b) Horizontal wipe. (c) Vertical wipe. (d) Circular wipe.

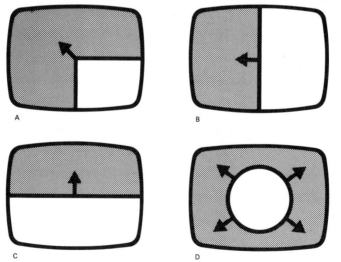

soft edges for the transition and the direction in which it will move across the screen. Wipes can be stopped at midpoint to obtain a split-screen or spotlight effect.

Keying. The switcher's special-effects unit also permits the insertion of one video source into another in a process called *keying*. The key is usually used to place titles into a background, but it can also be used to place one image into another.

There are basically four kinds of keys: the internal, or self, key; the matte key; the external key; and the chroma key. The internal key places titles from one video source into the background from another. The keying circuitry erases a space from the background that is the exact shape of the source being keyed. The titles are then fitted into the empty space like a key into a keyhole. Unlike a superimposition of titles over a background in which that background is visible through the letters, the internal key produces a solid composite image. (See Fig. 8-15.)

In a matte key, the space inside the titles can be filled with different colors or designs generated by the switcher's matte control. In the external key, the spaces inside the titles are filled with an image from a third video source.

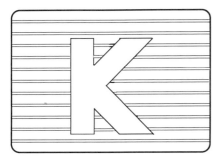

Internal Key

A

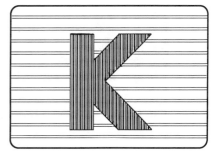

Matte Key

B

External Key

C

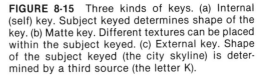

FIGURE 8-15 Three kinds of keys. (a) Internal (self) key. Subject keyed determines shape of the key. (b) Matte key. Different textures can be placed within the subject keyed. (c) External key. Shape of the subject keyed (the city skyline) is determined by a third source (the letter K).

Whether the third video source is a moving image or a design, it will appear in the spaces of the titles as though the viewer were observing it through the letters.

The chroma key enables the operator to place a second video image into a chroma-key window on the background. The window is created by the presence of a special color, usually blue or green, in the background image. A newscaster can be placed in front of a blue screen and the chroma-key effect will place the second source in all places where the color appears. The newscaster will seem to be standing or sitting in front of the source image.

Some switchers are capable of downstream keying. In this process, keying can take place after the signal leaves the switcher so that keys can be done over special effects or existing keys.

Digital video effects.   In combination with digital video effects (DVE) units switchers can provide an almost endless number of special visual effects, (Fig. 8-16). The DVE system first translates a video image into digital information. A host of intricate manipulations are then possible, including (1) changing the size of the image by compression or expansion, (2) positioning it anywhere within

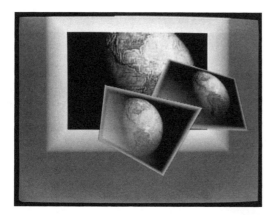

FIGURE 8-16 Digital video effects.
(Courtesy of The Grass Valley Group, Inc.)

the frame, (3) flipping it horizontally or vertically, (4) panning or tilting it, (5) twisting it, (6) peeling it off the screen, or (7) spinning it around. The DVE unit also enables the operator to break the image down into a series of small mosaic rectangles, change the contrast and colors of different segments, and manipulate the hardness or softness of edges.

Special features. A few special features found on some switchers including flip-flop controls, double reentry, and cascading, should be mentioned.

When a production situation calls for a rapid cutting back and forth between the same two video sources, it is possible to execute the transition quickly by means of flip-flop controls. The operator presses a cut or take button and the switcher "flip-flops" whatever is on preview to line. The image that was on the line now appears on preview. Pressing the button a second time will flip-flop preview to line and line to preview again.

A double reentry switcher permits the output to be fed back into the switcher several times. This allows the operator to key over an existing key (see downstream keying) or dissolve from one effect to another. In this process, the output of the switcher is treated as another video source. When reentry occurs several times, the process is known as cascading, as the effect passes down the switcher from one bank of busses to another.

The technology of switchers is developing rapidly. Many of them have become so complicated that the operator must rely on the assistance of a computer to execute difficult setups and transitions. At the same time, computer assistance is making switcher operation easier so that one person can carry out a number of functions at the press of a button. The computer can remember a sequence of transitions and execute them in order at a single command.

STORAGE AND RETRIEVAL

After a video signal has been processed by the production switcher, it can be either sent directly to a transmitter for instantaneous distribution to receivers or stored on a videotape or videodisc machine for later playback.

Videotape Recorders

A VTR is similar to an audiotape recorder in that it transfers incoming electronic signals into magnetic fluctuations which are captured by a plastic tape as it moves past the record head. A VTR records the video signal, up to three audio tracks, and a control track, which is used to synchronize the scanning of each video frame. One of the audio tracks can be used as a cue or address track, which records the director's commands, or a time-code reference, which assigns a number to each frame. VTRs can be classified according to the width of tape that they use and the arrangement of record heads in relation to the tape.

Tape widths.   Five videotape widths are available. The 2-inch and 1-inch widths are found in professional reel-to-reel broadcast-quality machines. These are often referred to as large-format or high-band systems because they can record high frequencies of video information. The 3/4-inch and 1/2-inch widths are found in cassette form only. The 3/4-inch U-Matic recorder is standard for ENG/EFP work and is common throughout the broadcast industry, although the format is less widespread than it once was. The 1/2-inch tape width is commonly used in small-format home video units. The fifth tape width is the 1/4-inch Technicolor format. It is used mainly in nonbroadcast, amateur units but has been adapted for broadcast use in the Bosch Quartercam.

Although it is tempting to correlate tape size with picture quality, as we do with motion picture film (the larger the base, the higher the quality of image), picture quality is more a result of the speed at which the videotape and the record heads move in relation to one another. Because so much information must be laid down on the tape, the VTR requires a large amount of tape surface passing over the heads per second. This could be accomplished by transporting the tape rapidly over the heads, but this method would result in a very short recording time even for large reels of tape. The necessary speed is accomplished in all VTRs by moving the record heads themselves as well as the tape. The combined speed of spinning heads and moving tape is known as the *writing speed.* Moving the heads as well as the tape provides the necessary speed for recording purposes without sacrificing playing time.

Tape-head configurations.   VTR manufacturers have devised two tape-scanning configurations—the transverse and the helical formats—which allow the record heads to rotate as the tape moves past them (Fig. 8-17).

Transverse Format.   Two-inch reel-to-reel VTRs use a transverse head configuration. Four record heads rotate 90 degrees to the tape path at a speed of approximately 100 inches per second across the tape, which moves through the machine at 15 inches per second. The resulting writing speed is approximately 1,500 inches per second. These four head machines are commonly known as quadruplex, or "quad," machines. A quad machine produces a high-quality broadcast image, but because each frame requires several passes of a head across the tape, it cannot produce slow motion, fast motion, or freeze frames.

Helical Scan.   A more widely used tape-head arrangement is the helical-scan format. The tape head rotates across the tape at an angle. This is accomplished by wrapping the tape around the head drum so that it lies at an angle in relation to the horizontally rotating heads.

One-inch reel-to-reel VTRs use two slightly different helical-scan formats. The Type C format uses one rotating record head which records one complete video field with each pass across the tape. The tape moves past the head at a rate of 9.61 inches per second, and the head moves across the tape at a rate of 1,007 inches per second. Because each sweep of the head contains the information to

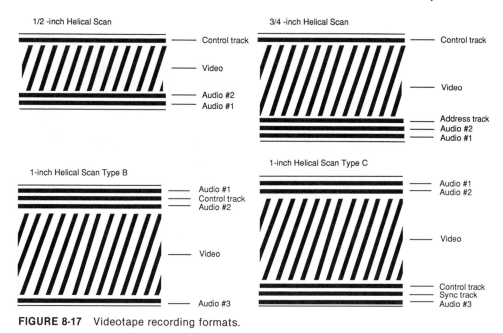

FIGURE 8-17 Videotape recording formats.

make up one complete video field (two fields make a frame), freeze frame and slow and fast motion are possible.

The other 1-inch format is Type B. This method uses two heads rotating past the tape. One head is always in contact with the tape, and it takes several scans to make up one video field. This means that the Type B machine cannot achieve freeze frame or slow and fast motion effects.

The 3/4-inch VTRs also use a helical-scan system, but the tape moves at a much slower speed of 3.75 inches per second. The resulting writing speed is 404 inches per second. Some machines use a higher tape speed to achieve a better picture quality. The 3/4-inch U-Matic VCR is widely used in the broadcast industry partly because the format is standardized—that is, all 3/4-inch U-Matic machines are compatible with one another (Fig. 8-18).

Home VCRs use either the Betamax (Beta) or VHS helical-scan formats with 1/2-inch videotape. The two formats are not compatible with each other. Beta and VHS units provide long recording times, but they do not produce broadcast-quality images. However, the Recam and Betacam cameras do use a high-speed 1/2-inch tape to produce a broadcast-quality image.

Video Disc Systems

A video image can also be recorded onto a metal disc which spins rapidly past a magnetic recording head (Fig. 8-19). Video discs usually record only a small amount of information (about one minute's worth), but this information can be

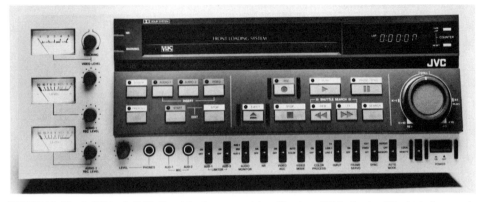

FIGURE 8-18   A 3/4-inch U-Matic videotape recorder. (Courtesy JVC Professional Products Company)

accessed very quickly. Video disc recorders are used for instant replay, freeze frame, and slow motion. They are ideal for use during broadcasts of sporting events.

SUMMARY

Individual pieces of video equipment function together as a total system to convert light into electricity, combine and alter signals from several inputs, and either transmit that combined signal or store it for later use. In addition, the video system has monitoring, amplification, and synchronization functions.

Inputs to the video system consist of cameras, character generators, animation systems, frame storers, and VTRs. Cameras gather light, convert it into electrical energy, and amplify the signal before it is sent to the rest of the system. Cameras vary according to

FIGURE 8-19   A video disc recorder. (Courtesy of Panasonic Industrial Company)

their resolution, the light levels they need, their contrast range and ratios, fall-off, and picture distortion.

A video camera consists of two main parts: (1) the camera head, which contains lenses, pickup tubes, and amplifiers; and (2) the CCU, which performs balance and shading functions. All modern pickup tubes are of the "vidicon" variety, and they are available in diameters from 1¼ inch to 2/3 inch. The CCD is a recent alternative to the pickup tube. It is a silicon chip approximately 1 centimeter square and covered with tiny light-sensing pixels.

Lenses gather light and focus it on the face of the camera's pickup tube. Video cameras once had several lenses of different focal lengths mounted on a turret. Most cameras today use zoom lenses, which provide a wide range of focal lengths.

Video cameras have several important operator controls, including zoom and focus controls, shading knobs for the camera's monitor, and volume controls for the studio intercom. Operators must be careful to set the zoom focus for each position of the camera.

Cameras can be classified both according to broadcast, industrial, and consumer categories and according to where they are intended to be used. Some cameras are designed only for studio operation; others can be converted from studio to location use; and others, such as ENG/EFP units, are designed only for field operation. Manufacturers have recently introduced broadcast-quality "recording cameras" with self-contained 1/2-inch VTRs. Other types of cameras are consumer units and "cinematography" cameras.

Studio cameras can be mounted on tripods, pedestals, dollies, and cranes. These camera mounts allow for smooth movement and steady images. Field cameras can be hand-held or mounted on Steadicams and other types of body braces.

Other important inputs into the video system are the film chain/telecine (which handles slides and motion-picture film), character generators, animation systems, and frame storers. These permit the creation of many kinds of computer-generated graphics and images.

The video signal is processed and mixed by the video switcher. This unit permits the operator to select the images that will be placed on line and the types of transitions between images. Switchers also permit the keying of images over one another and the generation of many special effects such as wipes and complicated digital transitions. Some switchers have flip-flop controls and double-reentry capability. Many modern switchers are computer assisted to allow the execution of complicated sequences of transitions and effects.

Video signals are stored on videotape and disc. VTRs are usually classified according to the width of the tape they use. The standard widths are 2 inch and 1 inch, which are found in open-reel machines, and 3/4 inch and 1/2 inch, which are found in cassette machines. The 1/2-inch format is common for consumer units, which are either VHS or Beta.

VTRs are also classified according to the scanning path of the tape heads. Two-inch open-reel machines use a transverse path in which record heads rotate at 90 degrees to the tape path. Other machines use a helical- or slant-scan path. This helical format is available in either Type C or Type B.

Video disc machines record a small amount of information, usually not more than a minute or so, but they can retrieve images very quickly. These machines are often used for replay during the telecast of sporting events.

FOR FURTHER READING

BURROWS, THOMAS D. and DONALD N. WOOD. *Television Production: Disciplines and Techniques,* 3d ed. (Dubuque, Iowa: Wm. C. Brown, 1986).

KINDEM, GORHAM. *The Moving Image: Production Principles and Practices* (Glenview, Ill.: Scott, Foresman, 1987).

PATTERSON, RICHARD and DANA WHITE, eds. *Electronic Production Techniques* (American Cinematographer Reprint, 1986).

WURTZEL, ALAN. *Television Production,* 3d ed. (New York: McGraw-Hill, 1986).

ZETTL, HERBERT. *Television Production Handbook,* 4th ed. (Belmont, Calif.: Wadsworth, 1987).

chapter nine _____

Video Writing
and Script Formats _____

INTRODUCTION

All video productions begin with ideas. These ideas range from the highly personal expressions of a video artist to a mother's desire to videotape her daugh-
ter's first birthday party. Most ideas for video productions are the result of a
response to a particular need. A network might need a new comedy series for
Thursday evenings; a local station might want to do an actuality on the community's drug abuse problem; the mathematics department at a university could need
a series of instructional videotapes; or a large corporation could decide to produce training tapes for sales representatives.

Some of these ideas require considerable research before they can be developed into a full script. The preparation of a script for a video documentary can
involve many hours of library research and on-site visits, for example. Other ideas
(such as the birthday party video) require little or no preplanning or scripting
and can be shot pretty much as they happen.

The development of ideas into a script is the job of the video writer. He is
a crucial person in the complex process of creating video programs because it is
almost impossible to produce a good video program without good writing. In
this chapter, we will discuss the role of the video writer, the processes of selecting
and developing ideas into script form, and the various types of script formats
that can be followed.

THE VIDEO WRITER'S ROLE

Writing for video is not the same as writing a novel, play, or collection of poems.
For one thing, video writers often work in a production team, which can include
other writers, producers, directors, and executives. Also, a video writer's work

must be designed to meet a specific need. In addition, a video script usually is not as personal as the works of a novelist or poet. By contrast, a novelist or poet often works alone, often producing a highly personal statement that might be read by a few thousand people.

Video writers must work with a number of conditions not faced by the isolated novelist or poet. They must always be conscious of the nature of the medium, which demands an ability to express ideas in visual terms and an understanding of the purposes of various video productions, audiences, production circumstances, and budgetary constraints. Also, the writers of video programs do far more than think up ideas and write scripts. They do research, write proposals, develop treatments, meet with production staff, and frequently rewrite extensively during actual production.

CONSTRAINTS

Video writers need to take into account several limitations when developing an idea into final script form. These constraints include the purpose of the production, the intended audience, the conditions of production, and the aesthetic characteristics of the video medium.

Purpose

Most video programs are intended to fill a specific purpose. Most commercial productions aired by networks and local stations are designed to entertain. Such productions would include situation comedies, police shows, and concerts. They often follow a well-established formula, and the writer must fit ideas into that fixed mold, shaping them to conform to established narrative devices and writing dialogue with established characters in mind.

Other programs, such as documentaries, newscasts, actualities, and discussions, are designed mainly to inform. Writing for such productions demands a considerable amount of research so that the writer can be very familiar with the subject in order to produce an accurate and credible script. The writing for such productions is often done by trained journalists who gather the information themselves and then appear on the air as reporters or news anchors. It is a fairly common practice at the networks and some larger local stations for on-air talent to write much of their own copy.

Some programs are intended mainly to instruct. Many stations broadcast instructional programs that can be taken for college credit. These programs might require that specialists in the field do the writing, or at least that the writer consult specialists to ensure the accuracy of the script.

Commercials and public-service announcements are intended to persuade, and most of them are written by experts who specialize in the writing of commercial copy. They usually work for advertising agencies and collaborate with other writers, producers, directors, and account executives in the development of advertising campaigns for particular products.

Audiences

A video writer must also take into account the intended audience for a particular script. A novelist who may reach only a few thousand people is relatively free to say what she pleases, but the video writer must be careful to tailor the script to the audience who will watch the final production.

Many broadcast productions are designed to reach a large audience made up of people with varying experience, backgrounds, and levels of education. The writer must create a script that can be understood easily. Such a script might avoid highly technical language, very abstract ideas, or controversial subjects.

On the other hand, some programs are designed for a particular audience. A writer might be asked to produce a script for a corporate training campaign or to do a series of instructional productions. In this case, the writer must be familiar with the specialized language and issues that are important to a specific audience. Ideally, the writer should spend a considerable amount of time becoming familiar with the backgrounds and interests of the audience that will be viewing this kind of program.

Production Circumstances

Video writers should keep in mind that all video productions are subject to some limitations. Often, the greatest limitation is time. An idea must be developed quickly, usually within a matter of days or weeks; sometimes, a production has to be written within a few hours. The writer must be able to work quickly, and this requires the ability to see the key issues of a subject, develop an overall approach, think visually, and write succinctly.

Another important production constraint is money. Even the most elaborate network productions are made within some kind of budget. Programs for local stations, schools, and some corporate settings are given very modest budgets, and the writer needs to know how much money is available for the actual production. Such information enables the writer to avoid requesting expensive location shooting, elaborate special effects, or large numbers of actors when there is no money to pay for them.

Equipment availability also presents a limitation to the writer's work. A production done at a major studio in New York can be much more elaborate than one done at a small studio on a university campus. The writer must shape the script to the available production facilities. Many student writers fail to recognize the limitations of the equipment at hand when planning their productions. They are inevitably disappointed when limited facilities do not allow them to do the special kinds of production work that they had envisioned while writing the script.

Aesthetic Considerations

Video writers also need to keep in mind the fact that they are writing for a visual medium. This requires that they think of ways to make their subjects visually interesting. This task can be particularly difficult for those who are trained to express themselves through words, yet it is an absolute requirement for successful video writing. Furthermore, the video writer must be able to write dialogue that is clear and to the point. Words must support and explain, rather than replace, the visuals. Student writers sometimes make the mistake of burdening their productions with long, loquacious passages rather than letting the visuals carry the ideas.

SOURCES OF SCRIPT IDEAS

Student writers often have difficulty coming up with ideas for video productions. The instructor might assign a 10-minute actuality or a 15-minute interview-demonstration, but then the student must generate suitable ideas. If you are stuck for a program subject, a few practical suggestions are presented here to stir your imagination.

Imitation

There are very few totally new ideas in the world, and most ideas for video productions are modifications of ones that have been used before. One way to get inspiration for a production is to turn on the television set and watch what networks, stations, and cable systems are actually broadcasting. Make a mental note of the kinds of people who are interviewed and the types of actualities that are produced. You might discover that a segment of the local "PM Magazine" could easily be adapted to fit the requirements of a student production. Remember that novelists, poets, painters, and musicians frequently modify the ideas of others. There is nothing unusual about taking inspiration from the work of another.

Adaptations

Another source of ideas is other media. Films, novels, short stories, plays, and magazine or newspaper articles are frequently used as sources for video productions. One student read an article in a local newspaper about a man who had just opened a museum for antique bicycles. The student called the man and made arrangements to videotape an interview and the museum itself. The result was a fascinating actuality about old bicycles.

Personal Interests

Every person has a wealth of experience and interests that can be the source of production ideas. Make a list of the things in which you are interested. Are you an amateur photographer, stamp collector, or musician? Have you recently taken a trip, sat in on an interesting lecture, or met an unusual person? Often, the subjects in which you have a special interest can be turned into successful video productions because you bring your knowledge and enthusiasm to their development.

A student fulfilled an assignment to produce a 10-minute interview by drawing upon her knowledge of astronomy. The student arranged for the director of a nearby planetarium to bring over a collection of old telescopes. The instruments were interesting to look at and provided an opportunity for the guest to tell fascinating stories about each one. What could have been a routine production turned out to be a stimulating and informative one because the student had tapped a subject for which she had special enthusiasm.

Contacts

If you cannot find something in your personal experience that suggests an idea for a production, you probably know someone who has an unusual interest, skill, or experience. Make a list of relatives, friends, teachers, community leaders, employers, and acquaintances. Perhaps several persons on this list would have interesting occupations or hobbies that could become the subject of a video production.

One student had a friend whose father spent his spare time making wooden toys for children. What made this especially unusual was that the man was almost completely blind. The student saw an opportunity to do an interesting actuality on the man's special dedication and skill. The production included an interview and a demonstration of how the man turned a block of wood into a finely crafted toy by using only his sense of touch.

Survey the Environment

Writers often dismiss the familiar in their search for program ideas, but artists have always known that some of the best ideas are found in the commonplace things around us. Novelists write about the people in their home towns; painters put on canvas the view from their kitchen windows; composers use folktunes as the basis for symphonies. In every community there are interesting people, colorful old buildings, and unusual events that can become the subjects of video productions. If you are stuck for an idea, take a walk around the neighborhood or down the main street of town. Keep your eyes open and let your imagination take over.

APPROACH

Once you have selected an idea for a production, you must decide how it will be developed. This step usually involves some research. If the production is to be an interview, for example, you will need to meet the guest and find out as much as possible. From this preinterview, you can establish the questions to be used during the actual interview.

It is sometimes best to approach a subject without any preconceived notions and spend time studying it until an approach suggests itself. A student once decided to do an actuality on historical preservation efforts in her home community, but she wasn't sure what her approach should be. She began by interviewing key people in the historical preservation movement and let them tell her what the important issues were. Next she went to several of the buildings that were being restored and recorded several hours of videotape. Her production did not take a final form until the postproduction stage. Just as some sculptors claim to see a form in the stone and perceive carving as an act of releasing that form, so the video writer needs to study a subject and perceive the natural approach to it rather than imposing an artificial one.

Early in the stages of developing an approach, the writer must decide upon the overall style of the production. Will it be a documentary, an interview, an on-site demonstration? Will it be shot in a studio, or on location, or will it be a mixture of the two? Will it use actors, experts, still photographs, slides, or film footage? The writer must also consider the practicalities of the production at this point. How long will the production take to shoot and edit? How much will it cost, and what facilities will be used? Careful planning at this stage can save a great deal of time, labor, and money later.

STRUCTURE

Most subjects can be treated in a number of ways, but the most appropriate one is often a function of the type of subject being dealt with or the writer's aims.

Let's take the example of an old movie palace that is being threatened with demolition. The subject is very visual and has sentimental appeal as well. The writer wants to communicate the idea that the building is worth saving.

One possible structure for the production is chronological. The program could present the history of the theatre and rely upon old photographs and perhaps interviews with former employees to show that the building had become an important part of the community.

Another structure is comparative. The script could discuss efforts to save movie palaces in other communities and show how other cities have benefitted from preserving such structures.

Perhaps the script could take an impressionistic approach. It could stress the beauty of the theatre's interior by using closeups of ornate details and supporting these with a voiceover narration and music.

The dramatic structure is another approach. The writer could treat the subject as a conflict between preservationists and developers. The program could contain interviews with representatives from each side and examine the ramifications of each point of view. Of course, all of these structural approaches can be combined in a variety of ways. A program need not limit itself to one or another.

Once a structural approach has been decided upon, the writer can lay out the segments of the production in order and begin to write copy. It is sometimes possible to develop a complete script in advance of shooting. At other times, it may be necessary to record footage and write the script only after viewing it.

Video writers have several script types from which to choose. They can prepare a full script that is a fairly complete written version of how the production is to look, or they might write a less detailed partial script or perhaps prepare a rundown sheet listing the order and timing of program segments. The rest of this chapter describes the various script formats that video writers can use.

THE SCRIPT

A script is a written master plan for a video production. It can be extremely detailed, or it might be merely a list of segments with a great deal of room for on-the-air improvisation. Regardless of their complexity, all video scripts are intended to (1) specify what materials will be used in the program, (2) indicate the order of these materials, and (3) communicate the overall approach to the subject.

Types of Scripts

Three general types of scripts are commonly used in video productions. The full, or complete, script is used for programs that must be executed with a great deal of precision and that have many complicated parts. A full script usually contains all dialogue and has indications for blocking, shot composition, and camera positions. Dramas, documentaries, newscasts, commercials, and public-service announcements usually follow a complete script.

Some programs do not lend themselves to a full script. Interviews, for example, cannot be completely scripted in advance. If they were, the conversation would be hopelessly stilted. A partial script, which contains some completely written portions and other unscripted sections, would be more appropriate.

If a program is done on a regular basis and follows basically the same format, a production crew can become so familiar with its routine that even a partial script is not necessary. In such a situation, a rundown sheet that lists the order of program segments with their timings is probably all that is necessary.

The full script.   The video industry uses two types of full scripts. The split-page type places audio (including dialogue, indications for sound effects, and music) on the right-hand side of the page (Fig. 9-1). The left side contains indications for the points where slides, film, and videotape can be inserted and the timings for these segments. The video column often contains suggestions for shot composition, camera movement, and transitions between shots. Sometimes the video column has the director's commands listed, with the exact points for takes indicated. The writer sometimes puts in this information, but it is usually added by the director in the process of marking the script (see discussion later).

Another type of complete script is the full-page format (Fig. 9-2). It resembles a film script in that dialogue is placed across the width of the page rather

VIDEO	FOCUS EMU	AUDIO
SLIDE	MUSIC: THEME, ESTABLISH, THEN UNDER & OUT	
LS STUDIO SET	SLIDE: TITLE	
	ANNCR: Good morning, and welcome to today's edition of Focus EMU, a program devoted to a discussion of issues and the people important to them at Eastern Michigan University and the Ypsilanti community. And now, here's our host John Fortune.	
CU HOST	HOST: Today, we are fortunate to have with us two members of the EMU School of Business faculty who will discuss the proposed move of the School to an off-campus location in downtown Ypsilanti.	
2-SHOT GUESTS	Let me introduce our guests Frank Jones and William Smith.	

FIGURE 9-1   A split-page script format.

than in a narrow column on the right-hand side. Individual scenes are sometimes numbered, and the writer provides a description of the location for each one and indications for how the scene can be shot. This information is often added later by the director. The full-page format is used for dramatic programs, while newscasts and documentaries use the split-page format.

The full script gives a director a great deal of control over the final program, and this is very important when the production is complicated. A full script allows for detailed preplanning, the orderly rehearsal of parts, and the polishing of all production elements. Writing a full script is a valuable exercise for beginning production students because it forces them to think through every aspect of the production in advance.

One disadvantage of working with a full script is that it permits very little flexibility during production. A beginning director can become so concerned about following a full script to the letter that he fusses needlessly over small deviations. Furthermore, if a mistake occurs during production, it can be difficult to get the program back on the script. This is less of a problem today than it was during the days of live television because the videotape can be stopped until the problems are corrected. Some beginning directors make the mistake of following the script so slavishly that they never have a chance to look at the cameras' monitors. Ideally, directors should be familiar enough with the script so that they can watch the monitors periodically during the production.

12 INT. LIVING ROOM—DAY

John is sitting at his desk by the window busily typing a manuscript. The telephone rings and he picks it up.

> JOHN
>
> Hello, Yes, this is he.
> No, she isn't in now, but
> I expect her back soon.
> OK. Goodbye.

John puts down the telephone, and his wife Sylvia enters screen left.

13 ANGLE CU SYLVIA

> JOHN
>
> Hi, You just missed a
> telephone call. Where were
> you?
>
> SYLVIA
> (uneasily)
>
> I . . . I was at the grocery.

14 CU- JOHN

> JOHN
>
> Sure you were! Listen, Sylvia,
> I don't care what you were doing.
> Just don't lie!

15 COVER SHOT

John rises. Turns off the typewriter and leaves the room.

16 EXT. GARDEN—DAY

John paces back and forth on the patio. He lights a cigarette and then carelessly tosses it away. John opens the door and goes back into the house.

FIGURE 9-2 Full page script format.

News scripts. News programs contain many elements that must be brought together with great precision. The entire newscast is usually unrehearsed, so the script must clearly indicate the relationship of all parts. The left hand "video" column of a news script contains indications for the insertion of slides, titles, and video or film footage. It shows whether that footage is silent,

silent with voiceover, read live, or whether it has its own sound (sound on tape or on film). Each insert is numbered, and the timing indicated (Fig. 9-3).

Each story is placed on a separate page headed by a title or slug for the story. In this way, stories can be quickly added or deleted from the copy. This method also allows the director to get a rough timing for the show by multiplying the timing of one page by the total number of pages in the script. The script copy is usually duplicated on a teleprompter so that readers can look into the camera rather than staring down at their scripts.

FIGURE 9-3 An example of a television news script. (Courtesy of WJBK-TV, Channel 2, Detroit, MI)

Partial scripts. Some programs do not require a full script. This would be the case when spontaneity is necessary or when the nature of a subject is such that it cannot be planned completely. In the latter situation, the director would watch the monitors and follow the action.

Interviews and discussions are usually partially scripted. Opening remarks and closing comments are often completely written out. The script might also contain a list of questions, but it would be understood that they might not be followed in order. During the interview or discussion, participants are free to follow the line of conversation, and the director calls camera shots to focus on speakers.

If a program contains a demonstration, it is not always possible to know exactly what will happen next. The partial script would contain specific instructions for the transitions into and out of the demonstration but would probably leave the demonstration itself unscripted. The director is then free to follow the action as it develops (Fig. 9-4).

FIGURE 9-4 A partial script.

FOCUS EMU (PARTIAL SCRIPT)	
VIDEO	AUDIO
	MUSIC: THEME, ESTABLISH, THEN UNDER & OUT
SLIDE	SLIDE: TITLE
LS STUDIO SET	ANNCR: Good morning etc.
CU HOST	HOST: Introduces guests and
CU GUESTS AS NEEDED	begins questions. Points to be covered include: 1) reasons for proposed move 2) new site location 3) timetable
	HOST: Frank, I understand that you've brought a model of the new School of Business building. Let's move over to the table and take a look at it.
MS MODEL	Continues to discuss model
CU GUESTS AND HOST AS NEEDED	HOST: Let's go back and sit down and find out more about how this move will benefit students. Continues questions.

```
FOCUS EMU (RUNDOWN SHEET)

VIDEO                                          AUDIO

                        MUSIC: THEME ESTABLISH,
                            THEN UNDER & OUT          (00:15)
SLIDE                   SLIDE: TITLE
                        OPENING ANNOUNCE             (00:15)
INTERVIEW SET           INTERVIEW                    (03.00)
DEMO SET                DEMO                         (03:00)
                        INTERVIEW                    (03:00)
SLIDES AS NEEDED        Slide Cue: Now,
                        let's take a look at some
                        slides of the construction
                        site.
HOST                    CLOSE                        (00:15)

                        MUSIC: THEME                 (00:15)

                        SLIDE: TITLE
```

FIGURE 9-5   A rundown sheet.

FIGURE 9-6   Standard symbols used in marking video scripts.

ELS (XLS)	Extreme Long Shot
LS	Long Shot
MS	Medium Shot
CU	Close Up
ECU (XCU)	Extreme Closeup
DI	Dolly In
DO	Dolly Out
<FI	Fade In
>FO	Fade Out
X	Dissolve
S or SUP	Super
2-SH	Shot of two people
3-SH	Shot of three people
R ①	Ready Camera ___(1)___ (straight cut or take)
T ①	Take Camera _____
R① to (DI)	Ready Camera ___(1)___ to ___(dolly in)___

Rundown sheets.   Many programs are done daily and follow exactly the same format. Directors, crew, and talent become so familiar with the program that there is no need to write out commands or even dialogue. What is needed is a list of program elements and their timing. From this rundown sheet, the program can be produced (Fig. 9-5).

Marking the Script

An important step in preparing a video production is marking the script. This is usually the director's task, and for some types of programs, such as dramas and newscasts, the marking can be quite extensive. For other kinds of programs, especially those that follow a set format each time, the marking can be less elaborate.

Marking the script serves several purposes. It enables the director to determine an overall visual approach to the program, permits the careful planning of complicated segments, assigns cameras to specific shots, indicates transitions between shots, indicates where shots and transitions will occur, indicates pacing, provides an opportunity to time segments, and puts in the director's commands to the crew.

FIGURE 9-7   Sample of a marked script. Opening readies are above the horizontal line.

FOCUS EMU

VIDEO   AUDIO

R FI MUSIC
R FI SLIDE
R MIKE ANN
R CUE ANN
R ⊗③ LS STUDIO
_____

                    FI MUSIC   MUSIC: THEME, ESTABLISH, THEN UNDER &
                                              OUT
                    FI SLIDE
SLIDE   MIKE ANN   SLIDE: TITLE
                    CUE ANN

LS STUDIO SET ⊗ ③____   ANNCR: Good morning, and welcome to today's
   R MIKE HOST   edition of Focus EMU, a program devoted to a dis-
   R CUE HOST   cussion of issues and the people important to
   R④ CUE HOST   them at Eastern Michigan University and the
                    FO MUSIC   Ypsilanti community. And now, here's our host
                    MIKE HOST   John Fortune.
                    CUE HOST
CU HOST   T④——— (HOST: Today, we are fortunate to have with us
   R② 2-SHOT GUESTS   two members of the EMU School of Business fac-
                                        ulty who will discuss the proposed move of the
                                        School to an off-campus location in downtown
                                        Ypsilanti.

2-SHOT GUESTS T②——— (Let me introduce our guests Frank Jones and Wil-
                                        liam Smith.

The first task in marking a script is to read through it and decide upon the overall visual treatment. For a studio production, script marking involves assigning shots to specific cameras and indicating camera movements. For a studio drama, it also requires the blocking of performers and the coordination of their movements with those of the cameras. In reading through the script, the director also notes any particularly difficult moments in the script and carefully plans how to handle them.

A director can use a number of symbols in the process of marking a script, but once a system is adopted, it must be applied consistently. Once marked, copies of the script must be distributed to members of the production team. All

FIGURE 9-8   Opening and closing readies.

```
                        FOCUS EMU (OPENING READIES)

VIDEO                                               AUDIO

Standby 60" to air                                            01:00
Standby 30" to air                                            00:30
Line in Black
Ready Roll VTR and Acknowledge
      Roll VTR and Acknowledge                                00:15
Ready Fade in Music
Ready Fade in Slide
Ready Mike Announce
Ready Cue Announce
                                                             00:00
_____

   Fade in Music                    MUSIC: THEME, ESTABLISH,
                                    THEN UNDER & OUT
   Fade in Slide                    SLIDE: TITLE
   Mike Announce
   Cue Announce                     ANNCR: Good morning. . . .


                   FOCUS EMU (CLOSING READIES)

Ready Close Host Mike             HOST: Thank you for joining us
Ready Fade in Music                 today on Focus EMU. We'll
Ready Dissolve to Slide             see you at this same time
   Close Host Mike                  tomorrow.
   Fade in Music                  MUSIC: THEME
   Dissolve to Slide              SLIDE: TITLE
Ready Fade Sound and Picture Out
(FSAPO)
   Fade Sound and Picture Out       BLACK
```

markings are usually made in pencil so that they can be changed as needed later. Figure 9-6 shows a standard set of symbols used for marking a script.

These are only some of the symbols that can be used to mark a script. The director can feel free to use additional symbols as the need arises. All symbols must be used consistently, and the meaning of all symbols must be clearly understood by members of the production team (Fig. 9-7).

Opening and Closing Readies and Transitions

The opening and closing of a video production can be difficult moments for a director. Also, transitions into and out of demonstrations and film or videotape inserts can be complicated. Beginning video directors might want to write out all their commands for these moments in the production. This is an especially good idea if the director has to give a number of readies and takes in quick succession. (Fig. 9-8.)

Shot sheets. For productions that require a number of different setups for each camera, it might be desirable to provide a list of shots for each camera. This shot sheet helps the camera operator anticipate the next required movement or framing. It is very important to transfer to the shot sheets any changes in camera directions that are made in the script. If this is not done, a conflict can result between the director's commands and the instructions on the shot sheet. (Fig. 9-9.)

Shot sheets are not necessary for every kind of video production. When it

FIGURE 9-9 A shot sheet.

```
                    FOCUS EMU (SHOT SHEET)

     Camera 1
     1. CU Host
     2. CU Jones
     3. CU Host and widen to follow to demo area
     4. CU Host and widen to return to interview set
     5. CU Jones
     6. CU Host

     Camera 2
     1. 2-shot guests
     2. CU Smith
     3. CU model
     4. CU Smith

     Camera 3
     1. LS Interview Set
     2. LS demo area
     3. LS interview set
```

FIGURE 9-10   A storyboard for a television public service announcement. (Courtesy of Steven Wextanen, art director, GM Photographic)

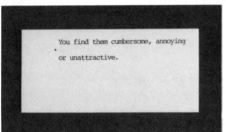

You find them cumbersome, annoying or unattractive.

But with the right eye protection over 90% of sports and work related eye injuries can be prevented

HELP SAVE THE SIGHTS OF AMERICA.

HELP SAVE THE SIGHTS OF AMERICA.

National Society to Prevent Blindness

Help save the sights of America.

FIGURE 9-10   (cont.)

is important for a cameraperson to follow unrehearsed action or to be creative in picture composition, a shot sheet can be a hindrance. Shot sheets can sometimes hamper creativity and limit flexibility.

Storyboard

When it is necessary for directors to have an exact idea of what each shot is to contain, they can be aided by a storyboard (Fig. 9-10). The storyboard contains drawings of each shot placed alongside or above the copy that accompanies them. The storyboard is often used in the planning stages of a production and is very useful in establishing the overall visual style of a program. Storyboard scripts are often developed for commercials and public-service announcements.

SUMMARY

All video productions begin with ideas. Some of these ideas are simple, and some are very complex. It is the writer's job to develop ideas into scripts. A video writer often works with a team of other writers and production personnel and must take into account a number of constraints in producing a script. Video writers usually do not have the freedom enjoyed by novelists and poets.

In writing a script, the author must consider the purpose of the production. Is it intended to entertain, inform, instruct, or persuade? The intended audience and production circumstances, including funds available and equipment to be used, are other important considerations. The video writer also must think visually and write succinct, clear dialogue.

Student writers frequently have difficulty coming up with ideas for scripts. They can often borrow ideas from existing programs, adapt them from other media, draw upon their personal interests, use their contacts with other people, and survey the environment for inspiration.

Once they have selected ideas, video writers must decide upon what approach they will use. They also must choose the methods of production and the types of facilities and talent they will use.

Video scripts may follow several possible structures, including chronological, comparative, impressionistic, and dramatic (conflict resolution). Once a structure has been selected, the writer can lay out the segments of the script in order and begin to write copy.

Video scripts may be full (or complete) or partial, or they may consist of a rundown sheet listing the order and timing of program segments. Scripts specify what materials will be used in a production, indicate the order of these materials, and communicate the overall approach to the subject.

Full scripts allow considerable control over a production and are useful when a program is very complex. They permit the director to think through every aspect of the production in advance. A drawback of the full script is that it can limit flexibility during the actual production. Full scripts are either split page or full page. The split-page format, which separates the audio and video information into two vertical columns, is used for newscasts, documentaries, and actualities. The full-page format, which resembles a film script, places dialogue across the entire width of the page. It is used for dramatic productions.

News scripts contain indications for the placement of slides and film or video inserts. Each story is given a separate page, permitting the director to add or delete stories quickly.

Partial scripts are used for programs, such as interviews, for which much of the content will be ad-libbed on the spot. Some parts of the production, such as opening and closing remarks, can be written out completely.

A rundown sheet lists the order and timing of a program's segments. It is used when the production uses an unvarying format with which the production crew and talent are familiar.

In preparing for a program, the director marks the script. This allows an indication of overall visual treatment, assignment of shots to cameras, blocking of camera movements, placement of transitions, indication of pacing, and timing of individual segments. Directors sometimes write out commands in the process of marking the script. The industry uses a standard set of symbols to mark scripts.

Beginning directors might find it useful to write out opening and closing commands and commands into and out of complicated transitions. They also might want to prepare shot sheets for individual camera operators.

Another kind of script is the storyboard, which consists of drawings showing the composition of shots. These pictures are placed alongside or above the audio copy. Storyboards are often used in the production of commercials and public-service announcements.

FOR FURTHER READING

HILLIARD, ROBERT L. *Writing for Television and Radio* (New York: Hastings House, 1962).

WILLIS, EDGAR E. *Writing Television and Radio Programs* (New York: Holt, Rinehart and Winston, 1967).

chapter ten _____

Video Aesthetics:
Pictorial Composition _____

INTRODUCTION

Video communicates meaning through a combination of pictures, speech, music, and sound effects. In making any video production, directors (perhaps along with the producer, writer, and other creative personnel) exercise control over the final product in a number of ways. First, they select a subject; then they develop an approach in a script. Next, the subject is rendered in visual terms at the shooting stage of production. Finally, that footage is arranged in postproduction editing. In this chapter, we will talk about pictorial composition and the aesthetic principles underlying it. In Chapter 11, we will discuss editing.

MISE-EN-SCÈNE

Mise-en-scène is a theatrical term meaning "having been put into the scene." It is used to describe the elements that are used to build meaning on a stage. These elements include performers, sets, props, costumes, makeup, and lighting. The director or designer of a play begins with an empty stage and, by carefully placing objects and people into that space, generates a meaning that is communicated to the audience. In the same way, a filmmaker or video director places subjects in front of the camera, lights them in a particular way, and selects a camera position and lens through which to view them. In this chapter, we will consider the following aspects of pictorial composition:

1. selection of subjects for placement in the frame
2. arrangement of subjects within the frame
3. subject–camera distance
4. lens selection
5. camera angle
6. camera movement

Selecting Subjects for Placement in the Frame

In Chapter 6, we discussed some technological characteristics of video and pointed out their effect on selection of subject matter and its treatment. These characteristics include the following:

1. Video can record movement.
2. The video screen is small.
3. The video frame has an aspect ratio of three units of height to four units of width.
4. The video image is low in resolution.

These technological features of the medium affect what the video director will select for placement within the frame. Here are some general guides:

Movement. Subjects that move take advantage of the medium's ability to record motion. If the subject itself does not move, motion can be introduced by camera movement or zooming. Unmoving, static shots can often be used as a relief or visual counterpoint to moving shots, but too many of them are boring to watch.

Large objects. Because the video screen is so small, objects placed within it must be large enough to be seen clearly. If the objects are small, they can be made to appear large by shooting them in closeup. You will notice that the closeup is widespread in video productions for that reason.

Interesting shapes and textures. Because video is a visual medium, the subjects within the frame should be interesting to look at. Viewers like to see unusual shapes, textures, and interesting movements.

Shapes that fit the video screen's aspect ratio. Shapes that depart radically from the video screen's three-by-four aspect ratio cannot be depicted without elaborate camera movement or framing. Subjects with extreme vertical or horizontal dimensions cannot easily be reproduced on the video screen. The video director should choose subjects that fit easily within the video screen's dimensions.

An uncluttered frame. A video screen's small size limits the number of subjects that can be comfortably placed within the frame. A simple, uncluttered composition is generally preferable to a busy one.

Arrangement of Subjects Within the Frame

Once suitable subjects have been chosen, they can be arranged so as to take maximum advantage of the space. Vertical, horizontal, and diagonal lines can be used as guides for the positioning of subjects.

Horizontal and vertical lines.   The horizontal frame line suggests rest and stability. The vertical frame line suggests force and power. The balance point of the frame is where the central vertical and horizontal lines intersect. An object placed here will appear to be at rest (Fig. 10-1).

Diagonal lines.   Diagonal lines across the frame generate a sense of unrest and tension (Fig. 10-2). A tilted, or "dutch," angle can suggest a crazed view of the world. An automobile's power can be indicated by showing it speeding up a hill. Viewers tend to assign directions to these diagonals. A diagonal from lower left to upper right is interpreted as moving up, while a diagonal from upper left to lower right is understood as moving down.

Look space and leading space.   When there is no need to suggest imbalance or tension in the frame, subjects can be placed in the central position of rest. An exception to this is when a person is looking off screen either to the left or to the right. As the person turns more to the full profile, more space is provided in the frame to offset the direction of the look. This is called "look" space (Fig. 10-3). When a subject moves horizontally across the frame, additional space is provided in front of the subject. This is called "lead" space (Fig. 10-4).

FIGURE 10-1   Vertical lines dominate this statue of a Spanish-American War soldier.

FIGURE 10-2 The roof of Holy Trinity Chapel in Ypsilanti, Michigan, cuts diagonally across the frame.

FIGURE 10-3 Look space.

FIGURE 10-4 Lead space. Subject moving to left is framed in right third of screen so that there will be space in front of her.

Symmetrical composition.   The most symmetrical position for a single subject is the midpoint intersection of vertical and horizontal lines (Fig. 10-5). Two subjects can be placed equidistant on either side of the midpoint to achieve a similar effect. Triangular and rectangular arrangements of subjects also create a symmetrical, balanced effect.

The golden mean.   The three-by-four rectangle in Figure 10-6 has been divided by a vertical line which creates two smaller rectangles within the original one. When properly placed, this vertical line creates a pleasing proportion among the three rectangles. The smaller one relates in size to the larger one as the larger one relates in size to the entire rectangle. This ratio can be used as a guide for the placement of vertical objects within the frame.

The powerful right side.   In small frames, viewers tend to concentrate on the right side. The most important information must be placed there. This tendency might be due to the fact that we tend to "read" past information on the left side of the screen and let our eyes come to rest on what is placed on the right side. For large frames such as a Cinemascope motion-picture screen, the opposite seems to be true, at least for members of the European and Western cultures. They tend to read a large screen from left to right and conclude that the first thing seen on the left is the most important.[1]

FIGURE 10-5 Symmetrical arrangements. (left) Triangular. (below) Horizontal.

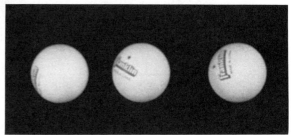

[1]See Herbert Zettl, *Sight, Sound, Motion: Applied Media Aesthetics* (Belmont, Calif.: Wadsworth, 1973), p. 128.

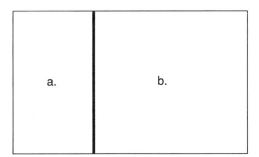

The Golden Mean

FIGURE 10-6 (above) The Golden Mean. (right) The tower of Pierce Hall at Eastern Michigan University is placed in the left third of the frame to emphasize proportions of the Golden Section.

Closure. When an entire object cannot be placed within the video frame, it must be placed in such a way that the rest of its shape can be suggested. Viewers will then have enough information to mentally complete or fill out the missing parts in a process called *closure.* For example, a person's body should not be framed at the natural division points. A shot of the head should also include the shoulders so that the viewer can fill in the rest of the body and not assume that the person has been decapitated (Fig. 10-7).

Suggesting depth. The video screen is a flat plane; it lacks the third dimension. Therefore, it is important to arrange subjects within the frame to suggest depth. This can be done in a number of ways.

Partial obscuration. When one object is placed in front of another so that it partially obscures or blocks our view of the one behind, viewers interpret this to mean that one object is closer than the other. Such an arrangement helps to give depth to the frame (Fig. 10-8). Video directors often use this technique when shooting a conversation between two people; they will frame one person over the shoulder of the other.

FIGURE 10-7 (above) Framing is too tight. (right) A looser composition is better.

Convergence lines. Realist painters were fond of emphasizing convergence lines to suggest depth. Parallel lines that recede from us appear to come together, or converge, at a point on the horizon. They are an important compositional tool for suggesting depth. Some studio sets exaggerate this phenomenon and "force" perspective, making the set appear to be deeper than it really is. On location, a cameraperson can choose a composition that takes advantage of natural convergence lines, such as railroad tracks or city streets (Fig. 10-9).

Foreground reference. Another way to suggest depth is to show the relationship between foreground and background objects. A shot of a desert landscape can look flat and uninteresting until a cactus plant is placed in the foreground (Fig. 10-10). This kind of composition gives the viewer a sense of depth.

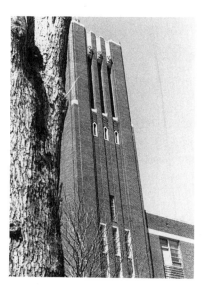

FIGURE 10-8 The tree in the foreground partially obscures the tower and gives a sense of depth to the scene.

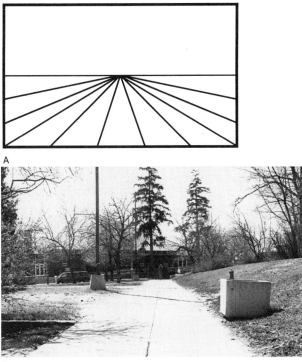

A

B

FIGURE 10-9 (a) Lines converging at a point on the horizon create a sense of depth. (b) A photographer can frame a shot to emphasize natural lines of convergence.

FIGURE 10-10 The plaque (right) provides a foreground reference that gives the scene on the right a greater sense of depth than the one on the left.

Size reference. We often determine an object's distance from us by judging its size. A universally recognized size referent is the human figure. Placing a person within the frame helps to clarify the size and distance of other objects in the frame with it (Fig. 10-11).

Subject–Camera Distance

An important compositional element is the distance between subject and camera. This distance can be either real or apparent. It is real if the camera is actually as far from the object as it appears to be. It is apparent when the distance is the result of a particular lens selection. For example, a camera can really be close to a subject or merely seem to be through the use of a closeup lens.

The long shot.   The long shot (LS) is the greatest subject–camera distance for a particular situation. A long shot could show the sweep of a landscape or the entire studio. The extreme long shot (ELS or XLS) gives an extremely wide perspective. The actual distance between subject and camera in the long shot is relative and depends upon the situation. On location, the camera could be miles from the subject, whereas in the studio it might be only a few yards distant; yet both would be called long shots. A long shot that covers the entire scene of the action is sometimes called a cover shot.

The opening or establishing shot of a scene is often a long shot. It shows the viewer the space in which the action is to take place. Video productions frequently begin with a long shot of the studio set or perhaps with an aerial view of the locale for a remote production.

The medium shot.   The medium shot is approximately 50 percent closer to the subject than the long shot. What the medium shot actually shows is relative and depends upon the amount of space defined in the original long shot. The medium shot directs the viewer's attention to what is most important in the space defined in the preceding long shot.

FIGURE 10-11   The human figure is a universally-recognized size reference. It helps viewers determine how far away the background buildings are.

The closeup.   If the long shot represents the outer limit of the subject–camera distance, the closeup (CU) represents the normal inner limit. A shot that is extremely close would be called an extreme closeup (ECU or XCU). A common closeup in both video and film is the human face. An extreme closeup would then be a shot of an eye, an earring, or other small object. The closeup is a powerful tool for directing the viewer's attention. The subject within the frame is so close that we can't see much of anything else (Fig 10-12.)

Lens Selection

The lens through which a subject is viewed affects apparent subject–camera distance, the rendering of spatial relationships within the frame, and focus. Lenses may be wide angle, normal, narrow angle, or variable focal length (zoom).

Wide angle.   The wide-angle lens has a short focal length and a wide field of view. It shows more than the eye would see if it were looking through the same-sized aperture opening. The wide-angle lens makes things look farther away than they actually are, and it tends to exaggerate distances between objects. A wide-angle lens also has a great depth of field. Thus almost everything is in focus, from a plane very close to the lens to infinity. On a wide-angle lens setting, a camera can move toward or away from objects, and they still remain in focus.

Some wide-angle lenses noticeably distort space. When viewed through a fisheye lens, vertical and horizontal lines can seem to bulge outward, creating an effect called *barrelling distortion.*

FIGURE 10-12   Long shot, medium shot, closeup sequence.

Normal angle.   The normal lens shows objects as the eye would see them through the same-sized aperture opening. Objects appear to be their normal size, and there is no distortion of perspective.

Narrow angle.   The narrow-angle lens shows less than the eye can see through the same-sized aperture opening. Objects within the frame appear to be larger than they actually are at that distance. A very narrow-angle lens functions much as a telescope does and is called a *telephoto lens.* A narrow-angle lens also flattens space, making things appear to be closer together than they actually are. A narrow-angle lens also has a shallow depth of field so that foreground and background objects cannot be in focus at the same time.

Variable-focal-length lenses.   The zoom lens combines the characteristics of lenses of different fixed focal lengths. At a wide setting, the zoom acts as a wide-angle lens. When zoomed in, it acts as a narrow-angle lens. The on-air zoom

A

B

C

FIGURE 10-13 Eastern Michigan University's Pease Auditorium in (a) wide angle, (b) normal, and (c) narrow angle.

is often used as a substitute for moving the camera, but the effect is not the same The zoom only alters the magnification of a subject while the moving camera actually changes our spatial relationship to it.

Depth of field.   A lens' depth of field is determined by subject–camera distance, focal length, and aperture opening. As the subject–camera distance increases, the depth of field increases. As the focal length increases, the depth of field decreases, and as the aperture opening increases, the depth of field decreases. Because f-stop numbers increase as the aperture opening decreases, higher f-stop numbers indicate a greater depth of field (Fig. 10-14).

Variations in depth of field provide the video director with an important expressive tool. By using a lens with a shallow depth of field, for example, the director can place foreground objects in sharp focus while throwing background objects out of focus. By doing so, the director draws our attention to what is in focus and deemphasizes what is out of focus. A defocused background also helps generate a sense of depth within the frame.

By adjusting the focus, the director can shift our attention from one object to another within the frame. We might see a foreground telephone in focus and a person standing behind it out of focus. As the telephone rings, the camera operator can "roll" focus to bring the person into sharp view as she picks up the receiver (Fig. 10-15).

Camera Angle

In addition to selecting the subject–camera distance, the type of lens, and the focus, the video director can also determine the angle at which the camera will view the subject (Fig. 10-16).

High angle. When the camera is placed above the eye level and shoots down at a subject, it makes that subject look small and insignificant.
Eye level. The normal viewing angle of a scene is eye level. This represents an objective, normal point of view. Camera operators usually match their cameras to the eye level of persons in the frame.
Low angle. When the camera is placed below eye level and shoots up at a subject, it makes that subject look strong and possibly threatening.

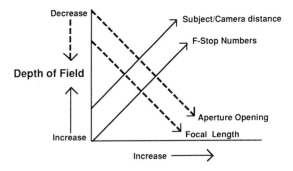

FIGURE 10-14 This diagram shows the relationship between subject/camera distance, F-stop numbers, aperture opening, focal length, and depth of field. As subject/camera distance and F-stop numbers increase, so does depth of field. As aperture opening and focal length decrease, so does depth of field.

FIGURE 10-15   Roll-focus can also be used to shift emphasis from foreground figure to background figure.

These camera angles imitate real-life situations. We usually talk to equals at eye level, but we look up at statues. On the other hand, speakers usually look down at audiences from raised platforms.

Camera Movement

An important way of introducing movement into the frame is by moving the camera itself. This movement can be motivated by the need to follow a moving subject, to reveal more of an object that is larger than the frame, to show hidden portions of a subject, or to suggest depth.

Camera movement can be divided into two types. First, there are those movements that can be executed without changing the position of the camera itself. Second, there are those movements that require some physical change in the camera's location.

The stationary camera.   There are three basic movements that can be executed without changing the camera's location: the *pan,* the *tilt,* and the *pedestal* (Fig. 10-17). Some camera mounts also permit the *tongue* and the *crane.*

The pan. The pan is accomplished by swivelling the camera from left to right or from right to left on its vertical axis. It can be used to keep a moving object within the frame or to show a panoramic (hence the term *pan*) view of a location. The pan mimics the way humans survey the environment by turning their heads and eyes from side to side. A pan that is executed so rapidly that the image is blurred is called a *swish* pan.

The tilt. The tilt is accomplished by swivelling the camera vertically up or down on its horizontal axis. It copies the human movement of looking up or down. A tilt

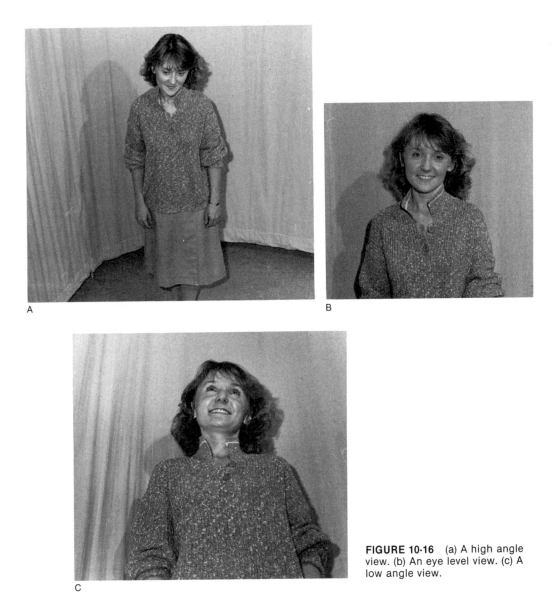

FIGURE 10-16 (a) A high angle view. (b) An eye level view. (c) A low angle view.

could be used to follow the movement of a helicopter as it takes off or to show the vertical lines of a tall building.

The pedestal. The studio pedestal mount allows the entire camera to be moved up or down while remaining in a horizontal orientation. It is similar to the movement of a person standing up or sitting down. The crane is a similar movement, but its range is somewhat greater. The tongue is a side-to-side movement of the entire camera head while the camera continues to point forward.

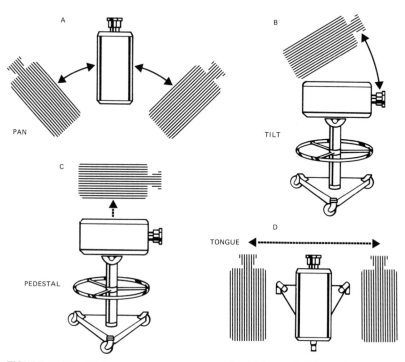

FIGURE 10-17   Stationary camera movements. (a) Pan. (b) Tilt. (c) Pedestal. (d) Tongue.

The moving camera.   If a camera is mounted on a base with wheels, or is handheld, another series of movements are possible. These include the *dolly, arc,* and *track* (Fig. 10-18).

> *The dolly.* This movement is accomplished by moving the camera closer to or farther away from a stationary subject. At one time, the dolly was very popular, but it has been largely replaced by the zoom. The dolly is a very fluid, graceful camera movement, and it helps to create a sense of space and depth in the frame.
>
> *The arc.* In the arc, the camera is moved in a semicircular path around a stationary subject. It is useful for revealing obscured portions of objects (such as a piece of sculpture), separating a foreground subject from the background, and suggesting depth within the frame.
>
> *The track.* Sometimes called a "trucking shot," this movement is accomplished by moving the camera parallel to a moving subject. While seldom used in a studio, it is a fairly common location shot. The movement gets its name from the fact that filmmakers would mount their heavy cameras on tracks or put them on a truck to follow a moving subject.

Point of View

The techniques described in this chapter give the video director ways of controlling how the viewer looks at a subject. By selecting a certain camera angle and by arranging subjects in a particular way, the director is trying to direct our

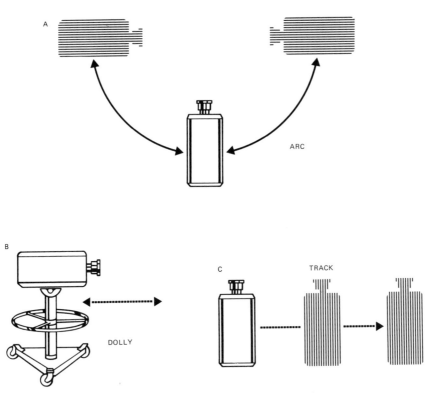

FIGURE 10-18   The moving camera. (a) Arc. (b) Dolly. (c) Track.

attention to what is important and attempting to shape our responses to the subject.

The director can establish two general types of viewpoint: either objective or subjective. Because video has traditionally been associated with realism and "live-as-it-happens" coverage of events, the objective viewpoint is the most common one. In this approach, the director wishes to show us the event as it happens. Excessive camera movement, unusual angles, and other highly noticeable departures from realistic frame composition are kept to a minimum.

In the subjective approach, the director hopes to communicate a particular interpretation of the subject. To do so, she employs the techniques discussed in this chapter in a highly creative and personal way. A subjective viewpoint can be communicated by highly unusual camera angles, unnatural lighting, asymmetrical frame composition, and other methods that are clearly not neutral.

Motion pictures offer many examples of the subjective point of view, ranging from the bizarre sets and lighting of German expressionism to experiments with first-person narration, of which Robert Montgomery's *Lady in the Lake* (1946) is an example. Although video tends to use the neutral third-person viewpoint, music videos and experimental works do contain examples of highly subjective approaches.

SUMMARY

The video director exercises creative control over a production by controlling the composition of subjects in the frame (the mise-en-scène). He can select subjects, arrange them, set lights, determine subject–camera distance, select lenses, and choose camera movements. Video technology suggests an uncluttered frame composition, a conformity to the three-by-four aspect ratio, and shooting in closeups. Subjects in the frame can be arranged so as to take advantage of the vertical, horizontal, and diagonal force lines within the frame and to suggest depth.

The director also selects distant, medium, or close positions for the camera and chooses which lenses are used for viewing the subject. Lenses have differing effects on depth of field and spatial arrangements. The director can also view the subject from different angles and can move the camera in several ways. All the compositional devices can be used to establish a particular point of view toward a subject. The point of view is usually objective, or neutral, but a subjective viewpoint can be generated by using unusual frame composition, camera angles, and camera movement.

FOR FURTHER READING

Boggs, Joseph M. *The Art of Watching Films* (Menlo Park, Calif.: The Benjamin Publishing Company, 1978).

Bordwell, David and Kristin Thompson. *Film Art: An Introduction* (Reading, Mass.: Addison-Wesley, 1979).

Zettl, Herbert. *Sight, Sound, Motion: Applied Media Aesthetics* (Belmont, Calif.: Wadsworth, 1973).

chapter eleven

Video Aesthetics: Editing

INTRODUCTION

In Chapter 10, we discussed how the video director controls the composition of subjects within the frame to communicate meaning. Another way in which a director can control the meaning of a production is through editing.

Editing involves several tasks, including the selection of particular footage from all that is available, arranging the footage in a specific order, determining the length of individual pieces, and deciding upon the transitional devices that will link the various pieces. A single uninterrupted piece of video footage is called a *shot*. Editing is the process of selecting, arranging, and connecting individual shots to make up a complete video production.

LIVE AND POSTPRODUCTION EDITING

Editing can be done either "live" in real time or during postproduction. When a video production is done live, the director makes editing decisions while the program is in progress and tells the switcher (or technical director) which shots to place on line and what kinds of transitions to use between them. In this situation, the director is basically selecting from among a number of simultaneously available views of the action. The director can do little more than select the best view. There is very little opportunity for highly creative editing. Live editing is essentially functional; that is, it serves to help us follow the action by showing us what we need to see when we need to see it.

The situation of postproduction editing is quite different. Here, the director is not selecting from among simultaneously available views of a live event but is choosing from prerecorded footage. The director is much more free to manipulate the material in a creative fashion. She can use editing to alter the time and space of the original event, create visual rhythms, compare and contrast images, and execute elaborate transitions between shots.

APPROACHES TO EDITING

There are several different approaches to editing, and they can be used in various ways.

Continuity Editing

This familiar approach has been used for many years in motion pictures and television. We will discuss it in detail later in the chapter. Continuity editing is designed to produce a continuous flow of visuals, showing viewers what they need to see, making time and space clear at all times, and minimizing breaks caused by the edits themselves. It results in a smooth, fluid, easy-to-follow progression of shots.

Editing for Dramatic Emphasis

Another approach is to use editing to heighten the dramatic intensity of a screen event by enhancing its tempo. A chase can be made more exciting by cutting quickly back and forth between the pursuer and the pursued, perhaps to the beat of accompanying music. This can sometimes be done during a live production, such as a sportscast. The editing can emphasize the rhythm of the pitch, the swing of the bat, and the ball sailing over the outfield fence.

Editing for Creative or Intellectual Purposes

Editing can be used to communicate ideas by linking two unrelated images in quick succession so that we make a mental connection between the two. Soviet filmmaker Sergei Eisenstein had a special interest in this kind of editing, and his works contain many examples of it. This approach is used in many commercials and music videos. It is also a standard tool for video artists.

WHEN TO EDIT

Editing can be motivated in many ways. Let's consider a simple production situation—a live studio interview-demonstration. Here are some instances that call for edits.

To Follow Dialogue and Action

The host introduces the program and turns to ask the guest a question. This entire action could be shown by a cover shot including both people. It is also possible to begin with a closeup of the host and then pan to a closeup of the guest. Another way is to cut from a closeup of the host to a closeup of the guest as she begins to answer the host's question.

If the guest gets up and moves to a demonstration set, the director could cut to a cover shot of the studio set as she gets up. The guest's movement serves to motivate the edit (Fig. 11-1).

To Show Details

The guest is shown in closeup on one camera, and she holds up a cooking utensil. To show the utensil better, the director could cut to a closeup of the item on another camera. It is possible to zoom in for a closer shot (Fig. 11-2).

To Show Something From a Different Angle

Suppose that the guest is demonstrating how to slice lettuce. The action is covered in closeup. The director could cut to a different angle so that the viewer can see it better (Fig. 11-3).

For Variety

In an interview situation, it is easy to get locked into a pattern of alternating closeups that follow the dialogue. The director could cut to a cover shot or to a reaction shot of the person who is not talking, just for the sake of variety. Editing

FIGURE 11-1 Cutting on action. Subject rises in shot on left, and director cuts during the action to the wider shot on right.

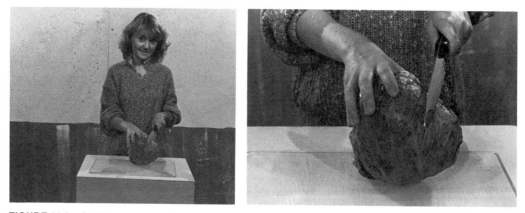

FIGURE 11-2   Cutting to a closer view. Director cuts from wide shot on left to a closer view of action on right.

for variety must be done with caution, however. Too much cutting without a clear motivation can be confusing to the viewer.

These are four good reasons for editing in a live studio situation, and all of them involve selecting among simultaneously available views of the same action. In this situation, editing is a matter of selecting which view permits the viewer to observe the action most clearly.

The editing of prerecorded materials in postproduction is a more elaborate process. Here the editor is not just selecting among a variety of views, but is reconstructing an event that happened in the past. This reconstruction can involve selection, rearrangement, elimination, and compression of footage. In this situation, the reasons for editing can become more complicated.

FIGURE 11-3   Cutting to a different angle. Director cuts from wide view on left to a closer view from a different angle on right.

To Manipulate Time

In the live studio situation, the time taken by the event and by the broadcast of it are identical. With prerecorded materials, it is possible to change the time of the video to make it shorter or longer than that of the real event. This lengthening or shortening is accomplished by adding or subtracting footage at the time of editing.

To Manipulate Space

Editing allows free movement in space. Shots recorded in different places can be edited together so that the viewer is transported quickly from one location to another. An opening shot can show the skyline of a city; the next can show a neighborhood; and the next, an apartment's interior. In a more extreme case, a nature documentary can take the viewer from Hudson Bay to an Amazon rain forest in an instant.

To Show Simultaneous Actions

A director can cut back and forth among two or more simultaneously occurring actions to show the relationship among them. D. W. Griffith used this technique during the concluding moments of *The Birth of a Nation* (1915) to show the Ku Klux Klan riding to the rescue of both the family trapped in the cabin and Elsie Stoneman frantically trying to escape the clutches of Silas Lynch. Griffith called the technique *cross-cutting*. It has been a standard device in movies and television ever since.

To Emphasize the Rhythm of an Action

Some screen actions can be edited to the beat of music or to their own inherent rhythmic pattern. This technique is often used in films, commercials, and music videos.

CONTINUITY EDITING

During the early years of the movie industry, there emerged a general set of rules about various aspects of film production, including editing. The continuity approach to editing has been widely practiced in motion pictures and television for many years. It offers one approach to editing, but it is not the only one.

Continuity editing is designed to keep viewers from being confused and to help them follow the story with a minimum of difficulty. It maintains a clear definition of time and space and minimizes the distraction caused by the edit.

Clear Definition of Space

Continuity editing allows viewers to know where they are at all times. This is accomplished by (1) a logical progression of shots, (2) adhering to the axis of action, or 180-degree rule, and (3) maintaining screen direction.

A logical progression of shots.   In continuity editing, we begin a scene with a cover shot. This shot shows us the entire space in which the action takes place. Once this space has been established, we cut to a medium shot, and then to a closeup of the subject of greatest interest (Fig. 11-4). For example, we could begin with a cover shot of a room in which a man and a woman are sitting on a sofa. We follow that with a medium shot showing the sofa and the two people, and finally cut to a closeup of the man. We could then cut back and forth, following the conversation. At some point, we might reestablish the overall space by returning to a cover shot. This logical progression of shots establishes the space and the relationships among objects within it.

An alternative to this editing pattern is the zoom. We could open with a cover shot and then zoom in to the subject of greatest interest. We could also do the reverse by opening with a closeup and then zooming out to show the entire space.

FIGURE 11-4   A logical progression of shots. Sequence begins with (a) shot establishing location, moves to (b) a close view, and continues with (c, d) alternating over-the-shoulder shots to follow dialogue.

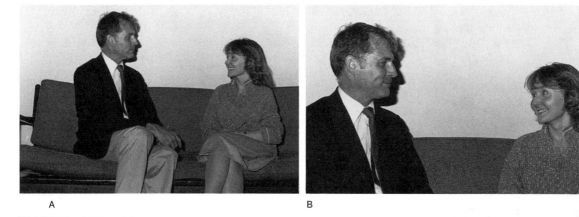

A

B

C

D

Axis of Action: Maintaining Screen Direction

Another technique of continuity editing that helps to maintain a clear definition of space is the axis of action, or 180-degree rule. It ensures consistent screen direction and placement of subjects in the frame. The rule requires that all cameras remain on one side of the action and that any camera movement be confined to a 180-degree space on that side (Fig. 11-5). If we cut back and forth between cameras positioned within this space, subjects maintain their spatial orientation from one shot to the next. If we are shooting a subject moving from screen left to screen right with cameras placed on the same side of the axis of that movement, the subject will continue to move in the same screen direction as we cut between cameras. If we cut to a camera on the opposite side of this axis, the subject will appear to reverse screen direction. This could be confusing to the viewer.

During a conversation between two people, the axis is drawn between them (Fig. 11-6). Placing all cameras on the same side of the axis guarantees that the subjects will retain their original left–right placement within the frame. Cutting

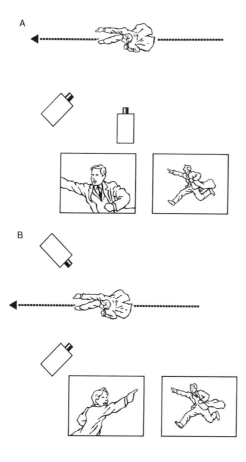

A

B

FIGURE 11-5 Crossing the axis of action for moving subject. (a) When cameras remain on same side of axis of action, subject moves in same direction. (b) When one camera crosses axis, subject appears to reverse direction.

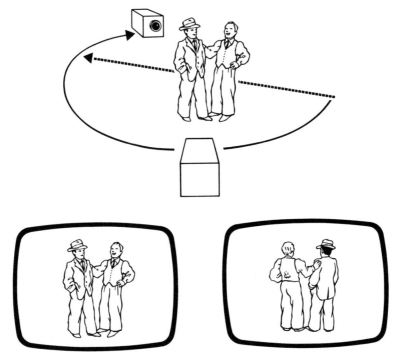

FIGURE 11-6   Crossing the axis of action between two people reverses their screen positions.

to a camera placed on the opposite side of the axis will cause the people to reverse their screen positions.

Sometimes it is inconvenient—or simply boring—to maintain a constant screen direction. The continuity system gives us two methods for reversing it. The first is to have the screen direction change within the shot. For example, we could see a car go around a curve and head in the opposite direction. Later shots could then show it moving in its new direction.

A second method is to insert a shot of the moving object in which the screen direction has been neutralized. We could cut from a shot of the car moving left to right to one of the car coming directly toward the camera and then to a shot of the car moving from right to left; this is called a *head-on* shot. We could accomplish the same effect by inserting a shot of the car moving directly away from the camera; this is called a *tail-away*. We could combine the two by editing to a head-on and then a tail-away (Fig. 11-7). These editing patterns permit a change in screen direction without confusing the viewer.

The axis of action and screen direction rules of the continuity system are only one way to define screen space. These rules can be broken for good reason. Television programs and motion pictures are filled with violations of these principles. The main point is that you should try not to confuse the viewer too much unless you purposely want to.

FIGURE 11-7 Head-on, tail-away sequence. Screen direction of a moving subject can be reversed with this sequence of shots.

Invisible editing. The continuity system attempts to hide the actual edits. That is, it strives to make them "invisible" by providing clear motivation and smooth transitions from one shot to another. Some techniques used are (1) cutting on action, (2) cutting on dialogue, (3) cutting on the look, and (4) matching frame composition.

Cutting on Action. One way to bridge a cut is to have an action begin in one shot and continue in the next (see Fig. 11-8). A talent opens a door and exits the room. We cut from the inside of the room to the outside as she opens the door and walks through.

It is sometimes difficult to match action in postproduction editing. When matching movement cannot be found in the footage, it is possible to make the mismatch less obvious by cutting away to a neutral shot and then back to the action. If we are editing footage of a parade and there are large gaps in the action, we can cut to an observer and then back to the parade footage. The mismatch is less noticeable because the viewer has been momentarily distracted. If

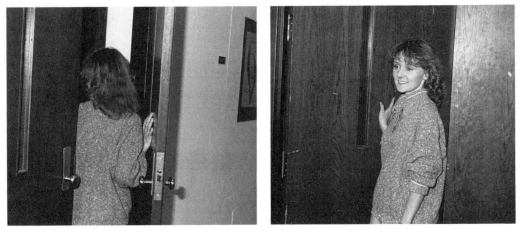

FIGURE 11-8 Cutting on action. The cut is made from inside the room to outside as the model walks through the door.

the mismatched footage were cut directly together, we would then have a *jump cut*, in which the subjects within the frame would suddenly appear to jump from one location to another location. In the continuity system, a jump cut is to be avoided. Inserting cutaway footage is the standard method for getting around a jump cut.

In the continuity system, cuts should not be made during a moving camera shot. The camera must come to rest and the action allowed to exit the frame (Fig. 11-9). The cut can come as the action leaves the frame of one shot and enters the frame of the next shot.

Cutting on Dialogue. Another method of hiding edits is to cut on dialogue. During a studio interview, the host asks the guest a question. We cut to a shot of her as she responds. We can continue in this manner, cutting back and forth to follow the conversation.

Although this is difficult to do during a live television program, it is a common practice in films and recorded video productions to cut to the next shot during the last word in the previous one. The audio follows the video by a split second. This "dialogue cutting point," as film scholar Barry Salt calls it, became a standard practice in feature films in the 1930s.[1] By avoiding an exact synchronization between video and audio, we make the edit less noticeable.

Cutting on the Look. Another strong motivator for cuts is the look or glance. A performer looks screen right, for example, and we cut to a view of what she is looking at.

As in cutting on action, it is important to maintain the correct screen direction of the look. If a host looks screen right to the guest, we would expect him

[1]See Barry Salt, "Film Style and Technology in the Thirties," *Film Quarterly,* 30, Fall 1976, p. 20.

FIGURE 11-9 Talent (left) exits frame left and (right) enters frame right in next shot.

o maintain the direction of that look. If he shifts it to screen left, we could assume either that he is looking at someone else or that the guest has moved. (See Fig. 11-10.)

Cutting on the look not only helps to motivate a cut, but it also helps to reestablish relationships among persons and things. The glance creates a strong bond between looker and the object of the look across edits.

Matching Frame Composition.   Edits can be hidden by carefully matching the content of one shot to the one following (Fig. 11-11). This can be done by matching pictorial composition, light levels, and shapes within the frame. Cuts from bright exteriors to dark interiors or from very cluttered compositions to

FIGURE 11-10   (right) Actor's glance to screen right could be followed by a cut to the object of his glance. (left) If he changes the direction of the glance, viewers could mistakenly assume that object of his glance has moved screen left.

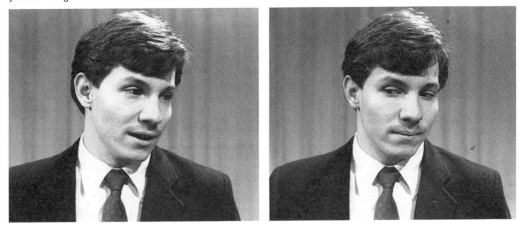

FIGURE 11-11 Matching compositions provide an easy transition from one shot to another.

simple ones can be jarring, and can be smoothed over by careful matching or by inserting cutaways between shots. Some directors purposely cut between objects that have similar shapes, such as a tall building and a statue, so that the strong similarity in composition of each shot makes the edit less noticeable.

ALTERNATIVES TO THE CONTINUITY SYSTEM

The continuity system is not the only approach to editing. It is common today to see jump cuts, reversals of screen direction, and other violations of the continuity system in feature films and on television. Overall, there is today a much more flexible approach to editing than in the days of the traditional Hollywood film. Viewers are much more familiar with nontraditional editing styles than they once were, and they are able to follow the visuals even when the editing is very noncontinuous.

It seems sufficient for directors today to establish the overall situation and then edit freely once the viewer is familiar with what is going on. Some interview shows have guests seated around a circular table, for example. Once this setting has been established by a cover shot, the director cuts freely among the participants without paying much attention to screen direction.

If an action is sufficiently strong and its location is made clear to the viewer, screen direction can be violated without creating serious problems of comprehension. Viewers know where they are and understand that they are following a single unified action. A classic example of this is found in John Ford's 1939 film *Stagecoach*. During the dramatic sequence when the stagecoach is being chased across the desert by Indians, Ford reverses screen direction. Viewers are not confused, however, because it is clear that there is only one stagecoach racing across the desert. The nature of the action makes this violation of screen direction acceptable.

In the last analysis, the principles of the continuity system should not dominate over good taste and common sense. The rules of continuity editing provide
one way of creating a smooth, coherent flow of visuals, and they can be violated
when the need arises. A director's good judgment in showing viewers what they
need to see, when they need to see it, is the final guide to all editing decisions.

TRANSITIONAL DEVICES

An important part of the editing process is selecting the transitional devices that
link shots. Video directors can choose from among traditional devices such as
cuts, dissolves, and fades, as well as a number of special digital effects.

The Cut

The cut is the most widely used transitional device. It is an instantaneous
replacement of one shot by another. Film editors literally cut the footage and
glue the ends together. In video, the cut is made electronically. A cut suggests
that no time has passed from one shot to the next. It can also suggest a cause–
effect relationship between shots. Viewers are so accustomed to seeing cuts that
they hardly notice them.

The Dissolve

The dissolve is a more gradual transition from one shot to another. One
shot slowly fades out while the next simultaneously fades in. At midpoint, both
shots are on the screen. The dissolve suggests that some time has passed between
the shots or that there is some poetic link between them. It can be used effectively
to bridge widely separated locations or mismatched actions. Dissolves are often
used during concerts or ballets to capture the mood of the event. The speed of
the dissolve can be adjusted to fit that mood.

The Fade

The fade is a more definite separation between shots. One shot fades completely to black before the next one fades in. A rapid fade out–fade in is sometimes called a "kiss black" or "touch black." Major segments of a program, such
as acts of a play, are often separated from each other by fades. Commercials are
often bracketed by fades so that the audience does not think they are part of the
program. A fade suggests that some considerable time has passed between shots.
Programs usually begin with a fade in and end with a fade out.

Defocus and Focus

Another useful transitional device is the defocus and focus. One camera
slowly goes out of focus and then we dissolve to another camera, which is also
out of focus. The second camera then brings its subject slowly into focus. The

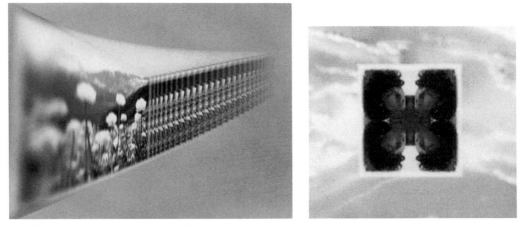

FIGURE 11-12   Digital video transitions. (Courtesy of The Grass Valley Group, Inc.)

defocus and focus can be done in the studio and requires no special electronic effects.

Special Effects

Many kinds of special effects are now available because of digital video technologies (Fig. 11-12). In addition to wipes, which can be done in several configurations, we now have the ability to twist images around, flip them over, or spin them off the edge of the screen.

Special effects are fun to use, and they create visual excitement. The choice of which ones to use and when to use them depends upon the type of production on which you are working. Special effects should enhance the overall meaning of the production and should not be used just for their own sake.

SUMMARY

Editing is the process of selecting, arranging, and linking video materials. During a live production, editing is a matter of choosing among simultaneously available views of the subject. Postproduction editing of previously recorded footage can involve a more complicated manipulation of the program materials.

Approaches to editing include the following: (1) continuity editing, (2) editing for dramatic emphasis, and (3) editing for creative or intellectual purposes. Editing must be motivated, and some reasons for editing are (1) to follow dialogue or action, (2) to show details, (3) to show a different view of the subject, and (4) to achieve variety. Screen time and space can also be manipulated by means of editing. In addition, it can be used to show simultaneous action and to emphasize visual rhythm.

Continuity editing is a standard approach that was developed in Hollywood and later used in television. It tries to define space clearly and to avoid confusing the viewer by (1) using a logical progression of shots, (2) adhering to the axis of action, or 180-degree rule, (3) maintaining screen direction, and (4) making edits less noticeable by matching picture compositions and cutting on action, dialogue, or the look. Continuity editing is only one approach, and its rules can be violated as judgment and taste dictate.

Several standard transitional devices can be used to link shots. The cut is the most common, but the dissolve, fade in–fade out, and the defocus and focus are also used. Digital video technologies provide a large number of elaborate special effects that can also be used to connect shots.

FOR FURTHER READING

BOGGS, JOSEPH M. *The Art of Watching Films* (Menlo Park, Calif.: Benjamin/Cummings, 1978).

BORDWELL, DAVID, JANET STAIGER, and KRISTIN THOMPSON. *The Classical Hollywood Cinema: Film Style and Mode of Production to 1960* (New York: Columbia University Press, 1985).

MASCELLI, JOSEPH V. *The Five Cs of Cinematography: Motion Picture Techniques Simplied* (Hollywood: Cine/ Grafic Publications, 1965).

chapter twelve

Video Production:
The Studio

INTRODUCTION

Video productions are made in a studio or on location, or a combination of the two. The studio is a space designed specifically for the production of video programs. It provides maximum control of lighting, sets, props, camera placement, talent blocking, and audio. An exterior location is a less controlled space, and production methods are somewhat different there. In this chapter, we will consider in some detail the production apparatus found in most video studios and the tasks of studio production personnel. In Chapter 13, we will discuss location production.

THE STUDIO ENVIRONMENT

Video studios come in many different sizes, layouts, and levels of production sophistication (Fig. 12-1). Some are rooms converted from other uses and are so small that they are suitable for only the simplest productions. Other studios are very large, with millions of dollars' worth of production equipment. In such facilities, dramas, concerts, and variety shows can be done with ease.

Regardless of their size and sophistication, most video studios have some characteristics in common. First, they provide a quiet, isolated space in which a video production can take place under controlled conditions. Second, they contain a few necessary pieces of production equipment such as lights, cameras, microphones, curtains, sets, and props. Third, there is nearly always a separate

FIGURE 12-1 A small video production studio.

room that functions as a control center where the director, switcher, and several other key production personnel can oversee the making of the program.

The creation of any studio video production involves a number of persons working in close cooperation as a production crew. A crew can consist of a few or several people, depending upon the number of individuals available and the complexity of the production being undertaken. One group of individuals functions as the creative crew, deciding upon the layout of lights, sets, props, camera placement, talent performance, and actual execution of the production. This crew includes the producer, the director, an assistant director, a switcher, and various control-room personnel. In the studio itself there is a second group of individuals who carry out the commands of the first group. These production crew members operate cameras and microphone booms, set lights, move sets and props about, and serve in a variety of other capacities.

In the early days of television, almost all programs (unless they were on film) originated from studios in which they were done live. Newscasts, interviews, quiz shows, and dramas were all broadcast from network or local station studios. With the introduction of portable video cameras, videotape recorders, and microwave relays, more television programs have "taken to the road." The studio remains an important location for many television productions, however, and you should become familiar with this type of facility.

Sets and Props

We can think of a studio without sets and props as a neutral space just like an empty stage. The moment sets and props are added, mood and meaning are created. Some video sets are very realistic; they try to recreate in every detail a particular location. Realistic sets, which are difficult to build, are useful for a period drama or similar program. Other sets can be very abstract, using only a few flats, risers, or other items to suggest a particular location. Most sets fall somewhere in between. They strive to suggest reality without actually re-creating it in complete detail. An interview program, for example, might use a set consisting of a few bookcases, a sofa, two chairs, and a desk. A few props, such as a vase of flowers, a lamp, and a globe would complete the suggestion of a person's study. The set is neither completely realistic nor totally abstract. It contains just enough detail so that the viewer can get an idea of what the location is supposed to be.

Hanging units.   Curtains, drops, and cycloramas are standard equipment in most studios. They are called *hanging units*. Studio curtains are drapes suspended from a traveller attached to tracks fixed to the studio ceiling. The traveller allows the curtains to be stretched out to their full length or bunched together out of the way.

Curtains are either pleated or flat. A flat curtain can be pulled taut so that it presents a smooth surface, or it can be arranged more loosely so that it forms folds. Taut curtains provide a ready background upon which various patterns can be projected from an ellipsoidal spot.

Curtains are available in various materials and colors. Velour is a popular fabric; it is durable and has a velvety texture. The less expensive Veltex is also widely used. Some curtains are made from canvas or muslin.

At one time, black was a popular color for curtains. Black curtains permit cameo effects (in which the performer seems to be standing in front of a black void), but they also absorb a great deal of light. Many studios today use lighter colors in addition to, or in place of, the black curtain.

Two popular colors are chroma-key blue and CBS grey. The chroma-key blue provides a backdrop for the keying effect on the video switcher. The curtain seems to disappear, and another background is electronically put in its place. The CBS grey color provides a neutral backdrop against which colorful set pieces can be placed. This curtain can sometimes be made to appear a different color when lit by colored spots. Curtain manufacturers today offer a wide choice of colors. A useful combination would be a chromakey- blue, a CBS grey, and perhaps a yellow or rust color.

A cyclorama is a special curtain found in some studios. It is a large piece of canvas or muslin that stretches around three sides of the studio without a break. Weights and ties along the bottom edge pull it taut. It presents a seamless surface onto which can be projected clouds, buildings, patterns, and other effects.

In addition to curtains and cycloramas, studios sometimes use backdrops, which are large pieces of canvas containing a painted scene. There are also chroma-key drops that can be lowered behind a performer who is to be keyed over a selected background.

Standard set units.   Flats, two-folds, and risers are known as standard set units, and most studios will have a supply of them.

Flats.   A flat is a light wooden frame 8 to 10 feet high and usually no more than 4 or 5 feet wide (Fig. 12-2). It can be faced with canvas, plywood, or some other hard material. The surface of either soft- or hard-faced flats can be painted,

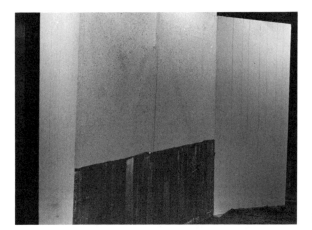

FIGURE 12-2 Studio flats.

and hard-faced flats can be textured or wallpapered and have pictures, mirrors, and other hangings attached to them.

Flats are designed so that they can be joined together to form two-folds (two flats) or three-folds (three flats). The vertical braces (stiles) of the flats are fitted with cleats to permit individual units to be lashed together. They may also be joined by hinges, but this requires exact positioning so that the connecting pin can be dropped into place.

Flats are usually fitted with a swingout brace (jack) on the unfaced side that can be weighted to the floor by a sandbag or stage weight (Fig. 12-3). Braced flats stand freely without additional support. Two-folds and three-folds stand freely if

FIGURE 12-3 Bracing for studio flats.

they are not extended to their full width. Additional bracing does ensure safety, however.

Flats are relatively easy to construct and, when not in use, can be stored behind curtains or in racks located in a nearby room.

Risers.   Risers are wooden platforms that are usually painted or carpeted (Fig. 12-4). They come in different sizes and are designed to raise a performer approximately six inches above the studio floor. Risers help to give a sense of depth and visual variety to a set. Risers are also easy to construct and can be stored easily.

Set Pieces.   Set pieces include doors, stairs, arches, fireplaces, and other items that can be used to make a set look more realistic. They can be purchased or built from scratch.

Furniture, Set Dressings, and Hand Props

Furniture and set dressings (books, lamps, flowers, and so on) can be added to a set once flats and set pieces are in place. They can add considerable realism to a set. Hand props include items that are actually picked up or touched by talent. Such items include maps, pencils, books, and cooking utensils.

It is unlikely that small studios will have a ready supply of furniture, set dressings, and hand props. However, these items can be purchased or borrowed from thrift shops, antique stores, and friends. A retail establishment will occasionally loan large items like refrigerators and sofas for dramatic productions in return for a mention in the program's credits.

Aesthetic and Technical Considerations

A set must be carefully planned to meet the aesthetic and technical requirements of a production. The set should be consistent with the purpose of the production and help to create the desired atmosphere. It should also accommo-

FIGURE 12-4   Risers provide different levels for a studio production.

date the technical needs of the production by allowing free movement of cameras and microphone booms.

The set should take into account unusual camera angles or lighting instrument positions called for in the production. A script that specifies low-angle shots might need a set with very tall flats so that the upper edges don't appear in the shot. Similarly, wide-angle shots might require a set built around three sides of the studio. Sometimes sets get in the way of lighting units. A very tall flat can block the beam of a back light. Also, improperly built or positioned set items can cast unwanted shadows.

The Floorplan

A floorplan is a scale drawing, like a blueprint, showing the location of all sets, props, flats, risers, and so on. It also shows the position of cameras, microphone booms, and studio monitors. Floorplans are usually drawn to a scale of 1/4 inch to 1 foot. Careful measurements must be taken of all set items so that they can be rendered in the correct scale on the floorplan.

The lighting scheme is usually drawn on a plastic overlay that can be positioned over the floorplan. The lighting overlay shows the position of all lights to be used in the production and the general direction of their beams. Accurately rendered floorplans and lighting overlays can help production personnel spot potential problems long before actual set construction begins.

LIGHTING

Video lighting has both technical and aesthetic goals. It must satisfy the technical requirements of the production by providing enough light so that the camera can register an image that does not contain too much contrast and in which the colors are correct. Aesthetically, the lighting must create a sense of depth, modelling, and texture. It should also help to create the proper mood for the program and direct the viewer's attention to what needs to be seen.

Lighting Equipment

The equipment for lighting consists of (1) lighting instruments, (2) hanging units, and (3) control devices. You need to be familiar with how this equipment works and how to use it safely.

Lighting instruments.   There are two categories of lighting instruments: *spotlights,* which produce a highly directional beam of light, and *floodlights,* which produce a more diffused beam.

Spotlights.   There are three types of spotlights: (1) Fresnels, (2) ellipsoidals, and (3) lensless spots.

Fresnels. The Fresnel (pronounced fre-nəl) spot is named after Augustin Fresnel, who invented the lens found on the front of the unit (Fig. 12-5). The lens

FIGURE 12-5   A Fresnel spotlight.

is shaped in a series of concentric rings which focus the light as a solid plano-convex lens does. However, the Fresnel lens is less bulky than a solid lens and allows heat to escape from inside the unit much more efficiently.

The Fresnel lens allows the light to be focused into a narrow beam. Behind the lamp is a reflector, and focusing is accomplished by changing the distance between the lamp/reflector and the lens. The position of the lamp and reflector can be changed by turning a knob or ring on the side of the instrument or by moving a lever back and forth. This method is called *sweep focus*.

There is some danger in moving the lamp because the filament could break. Some Fresnel spots are focused by moving the lens while the lamp and reflector remain stationary. This method is called *ring focus*.

When the lamp and lens are far apart, the beam is narrowed, or "pinned." When they are closer together, the beam is "spread." A pinned beam usually covers no more than 10 degrees of arc, while a spread beam covers up to 60 degrees of arc.

Fresnel spots come in a variety of sizes, and these are indicated by the wattage of the lamp and the diameter of the lens. Fresnels range in power from 150 watts to 10,000 watts and in size from 3 inches to 12 inches. A commonly found Fresnel is the 8-inch, 1,000-watt unit.

Ellipsoidal spots. The ellipsoidal spot, or leko, is a special-purpose unit that projects a bright, sharp beam of light with a hard-edged shadow (Fig. 12-6). The sharpness of the ellipsoidal's beam allows it to project patterns of different designs onto sets, curtains, and cycloramas. The patterns are stamped from metal discs called *cucaloruses*. They can be obtained in the shape of grids, bars, and many other designs.

Ellipsoidal spots come in several different sizes ranging from 500 watts to 2,000 watts. A commonly used ellipsoidal is the 1,000-watt size.

FIGURE 12-6 An ellipsoidal spot

Lensless spots. A lensless spot is similar to a Fresnel except that it does not use a lens (Fig. 12-7). Its beam can be spread or pinned by changing the distance between the lamp and the reflector.

Lensless spots do not have the range of beam control that Fresnels do. Because they are lightweight and efficient, these units can be used in many different lighting situations.

Floodlights. Floodlights are used to balance the concentrated, directional illumination of spots. The softer, diffused light from floods provides general illumination and fills in shadows cast by spotlight beams.

Floods use large reflectors to generate their diffused light. They usually do not have lenses. The beams of some floods can be widened or narrowed slightly, but the range of adjustment is not as great as that on spots.

The most common type of studio flood is the scoop (Fig. 12-8). It is so

FIGURE 12-7 A lensless spotlight.

FIGURE 12-8   A studio floodlight or scoop.

named because of its unique shape, which resembles an ice cream scoop. Scoops range in power from 1,000 watts to 2,000 watts and in diameter from 14 to 18 inches.

Broads are rectangular floodlights. Their beams can be adjusted somewhat, and they can be fitted with barn doors, which are hinged metal flaps used to partially close the front of the unit. Both scoops and broads can use scrims (spun-glass sheets) to further diffuse the light.

Softlights are similar to large scoops. They use reflectors and scrims to produce a very diffused illumination.

Lamps.   Most lighting units use quartz or tungsten-halogen lamps, but some use incandescent lamps. Quartz lamps are small and lightweight. They burn with a constant color temperature and strength. As they age, quartz lamps do not dim or change their color temperature. Incandescent lamps do both and are therefore not as suited to color video production.

Quartz lamps have a shorter life span than incandescent lamps. Quartz lamps also become very hot. Scrims, color gels, and even barn doors don't last too long in their presence. Lighting units that use quartz lamps can become very hot. They should be allowed to cool before they are handled. Lighting technicians need to wear gloves to protect against burns. Incandescent units operate at a much lower temperature and are somewhat safer to handle. However, they, too, must be allowed to cool before being touched.

Mounting devices.   Because video productions involve the movement of cameras, microphone booms, and talent, the studio floor must be kept clear of lighting instruments. This means that they need to be hung above the studio floor or mounted on devices that can easily be moved out of the way.

Hanging Units. A convenient method for mounting lights is to attach them to a pipe grid suspended a few feet below the studio ceiling. Some studios have a grid system that can be raised or lowered.

Lighting instruments are attached to the pipe grid by a C-clamp. The clamp allows the unit to be swivelled from side to side. For safety, the light is also attached to the pipe by a wire or chain so that if the C-clamp comes loose, the unit will not fall. It is sometimes desirable to set a light at a lower height than the grid, and this can be done by attaching it to a pole or a sliding rod which can extend downward from the grid. Another way to vary the height of the lighting instrument is to attach it to a pantograph which can extend down from the grid. Some pantographs permit the unit to be lowered almost to the studio floor (Fig. 12-9).

Floor Mounts. It is sometimes desirable to place a lighting instrument on a floor stand. Wheeled tripods with adjustable poles on top are often used for this. The instrument can be wheeled out of the way when no longer needed.

Safety Precautions. It is sometimes necessary to climb a ladder to aim or otherwise adjust lighting units. The ladder must be placed under the instrument and opened fully. A tall ladder must be steadied by a floor assistant. When moving a ladder about, make sure that the top does not strike lighting instruments. Crew members who adjust lights must wear heavy gloves and avoid looking directly into instruments that are turned on. Make certain also that the power to a particular unit is off before you attempt to unplug it. A burned-out lamp can fool you into thinking that the power is off when it is actually on.

Great caution should be used when you have to touch a lamp. Make sure that the unit has been off long enough for the lamp to cool. Always use heavy gloves to prevent the possibility of being burned. Also, lamps should not come into contact with the skin because oils found on the skin will be transferred to the surface of the lamp. This residue of oils will create hot spots on the lamp, causing it to burn out sooner.

Control devices. Sometimes, it is necessary to have additional control over the direction, intensity, or color of lighting instruments. This can be accomplished by means of barn doors, dimmers, scrims, and color gels.

Barn Doors. Barn doors are metal flaps that can be attached to the front of most lighting instruments (Fig. 12-10). They permit additional control over the spread of the beam. Barn doors can obstruct the escape of heat from instruments, however, and cause the lamp to burn out more quickly. Crew members need to wear gloves when adjusting barn doors.

Dimmers. Dimmers control the amount of electricity flowing to individual lighting units. Dimmer systems usually have some method of patching individual units to various circuits. In this way, several different lighting setups can be handled.

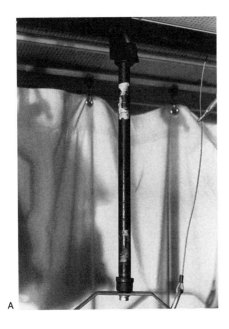

A

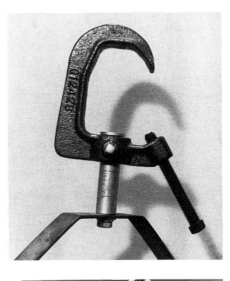

B

C

FIGURE 12-9 Mounting devices for studio lights. (a) Extender. (b) C-clamp. (c) Pantograph.

Scrims and Gels. These are used to diffuse the light from instruments. Scrims are spun-glass panels attached to the front of floods, and they soften the beam considerably. Some lighting instruments can also be fitted with color gels that alter the unit's color temperature. They can be useful in creating dramatic effects.

Lighting Setups

Now that you are familiar with lighting units and their auxiliary equipment, you need to know how to place them to achieve your lighting goals.

FIGURE 12-10 Barndoors mounted on a Fresnel spotlight.

The Three-Point Scheme. During the rise of the Hollywood studio system, standard lighting procedures were developed that were also used later in television. The system was borrowed from theatre and saw widespread application in film and television for many years. This "three-point" approach to lighting was designed to direct the viewer's attention to the performer who was the most important subject in the frame and to suggest depth (Fig. 12-11).

The three-point scheme uses lighting instruments positioned in a triangle around the subject. These lights are a *key*, a *fill*, and a *back light*. This layout is

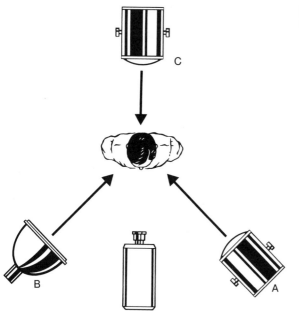

FIGURE 12-11 The three-point lighting scheme. (a) Key. (B) Fill. (c) Back.

only a starting point. It does not satisfy all lighting needs and must be modified somewhat for multiple camera productions (since it is basically designed for single-camera shooting).

The key light is the principal source of illumination for the subject. It is provided by a Fresnel or lensless spot with a partially spread beam. Barn doors can be used to adjust the spread. The key light is a studio substitute for sunlight.

If the key light is placed on a line with the camera, the subject will appear washed out. Moving the key to one side and up or down increases the shadows on the subject. It is usually a good idea to first place the key approximately 45 degrees to one side of the camera and about 45 degrees up from the floor of the studio. It can be further adjusted as is necessary.

The fill light is a studio substitute for natural ambient or reflected light which softens the harsh shadows cast by sunlight. The fill is provided by a flood or a Fresnel with a spread beam. The unit is placed on the opposite side of the camera from the key in a mirror-image position.

The fill light softens shadows and provides illumination to the other side of the subject. The fill needs to be about one-half the strength of the key.

The back light is placed behind the subject on a line with the camera and approximately 45 degrees above the studio floor. Its beam is directed down to the head and shoulders of the subject. The back light's main purpose is to provide modelling and to separate the subject from the background. It should be about the same strength as the key light.

The angle of the back light is important. If it is too steep, the beam will fall on the top of the subject's head, and the desired modelling will not occur. Subjects need to be a sufficient distance from the set so that the back light can fall at a suitable angle. If performers work too close to flats, the angle of the back light will be too steep to produce the desired result.

Additional Lights.   It is unlikely that a key, back, and fill alone will meet all your lighting needs. You may find it necessary to add more units before your setup in complete.

Side lights are Fresnel or lensless spots placed 90 degrees from the camera position and directed to the side of a subject's face. The side light adds sparkle and can serve as a key light if the camera moves in its direction. The side light also helps to reduce shadows and to increase the modelling on a subject's face.

The *kicker light* illuminates the subject from behind and is placed on either side of the back light. It produces a rim of light around the subject and helps to lighten shadows created by the key. A Fresnel spot is usually used for the kicker light.

Camera lights, also called "inky-dinkys," are small spots that can be mounted directly on the camera. These lights are especially helpful in eliminating shadows around the talents' eyes created by high-angle key lights. The camera lights add sparkle to the talents' eyes, making them more attractive.

Background or set lights are used to illuminate the set and not the talent. Since the three-point scheme is designed to illuminate the talent, the background is often cast into shadow. Most sets require some kind of special lighting. Background lights are very helpful in making an otherwise dull set look interesting. They can also help to establish a mood, indicate a time of day, or suggest a location. Ellipsoidal spots can be used to project various patterns against a cyc or curtains, and they can add considerable interest.

Special lighting situations. On occasion, you might have to light for cameo, silhouette, a rear screen, or chroma-key. These special lighting situations require a departure from normal practices.

Cameo and Silhouette. In cameo lighting, the talent is seen fully illuminated against a dark background. To achieve this effect, you must use highly directional three-point lighting aimed carefully so that there is no spill onto a background curtain. The curtain itself must be either black or some other very dark color. Cameo lighting was very popular in the days of monochrome (black-and-white) television, but is difficult to achieve with color. Silhouette lighting is the opposite of cameo lighting. It is achieved by placing the talent in darkness against a brightly lit background.

Rear Projector and Chroma-key. Some productions require the use of a rear screen projector in the studio. In order for images to appear clearly on the screen, the screen itself must be kept in relative darkness. This can be accomplished by carefully controlling the direction and spread of all light units and by separating talent from the front of the screen.

In order for the chroma-key effect to work, the chroma-key backdrop or window must be evenly lit. Any variation in light levels or shadows will cause the chroma-key effect to be uneven. The chroma-key backdrop must be lit by highly diffused floods or softlights to ensure the desired evenness. The chroma-key effect should be tried in rehearsal from a marked camera position to make sure that the lighting is correct.

Moving Talent and Cameras. There are two ways to ensure good overall lighting when there is to be considerable talent and camera movement. The first is to light the entire performing area with a general wash of light. This provides a base light for every camera position. The key areas can then be lit using the three-point scheme. A second method is to use cross-keying. The entire area is lit with overlapping three-point triangles. Keys are placed along two sides of the triangle and fills along the third (Fig. 12-12).

In developing any lighting scheme, you need to remember that the final measure of its success is how it looks on the video screen. Don't hesitate to depart from the three-point approach and to add any lights needed to achieve desired results. Also, set aside extra time in the studio so that you can experiment with and adjust your lighting setup until it is just right.

THE PRODUCTION

Studio productions are carried out by a team of individuals working together to form a production crew. While the size of the crew may vary somewhat from one situation to another, most crews have at least the following members: (1) pro-

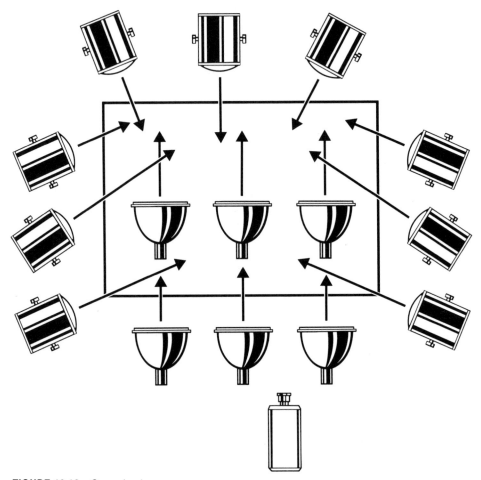

FIGURE 12-12　Cross keying.

ducer, (2) director, (3) assistant director, (4) switcher, or technical director, (5) audio operator, (6) VTR operator, (7) camera operators, (8) floor manager, (9) boom operator, and (10) lighting supervisor. More elaborate productions call for cable pullers, set and prop personnel, and a number of floor assistants.

Crew Positions

The producer is responsible for gathering all production elements before the actual production begins. The producer raises money, generates ideas, contributes to the overall program concept, works with writers and talent, and otherwise oversees the assembly of the production. The producer's functions can sometimes be combined with those of the director.

The director (who sometimes acts as producer) is responsible for actually re-

hearsing and carrying out the production of the program. The director partici-
pates in all preproduction planning and is the final authority once the production has actually begun. The director marks scripts, oversees the placement of
sets, props, and lights, rehearses talent, and selects the shots that actually go on
the air.

The assistant director can be assigned a variety of tasks at the director's discre-
tion. The assistant director usually helps the director during production by setting up shots, keeping time, and following the script.

The switcher, or technical director, operates the video switcher according to the
director's commands. Sometimes, when the production crew is very small, the
director can do the switching.

The floor manager is the director's representative in the studio during a production. The floor manager relays the director's verbal instructions to the talent
and crew during rehearsals and uses hand signals during the production itself to
give the talent timing and pacing information.

Other crew members operate specific pieces of equipment such as the audio
board, cameras, microphone booms, character generators, and VTRs at the instructions of the director. They must be able to follow the director's instructions
accurately and work quickly and efficiently.

Production Language

When a production crew has been working together for a long time, a director's instructions can be communicated easily. This is especially true if a program has an unvarying format from one episode to the next. The crew needs
very little instruction in what to do next.

Students often work with an inexperienced and unfamiliar crew, however.
In such situations, the director must be able to communicate instructions clearly
to each crew member. To make this possible, directors use a very specific language. Beginning directors need to know this language and use it when necessary,
realizing, though, that it is probably not used with such precision in typical production situations.

When giving commands to crew members, directors follow a few general
rules:

1. Crew members are addressed by position and not by name. The director will say
    "Camera 1, ready to zoom in to closeup of talent," rather than "Bill, ready to zoom
    in to closeup of talent." This minimizes the possibility of confusion if there is more
    than one crew member with the same name.
2. Every command is preceded by a "ready." This alerts the crew member to the com-
    mand that is to follow. The director will say "Ready, dissolve to Camera 1," rather
    than "Dissolve to Camera 1."
3. The director follows up commands with additional instructions when called for. If
    the director instructs a camera to zoom in, she needs to follow this command, if
    time permits, with an affirmation that the instructions have been properly carried
    out. The director might say, "Fine, Camera 1, that's what I wanted."

Ready Fade in Music
Ready Mike Talent
Ready Cue Talent
Ready Fade in Camera 1

Fade in Music
Mike Talent
Cue Talent
Fade in Camera 1

Ready Dissolve to Camera 2
Dissolve to Camera 2

FIGURE 12-13 Typical director's commands

FIGURE 12-14 Typical assistant director's commands

Prepare One Minute
Show One Minute

Ready Roll Credits
Roll Credits

Prepare 30 Seconds
Show 30 Seconds

Prepare 15 Seconds
Show 15 Seconds

Prepare Wrap
Show Wrap

Prepare Cut
Show Cut

A

FIGURE 12-15 Floor manager's hand signals. (a) Standby. (b) Cue. (c) Wave over. (d) Stretch. (e) Five minutes. (f) One minute. (g) Thirty seconds. (h) Wrap it up. (i) Cut.

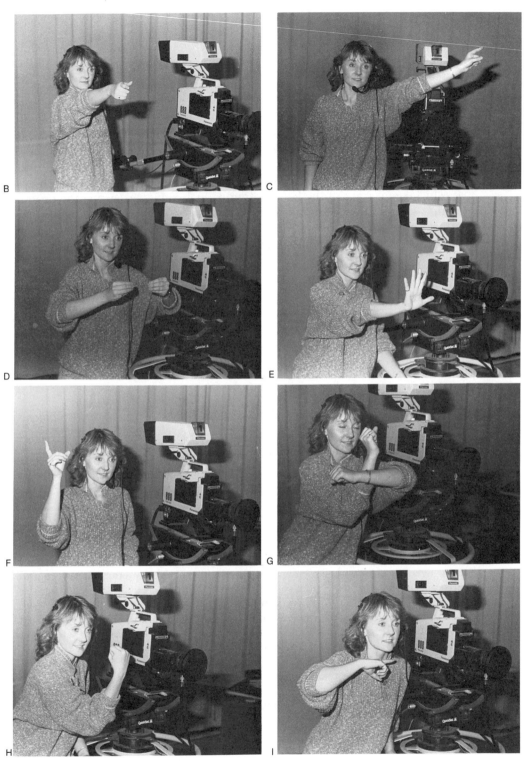

FIGURE 12-15 (Cont.)

247

Figure 12-13 provides examples of a director's commands to camera, floor manager, and switcher. Commands to other crew members follow a similar format.

Timing the Production

The assistant director is usually responsible for timing the production. The assistant director often keeps track of three different timings. These timings include *elapsed time*, which indicates the amount of time that has passed since the production began; *time remaining*, which shows how much time is left; and *segment time*, which keeps track of the length of individual segments. During the production, the assistant director reminds the director of how much time remains in the production so that this information can be passed on to talent and crew. Figure 12-14 lists typical time commands given by the assistant director.

Hand Signals

Because the director cannot talk directly with talent during the progress of an actual production, he gives instructions to the floor manager, who then passes them on to the talent by means of hand signals. It is important for both the floor manager and the talent to be familiar with the meanings of these hand signals. Figure 12-15 provides examples of typical hand signals used by studio floor managers.

Cards

The floor manager sometimes holds up cards for the talent to see. These can be used in place of hand signals to give timing and other information.

SUMMARY

The studio is a controlled space in which a video production takes place. Studio sets can range from the realistic to the abstract. They are made using curtains, flats, risers, set pieces, and other materials. Sets are often designed with the help of a floorplan and lighting overlay. A set must take into account both the technical and the aesthetic requirements of a production.

Studio lighting has two general functions: (1) to generate enough light to meet the technical requirements of the cameras and (2) to produce the proper mood for the production. Standard lighting units are the Fresnels, ellipsoidals, lensless spots, and floods. Lighting units can be suspended from a pipe grid above the studio floor by C-clamps and extended by sliding rods or pantographs. Lighting instruments can also be mounted on floor stands. Light intensity and direction can be controlled by barn doors, dimmers, scrims, and gels.

The three-point scheme is a common approach to lighting. It uses a key light as the main source of illumination, a fill light to soften shadows, and a back light to separate talent from the background. Additional lights are the kicker, side light, camera light (or inky-dinky), and the set light. Special lighting situations are cameo, silhouette, and lighting for rear screen and chroma-key backdrops.

A studio production uses a crew, or team, the members of which work together in close coordination under the supervision of the director. The director can use a precise language to communicate instructions to the crew. In addition to the producer and director, other typical crew positions are the assistant director, floor manager, switcher or technical director, and camera, audio, boom, and VTR operators.

The assistant director is responsible for timing the production. Commonly used timings are elasped time, time remaining, and segment time. The floor manager uses hand signals or cards to communicate the director's instructions to the talent during a production.

FOR FURTHER READING

ARMER, ALAN A. *Directing Television and Film* (Belmont, Calif.; Wadsworth, 1986).

BURROWS, THOMAS D. and DONALD N. WOOD. *Television Production: Disciplines and Techniques* (Dubuque, Iowa: Wm. C. Brown, 1986).

WURTZEL, ALAN. *Television Production* (New York: McGraw-Hill, 1979).

ZETTL, HERBERT. *Television Production Handbook* (Belmont, Calif.: Wadsworth, 1976).

chapter thirteen

Video Production: Location

INTRODUCTION

Video productions increasingly call for some or all of the shooting to be done on location rather than in the studio. Small, lightweight cameras with automatic setup procedures paired with small, lightweight VTRs, all operating on battery power, allow a camera crew to visit the most remote locations. Advances in technology have made location production possible. The note of realism captured by taping in the boardroom or the shipyard has made location production aesthetically desirable. In this chapter, we'll describe the most common forms of remote production and consider production techniques that are helpful in location shooting and postproduction.

TYPES OF REMOTE PRODUCTION

Electronic News Gathering

Electronic news gathering, or ENG, is a familiar form of remote production. Typically, a news reporter and crew are assigned to cover a news event. The crew may consist of a camera operator and an audio engineer, or the camera operator may also be responsible for audio. Because coverage of news events allows little time for preproduction planning, the crew must adapt quickly to conditions at the site of the event. For most assignments, the taped footage is brought back to the studio to be edited into its final form. For major breaking stories, the report may be microwaved back to the studio to be used live.

Electronic Field Production

Like ENG, electronic field production (or EFP) uses portable cameras and recorders. Unlike ENG, EFP productions are more thoroughly planned and scripted. Shooting is often done film-style, with a single camera. With this approach, the script is divided by grouping all the scenes requiring the same camera setup and location. These scenes are rehearsed and recorded. The camera and lights are then moved into position for the next group of scenes and those are recorded. Multiple takes are common. In postproduction, the best of the takes are edited into the proper order, sound tracks are completed, and titles and graphics are added.

Multicamera Remotes

Other location productions, such as sports events, make use of multiple cameras and mobile vans equipped with virtually all the support equipment found in the control room—audio mixers, switchers, character generators, VTRs, and all the necessary auxiliary equipment. These remote productions can be quite complex, using techniques borrowed from both studio production and ENG and EFP production. In this chapter, we'll concentrate on the requirements for ENG and EFP production, with occasional reference to how these might apply to multiple-camera remote production.

PREPRODUCTION

Preproduction planning varies, of course, with the type of remote production you are doing, but all remote productions require some consideration of scripting, surveying the location, and choosing the best equipment.

Script

For ENG productions, the reporter often scripts on the spot. On the basis of prior research and information gathered on location, a stand-up introduction may be planned to be followed by segments from an on-location interview or scenes from the event and a stand-up close by the reporter. Most of the final story is shaped in the editing process.

EFP productions, on the other hand, are usually carefully scripted. For example, a training video for a corporate sponsor may require approval of the script before the shooting begins. A film script format is often used for the shooting script. As illustrated by the sample script in Fig. 9-2, each scene is numbered and identified as to location and time of day. This makes it easier for the producer or director to identify all the scenes that are to be shot in one location and to plan the shooting schedule more efficiently by completing all the scenes in one location before moving on to the next location.

Because multicamera remotes are more likely to be for a regularly sched-

uled event, such as a baseball game or a Thanksgiving Day parade, these productions may use a format script. Such a script might include the standard opening,
a run-down of the segments, and the standard transitions between segments.

Surveying the Location

An important first step in your preproduction planning is surveying the
location. Seeing the actual space within which you will be working lets you plan
camera placement, audio pickup, and lighting setup. It also lets you anticipate
and plan for many potential problems.

Camera placement.   Many of the basic directing strategies you used in the
studio can be modified for use on location. If you are taping an interview, for
example, you may want to plan for an establishing two-shot, closeups of the interviewee, closeups of the interviewer reacting or asking questions, or over-the-
shoulder shots of each person. Using two or more cameras in the studio allows
you to frame those shots on separate cameras and switch between them during
the interview. With one camera, the camera will have to be moved for each new
angle. To keep the interview as spontaneous as possible, one strategy is to place
the camera so that you can frame an interesting closeup of the person being
interviewed and tape the interview from that position. The camera can then be
moved to frame a closeup of the interviewer repeating some of the questions and
listening. The camera might be moved to another position to frame an establishing shot for the introduction to the interview or the first question being repeated.

Looking at the room in which the interview will take place allows you to
judge whether the arrangement and the size of the room permit the camera
angles you want. In some situations you may be able to change the position of a
chair or move the interview away from a desk to another part of the room to get
better angles. Another factor to consider is whether the distance between the
camera and the subject allows you to use a variety of lenses or limits you to a
wide-angle lens. The kinds of shots and the perspective in the shots are affected
by the lens you can use. Try to visualize the framing of the shots from each angle,
and don't neglect to check the background of each for distracting visual elements.

In many location productions, it may be important for you to follow the
actions of a person. Again, strategies you used in the studio for following action
in long shot and closeup and techniques for cutting on action or dialogue are
useful, but the camera setup will have to be changed. For example, if you want
to show the exact procedure for operating a piece of equipment on the assembly
line, you will want to place the camera where you can tape a long shot of the
operator going through the entire procedure. You will then need to move the
camera into several other positions to record closeups of each step of the operation. By observing the actual operation carefully, you will be able to plan the
angles that will show clear, unobscured detail. In planning camera placement,
you should consider the axis of action and maintain consistency of point of view
so that the viewer does not become confused about the location of the pieces of
equipment shown in closeup.

In some situations, it is important for the camera to be as unobtrusive as possible. Most of us are a bit self-conscious when we know we are on camera. If you want to capture people responding naturally, the camera should be placed where it doesn't intrude or become a distraction. In these situations, rather than moving the camera from place to place, it may be wiser to find a location that allows you to cover most of the scene with small pans or tilts with zooms to allow you to change from wide shots to closeups.

After scouting the location, you may find that you want to modify your shooting script to take advantage of the location's unique visual qualities and to compensate for limitations imposed by the space within which you have to work.

Audio setup.   On location, take time to consider the audio setup as well. Although it is important to try to capture the actual sounds of that environment, it's also important to remember that a microphone does not discriminate between sounds that are important and sounds that are not. Listen carefully to all the sounds around you and try to anticipate what will be happening when you are actually recording. The coach's office may be quiet enough to record an interview early in the morning, but not in late afternoon when loud noise from an intramural basketball game filters in from the gym next door. The noise of the assembly line may be too loud for good audio pickup of the supervisor explaining emergency shut-down procedures. The intimate mood of an interview with the parents of a handicapped child may be broken by the noise of traffic and auto horns coming in through an open window.

Some of these problems can be controlled by careful scheduling of the time of the production or by turning off fans or by closing windows. However, you may decide that a particular location, essential for its visual elements, is simply too noisy for good audio pickup. In that case, you can record location sounds while you are recording the video. Then, in postproduction, that audio track can be mixed at low volume levels with voice-over narration or voice-over from an interview recorded under better conditions. The location sounds add authenticity to the visuals, and the voice-over provides the verbal information the viewer needs.

On location, you should also consider the number of microphones you will use and the placement of each. If the interviewer and interviewee are seated, placing a microphone on the desk between them may be acceptable. If that is too obtrusive, clip-on microphones are another option. Or, if you don't want the microphones to be visible in the shot, a microphone mounted on a fishpole could be used. Using a hand-held microphone or a camera-mounted microphone are other possibilities. If the talent moves, the microphone must move also. Can that be done quietly, without interfering with the action and the camera? In addition to all the factors discussed earlier in Chapters 1 through 5 on audio production, you must consider the visual factors as well.

On a multiple-camera sports remote, you may want several different sound tracks to mix during the telecast or taping. One or more microphones could be used to pickup the noise of the crowd. Separate microphones could be assigned to the announcer and commentator. Perhaps another microphone could be used by a roving announcer on the sidelines. Yet another microphone, a wireless, might be carried by a referee. All of these would be assigned to separate channels on the audio console so that the relative volume levels could be controlled.

Lighting.   Another consideration is lighting. Unless you are taping outdoors during the day, you may need to add additional lighting. Inside on a bright day with a good expanse of window, you might be able to make use of the natural light falling on the subject. But most interiors require some artificial lighting. Seldom is the normal light level in homes and offices sufficient for good, sharp video images. A light meter will give you a quick reading of available light levels. In your location survey, note the existing lighting conditions and the type of lights and reflectors you will need to bring along.

If you'll be shooting outdoors, visit the location at the time of day you intend to shoot. Note the position of the sun and the presence of shadows and other elements that will affect the lighting situation. Even outdoors, you may want to add light or use reflectors to fill shadows areas.

Other details.   Other very practical questions should be answered during the location survey. Will you be able to use existing electrical outlets for the equipment, or will you have to use battery power? Most of your equipment requires grounded (three-prong) outlets. Where are the electrical outlets and breaker box located? Will you need extension cords to run from the outlets to the taping site? Will the amp capacity of the circuits be adequate for your equipment? If you have problems with power, who should be called?

Observe the access to your shooting site. Where will you park? Will you encounter any problems moving the equipment from your car or van to the shooting location? Will arrangements have to be made to have doors unlocked?

The more detailed your survey of the location, the more complete your preproduction planning can be and the fewer surprises you'll encounter when you arrive for the shoot.

Permits and Permissions

Many, if not most, remote shoots require someone's permission. The city's police department and the shopping mall's security staff have legitimate concerns about the possible safety hazards or disruptions your activities might create. Owners of businesses may object to the inconvenience to their customers. Allowing you into an area implies that the owner has assumed liability for your safety. On most campuses no one would object to your setting up your camera for a scene outside your classroom building, but in other locations, you should check to see if a permit is required. Even where permits are not required, you should ask for permission. You may be turned down for any number of reasons, but many people are willing to cooperate once they understand the purpose of your project and your willingness to observe the limits they request. Restaurant owners may not allow you access during the noon rush hour, but they may let you tape in midmorning between the breakfast and lunch crowds or late in the evening after they close the doors to customers.

Equipment Checklist

Taking the time to make an equipment checklist will help you remember all the things you will need on location.

Cameras. In reality, your choice of cameras is limited to those available for your use. But when you have a choice, you should consider the operating characteristics of each. A three-tube camera may give you sharper detail than a single-tube camera will. In situations where you cannot avoid shooting directly toward bright lights, a camera with solid-state sensors rather than pickup tubes is less likely to be damaged by burn-in. In low-light situations, a camera with greater sensitivity would produce less noise in the images. If you anticipate needing to move rapidly from one shot to another to follow action, a camcorder rather than a separate camera and VTR might be lighter in weight and easier to manipulate.

Cameras may have different lens systems. Will the longest lens setting allow you to get the closeups you need from the place where you will set up the camera? Will the shortest lens let you get the widest shot you need? For some productions, a lens with a macro setting might help you to get extreme closeups of details.

Along with the cameras, don't forget a white card for setting white balance and the cables and connectors for the cameras.

Mounting devices. For most location shooting, a mounting device to help steady the camera is desirable. In some situations, a good shoulder mount and a steady arm will suffice. In most situations, however, a tripod is a more practical choice. If you anticipate needing to follow action with a moving camera, a Steadicam or a tripod mounted on a dolly is helpful.

VTRs. Unless you are using a self-contained camcorder, you may have a choice of VTRs. For professional applications, a 1-inch VTR will give you the best quality. For many broadcast and almost all industrial applications, 3/4-inch videotape is acceptable. The quality of standard VHS 1/2-inch format is adequate for many industrial and educational purposes. Other 1/2-inch formats, such as M-format and high-fidelity Beta, rival 3/4-inch quality.

Videotape. The performance of high-quality videotape is worth the extra expense. Estimate the shooting time you'll need and take along extra tape just in case.

Power source. Both the camera and the recorder require electrical power. Will you use batteries, or will you plug an adaptor into available outlets? Batteries allow you more freedom of movement. Make sure that they are charged and that you have enough to cover the shooting time you plan. An adaptor provides a more reliable source of power. Plan to take along extension cords to reach from the outlets to the camera location.

Audio.   The easiest way to record sound on location is with the microphone mounted on the camera. The quality of the audio track recorded with that microphone may be disappointing, however. If you are interested only in recording ambient sound to mix in with voice and music tracks, the camera-mounted microphone might be adequate. A better choice for most situations is an external microphone. An external microphone gives you more control over microphone placement. It also gives you more flexibility in choosing the microphone with the best pickup pattern and frequency response for a given situation.

Other items for your checklist include wind screens for the microphones; a head set for monitoring the quality of the audio being recorded; a microphone stand, fishpole, or other mounting devices; and all the necessary cables and connectors for the particular microphones and recorders you'll be using. If you plan to use more than one microphone, a Y-connector would allow you to run both microphone cables into the recorder, but a portable audio mixer would give you better control over the levels. If you're using a portable mixer, remember that its output is line level. If your VTR has only a microphone input, you'll need an adaptor to step down the mixer's line-level output to the recorder's microphone-level input.

Lighting.   If your location survey indicated that you would need to use portable lights, make sure your light kit includes not only the lighting instruments themselves but also stands and clamps for mounting them, extra lamps, diffusion screens or gels, power cords, and extension cords. In many situations, bouncing lights off a surface gives a more natural look than focusing the lights directly onto the subject. Bouncing the light off walls or ceilings is often possible, but reflectors may give you more control. A sheet of white foam core or matte board can be used. Even in natural lighting conditions, reflectors allow you to direct light to soften shadows or highlight areas.

Video monitor.   Just as headsets allow you to monitor the quality of the audio being recorded, a portable video monitor allows you to check the video signal. The small, black-and-white monitor in the camera's viewfinder is adequate for judging framing. A portable color monitor allows you to make better judgments about the overall quality of the video image being recorded.

PRODUCTION TECHNIQUES

Although each production situation is different, there are some general guidelines that may help you get better footage on location. One that seems obvious but is often overlooked is simply to take the time to become familiar with the camera you will be using. Read the manual and shoot test footage under conditions similar to those you expect to encounter. The more familiar you are with white balancing and other setup procedures, the operation of the focus and zoom controls, and the camera's operation under various lighting conditions, the less time you'll waste on location. Even if you are familiar with the equipment, allow enough time to make sure everything is working properly before each shooting session.

Adapt to lighting conditions.   Most portable cameras have an auto-iris function, which sets the aperture opening according to the average light level entering the lens. This is a real convenience, but it can also create conditions to which you must be alert. If your subject is placed against a very light background (a highly reflective light-colored wall, a bright window, or a sunny sky), the auto-iris will adjust for the light level of the background, leaving the subject underexposed and too dark. In such a situation, one option is to change the background by moving the subject. If you must shoot toward the bright window, you can reduce the light level by closing the draperies or covering the window with a neutral-density filter. Another option is to disengage the auto-iris function and open the aperture until the subject is properly exposed. In this case, the background will be overexposed and look washed out.

The auto-iris, when it is engaged, is constantly monitoring the light level and adjusting to accommodate any change. If light or reflective objects move through the frame or within the frame, the amount of light they reflect toward the camera will change. As the aperture opens or closes in response, the change in exposure will be noticeable. The same thing occurs when a zoom in or out alters the average light level entering the lens. If, in editing, you will eliminate those frames in which the aperture opening or closing is obvious, this need not be a concern. If you don't anticipate editing out those sections and find them objectionable, you can disengage the auto-iris function and set the exposure for the optimum level for the most important shots.

Many portable cameras have a gain, or sensitivity, switch. This function boosts the gain of the video signal so you can record images in low-light situations. Increasing the gain also increases the noise in the image and reduces resolution.

Use a tripod.   From an aesthetic point of view, the unsteady shots typical of a hand-held camera may lend authenticity to news or documentary footage. In many cases, however, the unmotivated camera movement is distracting. For times when you must hold the camera, practice until you find the positions (sitting or standing) and postures that are comfortable and that you can hold without wavering. Because camera movements are more obvious on the telephoto lens, try to plan your camera placement to allow you to use a normal or short lens.

For most productions, using a tripod is more satisfactory because it provides a steady base for the camera. Most tripod mounting heads also allow smooth pans and tilts. For moving shots, a tripod can be mounted on a dolly. You can improvise by seating the camera operator in a wheel chair or an office chair that not only rolls but also swivels smoothly for pans. Keeping moving subjects in focus can present problems. Use a lens with a large depth of field to minimize this problem.

Make the shot long enough.   When recording each take, remember that most recorders need a few seconds to come to speed before they begin laying down a steady video signal. In editing, you'll need several seconds of unbroken control track or time code for the pre-roll ahead of the first frame you actually use. Therefore, a good habit to develop is to roll the tape about 15 seconds before calling for the action to begin. At the end of the shot, allow the tape to continue recording for another 10 to 15 seconds to be sure the shot will be long enough. Editing out extra footage is easy. Adding footage means going out on location again.

Shoot for the edit points.   In planning your shots, try to shoot for the edit points. That means visualizing the action and how the first and last seconds of each shot should be framed. For a scripted production, your storyboard can help. As you sketch each frame, you can test how the shots will look when they are cut together. Are you maintaining continuity of screen direction? Are the shots that will bridge the edit framed so that they are matched in terms of focus of attention or mass or composition? Is the flow of action consistent? Or, if you are deliberately trying for a jarring effect, are the shots mismatched in such a way that the cut produces the visual effect you want?

Good notes will help you avoid many continuity problems. For example, if you were shooting a sequence involving the use of a computer, you might plan to shoot the entire operation in a long shot and then shoot closeups of particular segments to insert as specific procedures are being explained. For continuity, the information on the computer screen or the position of the operator's hands would have to match. The production assistant's notes would help you make sure that they do match up. Experienced actors are more likely to remember how they were holding an object or how their costumes were arranged at the beginning and the end of a scene than less experienced performers; but even they may need to check your notes if some time has elapsed between the segments.

For an unscripted production, try to anticipate how the shots will cut together. That may be difficult to do when you can't ask talent to repeat an action or wait while you set up for another camera angle. In general, moving shots or zooms are hard to edit together while maintaining a pleasing visual rhythm, so try to eliminate pans, tilts, or zooms, especially at the moments you anticipate using as an edit point. If you pan, tilt, or zoom, end the movement and hold a steady shot for a few seconds. Rather than panning to follow action, allow the moving subject to exit the frame. Then set up the next shot with an empty frame into which the subject moves.

Shoot cut-aways. Remember to shoot plenty of cut-aways. Look around the location and identify objects that can be shot in closeup and used to cover an edit point. In an interview situation, shoot "listening" footage of each person. Look for objects on the desk—a name plate or a book—that tell the viewer something about the person or the topic of the interview. At a sporting event, closeups of spectators' faces, pennants, the referee's whistle—any of these might provide the right visual insert to cover an edit point and help tell the story.

Record ambient sound. For the audio track, unless you have recorded plenty of ambient sound with the video, take the time to record several minutes of wild sound. Once you're in the editing suite, you may find that you'll need location sound to smooth transitions or to replace sections that aren't useable because of the crew members' voices or other audible intrusions.

Label the footage. Keeping good records during the production will save time in postproduction. Recording a few seconds of a slate with information identifying the production, scene or shot number, and take number at the beginning of each shot will help you locate individual takes quickly. If you don't have a slate, the information can be written on a card or a crew member can read it. Each tape should be clearly labeled with the title of the production, the date of shooting, and the tape number. Then a written log can list the details of what is on each tape as well as notes about which takes are good and which ones can't be used.

Take care of the equipment. Handling the equipment with care can prevent problems on location. Capping your camera except when it's actually in use is probably more important on location than in the studio. When lights are being moved around or when the camera is being carried, you might not notice that the camera is picking up bright lights and suffering burn-in.

Be alert for extremes in temperature. The condensation that happens when moving equipment and tapes from warm to cold or from cold to warm areas can cause problems. Allow enough time for the equipment to adjust to the location temperatures before starting to record. Remember, too, that cold temperatures shorten the operating life of batteries. Anticipate weather conditions so you'll be prepared to protect all the equipment from rain, snow, or blowing dust and sand.

POSTPRODUCTION

Once the location shooting is finished, the postproduction work begins. Postproduction includes all the steps needed to turn the raw footage into a finished master tape. Depending upon the individual production, this process can be as simple as reviewing the footage, deciding upon the particular takes, and editing them together. Or it might involve more complex steps, such as generating computer graphics and titles, mixing and sweetening the audio track, and inserting special effect transitions at the edit points.

Logging the Footage

In either case, the first step is to review the footage and log each tape. Logging the tapes involves making a list of each take, indicating where it begins and ends on the tape, noting any problems with the video or the audio, and jotting down comments that will help you decide which takes or shots to use. Identification of the exact location of each take on the tape varies with the particular viewing system you're using. Some VTRs have counters that count tape revolutions. These counters give only an approximate location on the tape because the numbers differ as you move the tape from one recorder to another. Other VTRs count the sync pulses on the control track and translate those into a number representing hours:minutes:seconds:frames. This provides a more reliable method of locating specific shots if you remember to reset the counter to zero at the beginning of the tape each time. SMPTE time code provides the most accurate method for identifying individual frames of video. SMPTE time code assigns a specific number (in hours:minutes:seconds:frames) to each frame of video. This number can be recorded during production by using a time-code generator and recording the time code on the videotape in the vertical blanking interval or on an address track. If SMPTE time code was not recorded on the tape during production, it can be added after production by recording it on one of the audio tracks. In ordinary playback, the time code is not visible. In editing, the SMPTE time-code reader displays the numbers, or you can make a work print of your original tape and have the time-code numbers burned-in (superimposed over) the video so that they can be seen on the monitor. See Fig. 13-1.

On-line and Off-line Editing

On-line editing refers to the process of creating the final edited master tape. For a simple production, you might move directly to on-line editing, making final decisions about the exact edit points as you go. In many production units, this process involves using sophisticated computer-assisted editing systems. This is a more expensive process; therefore, in order to save time, all the decision-making usually occurs during off-line editing.

Off-line editing can be done on paper by making a list of the SMPTE time-code numbers identifying the edit points for each shot from beginning to end. In some production units, off-line editing goes beyond compiling this edit list to include the preparation of a rough edit (usually a "cuts only" version) from work copies of the original tapes. With all the creative decisions made, the precise edit points identified, and any special-effects transitions noted, the time and, therefore, the expense needed for on-line editing is considerably reduced.

FIGURE 13-1 Frames can be located using (left) control track numbers from the status display monitor or (right) SMPTE time code numbers displayed on a time code reader or burned-in the image on a work print of the tape.

Videotape Editing Systems

A basic videotape editing system includes a source deck (for playback), a record deck, a controller, a status display monitor, and video and audio monitors. A more complex system might include two or more source decks, provisions for routing the video signals from these plus other video sources (cameras or character generators) through a switcher or digital-effects generator and the audio signals through a mixing console, a record deck, a computer-assisted controller, and monitors for video and audio.

The single-source system provides cuts-only transitions at the edit points, although some controllers used with these systems do provide a fade in–fade out function. The multiple-source systems, by routing the video signals through a switcher, allow for a full range of wipes, dissolves, and other special-effects transitions (Fig. 13-2).

Videotape Editing

Unlike audiotape editing, in which you cut and splice the tape, video editing involves selecting the individual segments to be used and then rerecording them in the proper order onto another tape. With audiotape, finding the precise edit point is a fairly simple process of listening as you turn the reels by hand, moving the tape back and forth across the playback head. With videotape, manually locating the precise point on the tape where one frame of video, along with

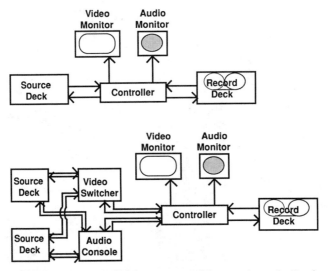

FIGURE 13-2 (top) Single source editing system. (bottom) Multiple source editing system.

its audio and control track information, ends and the next begins is almost pure chance. However, this task can be done electronically by the controller.

Controllers perform the edits in one of two modes: the assemble mode or the insert mode (Fig. 13-3). The basic difference between the two modes is the way in which the control track is recorded onto the master record tape. In the assemble mode, all tracks (audio, video, and control tracks) are transferred from the source tape to the record tape for each shot. In the insert mode, a continuous

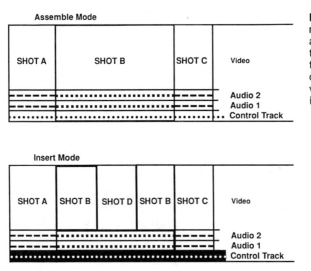

FIGURE 13-3 In the assemble mode, all tracks (video, audio, and control) are transferred together from the source tape. In the insert mode, a continuous control track is laid down. Then video and audio tracks are inserted.

control track must be laid down on the master record tape before editing begins by recording an uninterrupted video signal, usually a black signal, onto the tape. Then only the audio and video tracks are transferred from the source tape to the record tape for each shot.

In the assemble mode, because the control track comes from each individual shot, there is a chance that the control tracks may not match up precisely. This can produce video breakup at the edit points. In the insert mode, because the control track is continuous, there is less likelihood of glitches or breakup at the edit points. In addition, in the assemble mode, correcting a mistake means going back to that spot in the tape and redoing that edit plus all that followed it. In the insert mode, new audio or video can be inserted at any point in the tape to replace what is there.

In getting ready to edit, it is important to remember that there is a difference between a blank tape and a black tape. A blank tape has no video signal recorded on it, while a black tape has a black video signal on it. This black signal includes a control track. If you are using the assemble mode, you can use a blank tape with a few seconds of black at the beginning. If you are using the insert mode, you must use a black tape or a tape with another continuous video signal, such as color bars, on it. The black signal is recorded in real time, so allow enough time to black the record tape before you start to edit.

Leader. The leader should be recorded onto your master tape first (Fig. 13-4). Although the exact requirements for the leader may vary, all leaders include a few seconds of black for threading, at least 30 seconds of color bars and audio tone as a reference for setting playback levels, 15 seconds of slate to identify the production, countdown numbers and audio beeps from 10 through 2 for cueing the tape, and 2 seconds of black.

Assemble editing. When recording the leader onto the record tape for assemble editing, continue recording about 10 seconds of black after the last countdown number. In the assemble mode, the control track is recorded along with the video and audio from the source tape. To synchronize the tapes when performing an edit, the controller must read control-track pulses from both the source tape and the record tape. Thus, in the assemble mode, edits are overlapped.

For the first edit, then, find the first frame of the first shot on the source

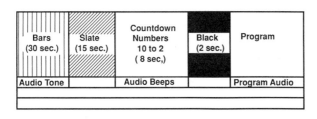

Bars (30 sec.)	Slate (15 sec.)	Countdown Numbers 10 to 2 (8 sec,)	Black (2 sec.)	Program
Audio Tone		Audio Beeps		Program Audio

FIGURE 13-4 Leader for video-tape productions.

tape and set that as the "in" point. Then find the last frame of the shot and go beyond that frame about 10 seconds before setting the "out" point. You'll need that extra footage as overlap for the second edit. On the record tape, find the last frame of the last countdown number (the number 2), then advance the tape 2 seconds and set the "in" point.

Now you can preview the edit. When you activate the preview operation, both tapes rewind to a pre-roll position and then begin the preview, stopping automatically at the "out" point. If you are satisfied with the look of the preview, let the tapes rewind to their starting position and perform the edit. If you want to change the beginning or the ending points, simply find and set the new in and out points. Preview those changes and then perform the edit. After completing an edit, review it to make sure that it is clean and that the in and out points are correct. If so, you're ready to find the in and out points for the next segment on the source tape and the new in point on the record tape and preview your next edit. As the term "assemble editing" implies, you assemble the final master tape segment by segment.

If you're using control-track editing, the numbers used as in and out points are coming from counting the control-track pulses. The sensing device may not detect every pulse as you shuttle the tape back and forth looking for the edit points, especially at slow speed; or the control track itself may have been damaged so that some pulses are missing. Some editing systems are more accurate than others, but whenever you're using control-track editing, don't expect to be frame accurate. In assemble editing, since you are overlapping edits, this is generally not a problem. Using SMPTE time code does give you frame accuracy because the numbers used to set in and out points are the numbers assigned to individual frames. SMPTE time code allows you to take full advantage of the possibilities offered by insert editing and computer-assisted systems.

Insert editing.   As with assemble editing, the master tape should begin with a leader recorded at the beginning of your black tape. From there, you might continue as you did in the assemble mode to edit the tape in sequence from beginning to end. (If you're using control-track editing, it's a good idea to overlap edits a few frames in order to minimize the risk of leaving a black frame between edits if the pulse count is off.)

Insert editing allows you more options, however. You can insert any piece of video or audio at any place on your master record tape, so you don't have to edit in sequence. Moreover, insert editing makes it possible for you to work with audio and video separately. This opens up the possibility for other editing strategies.

For example, suppose you're editing a news feature about the new tigers at the zoo. You might begin with the reporter's stand-up introduction and the beginning of the interview with the director of the zoo. Because the information about the tigers comes from that interview, you might continue editing together the segments of the interview that provide the comments you want. Then, using the "video-only" mode, you could replace some of the interview visuals with closeups of the tigers, shots of visitors watching, and other images as the director comments on them. In the video-only mode, only the video track is erased and replaced with the new video from the source tape. The audio track is untouched.

In that news feature, you edited the audio track along with its video first and then corrected the video sequence. Another time you might lay down the audio track first is when you're editing a fast montage of images that cut on the beat of music. To accomplish this, you would edit the music onto your record tape and then edit the video to match the rhythm of the music.

Often you may want to do the reverse: Edit the visuals first and then add the audio. Many visuals have a rhythm of their own. This is particularly true of shots containing movement of objects within them or movements of the camera itself. Other visuals are complex enough or interesting enough that the viewer needs time to look before going on to the next. Cutting the shot before a movement is finished just to conform to an audio track often looks awkward. Cutting before the viewer is ready can leave the viewer confused or irritated. In cases like these, editing visuals first and then inserting the audio produces more satisfying results.

For example, many instructional videotapes use voice-over narration to explain the procedures being shown. Because the visual information is so important, it's preferable to edit that first and then match the verbal explanations to the video. This may require rewriting portions of the narration or rehearsing the talent so that they can match their timing to the visual sequence.

Insert editing also allows you to work with the audio tracks separately (Fig. 13-5). For example, if the interview about the new tigers at the zoo had been recorded in a quiet office, all the sounds of animals and people we associate with a trip to the zoo would be missing. When images of the zoo exhibits are inserted, sounds recorded on location could be added to the other audio track. Working with two audio tracks requires careful planning so that the relative volume levels are correct. Overlapping sound also helps bridge the edit points and makes the transition seem more natural.

A-B roll editing. *A-B roll* is a term borrowed from film editing. It refers to the technique of assembling even-numbered segments on one reel and odd-numbered segments on a second reel, with the spaces between the segments on one reel matching the exact length of the segments on the other reel.

Track Separation

Interview	MS Tigers	CU Tigers	MS Children Watching Tigers	Interview	Video
Continuous Interview Audio on Audio 2					Audio 2
	Ambient Sound From Tigers				Audio 1
· · · · · · · ·	· · · · · · ·	· · · · · · ·	· · · · · · · · · · ·	· · · · · · · · ·	· Control Track

FIGURE 13-5 Insert editing allows you to combine visual images and audio tracks in creative ways.

Editing is done by rolling the two reels at the same time and dissolving or cutting between them.

In A-B roll video editing, two source decks are used, with the segments divided between the source tapes. The video output of the source decks feeds through a switcher, so dissolves, wipes, or other special-effect transitions can be done at the edit point. The audio output feeds into an audio console, allowing manipulation so that the audio track can be sweetened by mixing in other sources as well.

SUMMARY

Video productions that are done outside the studio fall into three general categories: electronic news gathering (or ENG), electronic field production (or EFP), and multicamera remotes. These types of production differ in the extent of preproduction planning, in shooting styles, and in the complexity of postproduction work.

Preproduction planning includes developing a script, surveying the location, and selecting the most appropriate equipment. Scripts for ENG productions are often written on the spot as information is gathered and combined with prior research. EFP productions are usually carefully scripted in advance. Multicamera remotes are more likely to use a format or partial script with complete run-down sheets for all the elements to be used in the broadcast.

A survey of the location includes noting where cameras can be placed, checking the environmental factors that will affect your audio, and observing existing lighting conditions. Other details such as access to the location, availability of electrical outlets, and the need for permits and permissions should also be checked.

In making an equipment checklist, decisions about the best equipment for the particular production situation are made. This list also serves as a reminder about all the equipment and accessories that are needed on location.

Familiarity with the camera and its features is important if you are to obtain the best possible footage under the various lighting conditions found on location. For steady shots, use a tripod. Allow time for the video recorder to come to speed before beginning a shot, and allow extra time at the end for editing purposes. In planning shots, shoot for the edit points. Record cut-aways and location sound to use during the editing process. To locate individual shots quickly, record a slate or make a log and label each tape.

In postproduction, footage is reviewed and decisions about the exact edit points are made during off-line editing. During on-line editing, the final master tape is created.

Editing is done in one of two modes: assemble or insert. In assemble editing, shots are edited in sequence, with the control track for each shot transferred with the shot onto the record tape. Insert editing requires the use of a black tape, which provides a continuous control-track on the record tape. The video or the audio, or both, for each shot can then be inserted in the proper place on the record tape. Additional audio can be added onto the second audio track. To determine in and out points, control-track editing counts pulses on the control track and converts those into hours:minutes:seconds:frames. Since SMPTE time-code editing uses the address number assigned to each frame of video, it is more accurate. A-B roll editing by using alternate shots on two source tapes allows for dissolves, wipes, and other special-effect transitions between the two tapes.

FOR FURTHER READING

COMPESI, RONALD J. and RONALD E. SHERRIFFS. *Small-Format Television Production: The Technique of Single-Camera Television Field Production* (Boston: Allyn & Bacon, 1985).

FULLER, BARRY J., STEVE KANABA, and JANYCE BRISCH-KANABA. *Single-Camera Video Production: Techniques, Equipment, and Resources* (Englewood Cliffs, N.J.: Prentice-Hall, 1982).

chapter fourteen _____

Video Production: Applications _____

INTRODUCTION

As we've suggested throughout this section, video production is being done in a variety of settings. In gathering materials for this chapter, we talked to professionals working in corporate, cable, biomedical, commercial, and public broadcast facilities. They ranged in experience from relative newcomers to seasoned veterans, but all of them shared several important characteristics.

All of those we interviewed think in terms of the audience they are trying to reach. From selecting an idea for a program to deciding the order in which information will be presented or the way in which that information will be turned into visual images, they all have a specific audience in mind and care about communicating clearly to that audience. Although they all work hard to maintain good technical quality, what the video program communicates is ultimately more important to them.

All of them, too, are creative. They see new possibilities to keep standard program formats fresh and interesting. They are willing to experiment. They know that some experiments will fail, but they are willing to take creative risks.

In addition, all are enthusiastic about their work. Despite the pressure that comes with their jobs, they enjoy being a part of the television production process. As they talked about specific situations and events, it was obvious that they find a great deal of satisfaction in what they do. For them, the payoff for all the hard work is that moment when they capture on tape a spectacular play during a game, or win an award for a video they produced, or help coordinate the coverage of a major news event, or put together a program that makes viewers face critical issues in their communities.

SPORTS EVENTS ON CABLE

Like many cable companies, Maclean Hunter Cable Television, in Taylor, Michigan, airs several locally produced television programs each month. Some of these are produced in the studio; some are live remotes. For program director Ken Schramm, directing remote broadcasts of sports events is an exciting challenge. To explain how he approaches these broadcasts, he described the procedure followed for most basketball games.

The crew call is set for 5 hours before the game, but as the director, Schramm is at the studio even earlier to make sure that the remote truck is ready and to go over the equipment checklist (Fig. 14-1). Once the crew is assembled, the remote truck is driven to the location. Schramm likes to arrive on location at least 4 hours before the game to allow plenty of time to set up for the broadcast. Following a list of setup priorities allows the engineering and production crews to work quickly and efficiently (Fig. 14-2).

Four cameras are used to cover the action on the court. Two of these are placed on the center line—one high in the press box to follow the ball on a wide shot and the other to get closeups of individual players. Both of these cameras

1. Make sure truck is road ready.
   a. No flats.
   b. Gas and oil.
   c. Troubleshooting kit.
   d. All equipment is bolted down or loaded. Cameras, cables, AC cable, audio cable, tripods, mounts.

2. Check accessories.
   a. Extra tape decks.
   b. Mics.
   c. Table and chairs.
   d. Mic flags.
   e. Banners.
   f. Monitors.

3. Check tape.
   a. Pre-recorded material.
   b. Audio carts.
   c. Replay tape.
   d. Mastering tape.
   e. Record buttons.

FIGURE 14-1 Director's check list.

LIVE REMOTE SET-UP PRIORITIES

ENGINEERING AND PRODUCTION

1. Get power to trucks.
2. Get bars and tone to AT&T and get confirmation from any receive site possible.
3. Get all necessary cameras up, registered, and color balanced. This does not include beauty shots.
4. Get announce audio confirmed. This includes announcer's headsets, interview mics, P.A. mics, all non-ambient mics.
5. Confirm intercom to all crucial areas: cameras, floor director, extra trucks, graphics, replays.
5a. Confirm pics/audio from slo-mo or other outside sources.
6. Ambient sound: parabolics, crowd, baskets, camera mics. Confirm I.F.B. to announcers.
7. Beauty shots: clock, 5th or 6th camera. This step can be scratched if too time consuming.
8. Pre-taping. Check tapes while recording and again before talent is released from set.
9. Camera call.

FIGURE 14-2   Set-up priorities.

are mounted on studio tripods. The other two cameras are hand-held by camera operators positioned at either end of the court. These cameras roam between the sidelines and the basket. To maintain continuity of action, all four cameras stay on one side of the axis of action drawn down the court from one basket to the other. For some games, a fifth camera is used to cover the scoreboard. A sixth might be used for beauty shots of the crowd and other interesting activity.

For audio, the play-by-play announcer and the color announcer use headset microphones. Ambient sound comes from lavaliere microphones taped to each backboard out of the area of play, a 635A omnidirectional microphone for general coverage of the crowd, and a shotgun microphone, which follows the movement of the ball. The microphones covering the baskets and the crowd are mixed down to a submaster. Sometimes a submaster is also used for the shotgun microphone on the ball. The 12-channel audio system has the capacity to handle a spare microphone, plus audio and videotape playback, and tone or return feed.

Two videotape players record master tapes of the game. Two others are used to play back commercials, clips or stills of stars, and replays. The two VTRs assigned to replays of the game cover different views of the game. One switches between the two roaming cameras, while the other takes the program video minus the keys or the wide shot of the court.

The character generator (CG) used has a 700-page memory capacity. This allows the graphics producer to program shell pages for each player before the game. During the game, statistics can be added and updated quickly.

Depending upon the number of cameras used, the size of the crew may range from 19 to 21 members. Stationed in the truck are the director, the technical director, the engineer, the audio board operator, two videotape operators, the graphics producer, the CG keyboard operator, and a statistician. Working with the play-by-play announcer and the color announcer in the press box are an assistant director, a spotter, and a statistician. Positioned within the stadium are the camera operators and the audio assistant assigned to handle the shotgun microphone.

As Schramm points out, each sport has its own format, or set of unwritten rules that directors follow. The basic four-camera setup was established in the 1950s. As minicameras added to production possibilities, this setup was refined during the 1960s and 1970s. Because the playing field in football and basketball is basically the same, the look of the television coverage is the same. The baseball stadium is different, so camera placement and the look of the coverage is different.

In each sport, every play has a specific pattern or sequence of shots that is typically used to cover that play. To Schramm, the difference between a beginner and an experienced director is that the rookie tends to follow the "rules" in covering the game while the good director concentrates more on following the game. The shots the director chooses determine how the viewers see the game and how they perceive what happened. These differences are what distinguish one director's style from another's.

As an example of two patterns commonly used in basketball, Schramm described the sequence of shots used for a foul shot and for the action following a basket. When the players are set for a foul shot, the viewers are shown a closeup of the shooter. A graphic with statistics is then keyed over the shot. As the shooter raises the ball, the video cuts to a wide shot. If the remaining game time is under 2 minutes, the time will be shown as often as possible. When the ball is in play, the action is followed in a wide shot until the basket is made. Then, the shot cuts to a closeup of the hero while the ball is out of bounds. As the ball comes in bounds, it cuts to a wide shot with the score keyed over.

As a directing strategy, Schramm keeps one camera on a wide shot so that there is always a shot of the total action available. The other three cameras are used to add different views of the action.

Replays are added only when the action on the court stops. The videotape operators often try to sell particular shots they have on tape. As director, Schramm chooses a replay that shows the viewer something different. It might be a spectacular play or a fantastic effort, a different angle on the play, or a view that clarifies confusion about what happened.

For Schramm, directing sports is fun because you never know what's going to happen next. At any time, you could be the one to capture an outstanding moment in sports history. And in cable, there's the extra incentive to look as good as the commercial networks that your viewers also watch.

There are problems, however. Some are those associated with all remote broadcasts, such as the unpredictability of shooting in a remote location and the potential lack of cooperation from people there. Technical problems also occur, especially in hot or cold climates, with the breakdown of cameras or other equipment. There is also the potential for loss of power, and not all stadiums have the necessary 200-watt, 80-amp generator to get back on the air. Other problems grow out of budget limitations. The most pressing problem is the high turnover of personnel, which means working much of the time with inexperienced crew members.

Schramm offered several suggestions for anyone interested in sports broadcasting as a career. First, get as much experience as you can and practice to be good. Be ready to challenge yourself. Rather than limiting your experience, have the confidence to volunteer to do a job even if you're not sure how. Second, learning to be a good camera operator is one way to get a start. In sports, camera operators have to be proficient because they have one chance to get the action. Shots must be well composed, moves must be smooth, and the shot must stay in focus. Third, learn to dissect television by watching with the sound turned off. Instead of getting lost in the sports event, concentrate on the way the event is covered so that you're watching the show, not the contest. Watch for the changes that new technology makes possible. Fourth, learn about trucks because remote broadcasts happen from trucks. Production people are proud of their trucks and expect everyone involved to keep them neat, tidy, and well maintained.

BIOMEDICAL COMMUNICATION

Biomedical communication departments in healthcare facilities provide a wide range of services. At the University of Michigan Medical Center, for example, these services include graphics, writing, photography, medical illustration, and media production. The television production unit in that department works with both audio and video, producing slide-audiotape programs, audio recordings, and videotape recordings.

The videotapes produced in this biomedical communications department are used for several purposes. Some are designed as instructional tapes that are available to be checked out for study by medical students. Portions of tapes documenting an unusual case might be shown in the classroom. With the trend toward shorter hospital stays and more outpatient treatment, other tapes are intended for patient information. These educational tapes are accompanied by a summary brochure that the patient can keep for reference. The majority of the tapes produced by the department are intended for postgraduate use to update practicing physicians. Some of these are designed to allow the physician to earn Continuing Medical Education credits. They are distributed in the United States through the media library and in Europe and Asia through a distribution network that is granted translation as well as distribution rights.

Greg Lyon, production manager in Biomedical Communications at the medical center, described how a videotape program is developed (Fig. 14-3). The process usually starts when a client, in most cases a physician or nurse, comes in with an idea. During the initial contact, a meeting is set up with an instructional designer and the production manager to develop the overall concept for the program. Once the concept is clear, a producer is assigned to the project and script development begins, with the client functioning as executive producer and content expert. At this stage, instructional development is carefully monitored to be sure that the script is instructionally sound.

FIGURE 14-3 Flow chart of the production process.

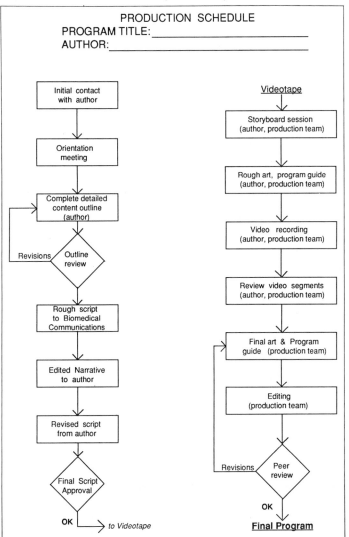

PRODUCTION SCHEDULE
PROGRAM TITLE:_____
AUTHOR:_____

Initial contact with author

Orientation meeting

Complete detailed content outline (author)

Revisions — Outline review

Rough script to Biomedical Communications

Edited Narrative to author

Revised script from author

Final Script Approval

OK → to Videotape

Videotape

Storyboard session (author, production team)

Rough art, program guide (author, production team)

Video recording (author, production team)

Review video segments (author, production team)

Final art & Program guide (production team)

Editing (production team)

Revisions — Peer review

OK

Final Program

Once the script is finished, a storyboard session is scheduled. At this meeting, the client, the instructional designer, the producer, and the medical illustrator or graphic designer refine the order in which the information is presented and fine tune the script and dialogue. With the script in final form, production responsibilities are assigned. A schedule is established for the location shoots. Specific patients to appear in the video, as well as additional actors and a narrator, are located.

Lyon finds that it is helpful to use index cards to record the specifics for each scene. These cards contain details about costumes, props, sets, the physical environment, colors, and so on. Cross-references to other scenes are noted. These cards are used in dissecting each scene so that no detail is overlooked in planning a taping session. They also aid in maintaining continuity. If, for example, a person is moving from one room to another and there are clocks in both locations, a note on the scene cards about the time of day is a reminder that all clocks need to show the same time. When sequential scenes are shot several days apart, notes on makeup and costume help avoid obvious changes in the actors' appearance. Notes about technical details, such as whether the cameras were balanced for daylight or for tungsten lights, minimize color differences in the video image recorded at different times.

Then production begins. The cast is selected, graphics are made, and locations are scouted. Decisions are made about lights and equipment. Arrangements are made for transportation. A composer is given a contract to write original music, or selections are made from the music library.

During the actual shooting and editing, the clients are encouraged to be present. Since they are the content experts, their approval is important for ensuring the accuracy of the portrayal of medical information and medical situations. Once the tape is completed, it is shown to the client, and any requested changes are made (Fig. 14-4).

The process just described is similar to the production process that might occur in many corporate or independent production units. One situation that is unique to medicine is videotaping surgical operations. These tapes are made to document an unusual case, to use in teaching students, or (in rare instances) to record the procedure as protection against a potential law suit by the patient. As Lyon points out, the videographer's purpose is to show what the surgeon wants shown to keep the viewer oriented. The camera is often positioned to shoot over the surgeon's shoulder. A monitor is placed across from the surgeon. During the taping, the surgeon can check the framing of the shot and ask for a closer or wider shot. Taping starts and stops on the surgeon's orders, so during a 4-hour operation, only 40 minutes of taping might be done.

A major concern in videotaping in the operating room is to avoid compromising the sterile field. Although the videographer wears a scrubsuit and the equipment is all thoroughly dusted and cleaned, none of it is sterile. Thus care must be taken that nothing touches the sterile field. Another strain is being confined to a small area during lengthy procedures. Recording begins when the surgical site is open and the procedure is ready to start. But the videographer must

Date: _____

Program #: _____

Program Title: _____

How many people participated in completing this form? _____

   Viewer(s): ____ Physician   ____ Nurse
               ____ House officer   ____ Allied health professional
               ____ Medical student   ____ Nursing student
               ____ Other (please specify): _____

Please circle the number on the scale which represents
your evaluation of each item.

Section I: Educational Standards	Excellent				Poor	N/A
1. Material accurate?	5	4	3	2	1	___
2. Content current/up-to-date?	5	4	3	2	1	___
3. Content appropriate for intended audience?	5	4	3	2	1	___
4. Content free from extraneous material?	5	4	3	2	1	___
5. Objectives clear?	5	4	3	2	1	___
6. Content relevant and sufficient for stated objectives?	5	4	3	2	1	___
7. Logical flow (sequence)?	5	4	3	2	1	___
8. Length appropriate to amount of content and audience?	5	4	3	2	1	___
9. Medium effective in communicating content?	5	4	3	2	1	___
10. Accompanying print relevant and helpful?	5	4	3	2	1	___
11. Improved understanding of subject?	5	4	3	2	1	___
12. Production unbiased?	5	4	3	2	1	___
Section II: Production Standards	Excellent				Poor	N/A
13. Holds viewer's interest and attention?	5	4	3	2	1	___
14. Sets/visuals enhance educational content?	5	4	3	2	1	___
15. Pace of presentation appropriate?	5	4	3	2	1	___
16. Visuals easily read/understood?	5	4	3	2	1	___
17. Talent credible?	5	4	3	2	1	___
18. Words pronounced correctly/narrator quality?	5	4	3	2	1	___

FIGURE 14-4 Evaluation form for peer review.

remain in place until the procedure is over and the site is being closed. Tension builds up because it is important to do a thorough job without interfering with the surgery.

In discussing the skills needed to work as a producer and director in biomedical communications, Lyon mentioned the importance of learning as much as you can about all aspects of video production and being willing to experiment. For example, the character generator in his facility is an older model with limited capacity, so he often generates graphics on his Macintosh computer and reverses to get white on black, then shoots these with a camera for keys and titles.

Lyon also stressed the importance of understanding both technical and aesthetic factors that contribute to the look of a production. He works with late-model equipment and with a skilled engineer who believes in preventive maintenance to minimize technical problems. He also pays particular attention to lighting on location, using a light kit and filters as needed to correct for color differences.

For Lyon, learning to be a good producer or director involves being interested, reading, talking, experimenting, learning from mistakes, and getting as much experience as possible.

LOCAL NEWS

Regardless of the size of the market, an important part of a television station's programming is local news. The production process—from the time that an idea for a story is generated until the story is aired—requires the skills of many people. As an assignment-desk editor at WKRC-TV, Patti McGeever is one of those whose work contributes to the local news coverage on which viewers rely for information about important events in the community and the surrounding area.

Ideas for news stories come from many sources. At the assignment desk, McGeever takes calls from public relations people representing all kinds of organizations and events, as well as calls from individuals passing on news tips about things that are happening in the area. She screens the mail and the newspapers for possible ideas. Someone is constantly monitoring the scanners to pick up information about police and fire department calls. Reporters contribute their own ideas based on the sources of information they have developed in their domain. Each reporter, for example, tends to concentrate on one area—city hall or the police department or a neighboring community. In brainstorming sessions, producers, reporters, and assignment-desk people discuss the ideas. Decisions are then made about which stories to cover.

Once those decisions are made, the assignment-desk editor is responsible for scheduling a reporter and a photographer to cover each story. If the story is to be broadcast live, a live truck and crew must also be scheduled. With news, however, those schedules can change instantly. As an example, McGeever described the afternoon when a report came over the scanner at about 5:00 PM. Shots had been fired at the bus station. Because some of the talk on the scanner is in code, there was confusion about what had happened. A reporter and a photographer were sent to the bus station immediately. A live truck followed. By 5:20 PM the reporter on the scene was still not certain about who had been shot and who had done the shooting. By air time at 5:30 PM, enough information was available to lead with the story live from the bus station. With the reporter and crew still on the scene, the producer and director were able to break into the local newscast with updates on the story as more information became available.

Local news is very competitive, with every news department wanting to be on the air first with stories important to the community. In many cases, the new technology provides an edge. Although there is disagreement about the importance of live reports, the shooting incident McGeever described is a clear example of how a report from the scene microwaved back to the studio saves time. The report can go on the air immediately. Recording the story and bringing the tapes back to the studio to edit takes time. In addition, the visual impact provided by the on-the-scene video is much different from the visual impact of the same story telephoned in by the reporter and read by the news anchor on the set.

To increase its range, WKRC-TV uses a satellite truck to feed reports back to the studios from a three-state area, to cover national spot news that's happening close to home, to provide election night reports from all over the state, and to cover other important state events quickly.

The staff is constantly aware of the need to update equipment if this will help keep that competitive edge. For example, even the bulk and weight of ENG cameras and recorders can make a difference. Compact, self-contained units allow the photographer to move faster to follow a subject or to get a better angle for a shot.

In talking about her job, McGeever emphasized the importance of knowing how to work with people. The reporters and photographers she schedules for assignments have different personalities and preferences. Gaining their cooperation and maintaining good working relationships is important. Individuals who call in wanting to get news coverage for particular events and viewers who call in with news tips may be offering newsworthy information or useless trivia. Dealing with all of these people tactfully is necessary.

McGeever also stressed the importance of getting as much experience as possible. For her, writing for the high school newspaper and working in the news department at the campus radio station while she was in college were valuable. So, too, was her work as an intern at a television station. Working as a part-time production assistant gave her a chance to be where things were happening and to learn how productions are done. She believes that experience was good preparation for her job in the news department.

STATION PROMOTION

Broadcast stations are concerned with audience ratings, so they are all involved with promoting the station as well as individual programs on that station. Kenneth Horning, former promotion director at KEZI-TV, described a news promotion campaign used to move KEZI's local news programming up in the ratings against the competition in Eugene, Oregon.

The first step was to analyze the station's position in the market. The competing television station had gone on the air several years before KEZI. Even though KEZI had been broadcasting for many years at the time this campaign was being developed, the station was still thought of as the newcomer in town. The theme developed for the campaign attempted to turn this newcomer image into an advantage by portraying KEZI reporters as active, energetic, and out on the street where the news was happening. Building on the reputation KEZI was acquiring from investigative news successes, their campaign slogan was "Get your news from the newsbreakers."

Advertising in a mix of media is the best way to reach a broad spectrum of the population, so promotional materials were produced for newspaper, radio, and television (Fig. 14-5). For television, two basic styles of promotional spots were used (Fig. 14-6). One was a generic Eyewitness News promo emphasizing the idea of KEZI reporters as a team. These promos used action-oriented video footage that showed the news anchor on the street. Some also included mentions of the awards the news team had won and personalized statements by network news personalities.

The other type of promotion was episodic. They featured the news anchor on the news set profiling the major stories in the upcoming newscast. The standard format for these promo was as follows:

I'm ...
Tonight on Eyewitness News we'll tell you ...
And in sports we'll find out ...
And ... with weather. Join us tonight.

After 2:30 PM, when the line-up of stories for the evening news had been decided, news anchors recorded an audio version of the episodic promo for radio. Production personnel combined it with the opening news theme music and

FIGURE 14-5 Newspaper ad for the KEZI-TV news promotional campaign. (Courtesy of K. Horning)

FIGURE 14-6 An animated logo was used in the television promotional spots for KEZI-TV news. (Courtesy of K. Horning)

closing campaign slogan. Dubs were then made onto audio carts, which were delivered to six radio stations by 4:00 PM.

Scheduling was also important in the promotional campaign. On KEZI, the episodic news promos started running at about 2:45 PM to alert viewers to the lead stories coming up at 5:30 PM. In "People's Court," the show which immediately preceded the news, one generic and one episodic promo were inserted. During the closing credits for "People's Court," a voice-over reminder to stay tuned to the news was used. In the evening, during the 10:00 to 11:00 PM network programming, promos were scheduled in the available breaks to keep listeners watching for the 11:00 PM news.

In talking about the skills needed for producing promotional campaigns like this, Horning stressed the value of having a news background. Condensing the major stories of the day into 20 seconds of copy requires experience in news writing. Staying abreast of news developments and being a news critic helps. Of course, watching the news with a critical eye also is important in identifying footage that can be used in the promos.

As is the case in all production work, preplanning is necessary. The success of the preplanning stage often determines the success of the final campaign.

Another useful skill Horning mentioned is the ability to work well with people. News reporters often see a request to record promotional materials as an interruption in their job of gathering and reporting news, but their cooperation is essential. So, too, is gaining the support of management. Because many departments at a station may be competing for the use of production studios and equipment, the ability to communicate both the needs of the promotion personnel and the importance of their work is important.

INTERVIEW SHOW

The interview show has become a standard program form in television. At the network level, programs such as "This Week with David Brinkley" or "Wall Street Week in Review" rely heavily on interview segments in which guest experts are questioned on topics of current interest. Even the morning programs aired by the three commercial networks use the interview format for many of their segments. On the local level, stations find the interview show a useful format for local public-affairs programming.

At WTVS-TV, that format is working well for the nation's longest-running minority affairs series, "Detroit Black Journal." Aired live and taped for a repeat showing, this half-hour program features host Ed Gordon interviewing one or more guests, with additional questions from viewer call-ins. Overall responsibility for this show is shared by host Ed Gordon, series producer Trudy Gallant, and director Cato Weatherspoon.

WTVS-TV is a public television station with budget limitations; therefore, rather than working with a program staff, as is usual in major markets, Gordon serves as his own producer. Ideas for the show come from many sources—from newspapers, from what he hears on the street, from his own experiences, and from stories in the news. These ideas generally involve social and political issues, celebrities, or newsmakers. The topics chosen must fit the format of a live, half-hour, call-in show. Some simply aren't suited for that. Topics, too, must be of interest to the audience. The show is targeted to the black viewers, so issues are dealt with from a black perspective. In addition, Gordon tries to gear each issue to the interests of the local Detroit community.

Gordon spends much of the week on the telephone getting information and lining up potential guests. He compares the research process to that involved in doing a college term paper or research paper. It means going beyond surface information to obtain detailed facts and figures. Although an intern helps with the library research, Gordon makes the phone calls and collects background information from many sources. He talks with people and makes judgments about which individuals will be best on the show. Not everyone who is an expert on a particular issue will come across well on television. In addition, the right mix of guests helps to ensure an interesting discussion.

The overall format of the show includes an introduction to the topic. Sometimes the introduction is a taped piece produced by Gallant or Gordon. The introduction is followed by some exchange with the guests. Viewers are then invited to call in with their questions. For some shows, Gordon may work without a list of questions and simply go with the flow of the conversation. For others he may begin with a few prepared questions and then follow the flow. Alternatively, he may work from a more detailed list of questions with notes on statistics or specific facts related to the topic. As an interviewer, Gordon tries to be as quiet as possible. He thinks of himself as a conduit for the discussion.

During the show, Gallant functions as line producer. Working in the control room, she is responsible for making sure everything goes smoothly. As calls come in, Gallant and her assistant talk with each caller to determine the questions they want to ask and to decide which calls will be answered on air.

As director, Weatherspoon feels that 80 percent of his work is done in the planning stage. He tries to visualize what the show should look like and then works through the mechanics that will make it happen that way. Working with three cameras (plus a fourth high camera set on a long shot of the entire set), he tries to use the cameras to dupiicate what happens in typical conversation. As we begin talking with strangers, we tend to keep our distance and look them over. Then, as the conversation continues, we become psychologically more familiar with them and focus in. For this type of show, a full rehearsal isn't possible. But Weatherspoon does rehearse the opening sequence and other segments that can be rehearsed. Since the camera operators know his style, he allows them a great deal of freedom in changing shots to follow the flow of the discussion.

In talking about skills that are important for a director, Weatherspoon emphasized the ability to communicate clearly so that the crew understands and responds accurately. As Weatherspoon noted, from hearing to doing takes only seconds, and there's no time for discussion about what was meant. It is important, too, to be able to react quickly, to make a move without thinking about it, and to be right. Developing good habits from the beginning helps. Weatherspoon also believes that being a leader requires an understanding of all crew positions. Having worked as camera operator, technical director, and audio technician, he has a comprehensive understanding of the technical end of producing a show.

For a producer, good writing and telephone interviewing skills are essential. As Gordon pointed out, preparing for a show of this type requires working hard and doing your homework so that you're prepared. As talent on a talk show, you have to be quick and able to think on your feet because so much of the show is not scripted. And, because it's show business, you must be able to accept criticism and live with rejection.

CORPORATE VIDEO

Domino's Pizza Satellite Network is the department responsible for live satellite broadcasts and film and videotape production for Domino's Pizza and other clients. About half of this unit's productions are done in the studio, which is equipped with permanent news and interview sets. The other productions are shot on location and edited into their final form. These productions range from educational and motivational programs to corporate news and documentaries. Some are distributed live via satellite. Others can be purchased on videotape (Fig. 14-7).

Producer Gary Rieck believes that, although its goals are serious, corporate video can be fun. As an example of that philosophy, he described the production of "Lifestyles of the Clean and Famous," an educational videotape, made for Domino's Pizza, that won the Golden Cassette Award of Excellence from the Detroit chapter of International Television Association (ITVA) in 1986.

Rieck's job was to produce a tape to meet a specific need. The tape was to explain sanitation techniques that were to be followed by the employees in the stores. In thinking about those employees, he realized that the tape would not only have to teach sanitation techniques, it would also have to change attitudes. The audience for the tape was very narrow: employees between 18 to 24 years of age. For that age group, sanitation is boring and definitely not "cool."

In a brainstorming session with coproducer Barbara Schmidt and technical

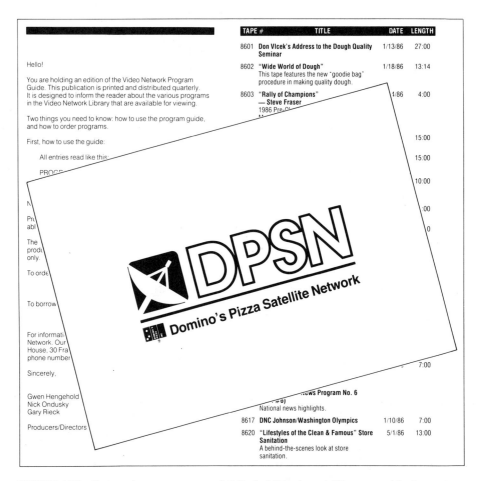

TAPE #	TITLE	DATE	LENGTH
8601	Don Vlcek's Address to the Dough Quality Seminar	1/13/86	27:00
8602	"Wide World of Dough" This tape features the new "goodie bag" procedure in making quality dough.	1/18/86	13:14
8603	"Rally of Champions" — Steve Fraser 1986 Pre	4/86	4:00

Hello!

You are holding an edition of the Video Network Program Guide. This publication is printed and distributed quarterly. It is designed to inform the reader about the various programs in the Video Network Library that are available for viewing.

Two things you need to know: how to use the program guide, and how to order programs.

First, how to use the guide:

All entries read like this

PROG

N

Pr
abl

The
prod
only.

To orde

To borrow

For informati
Network. Our
House, 30 Fra
phone number

Sincerely,

Gwen Hengehold
Nick Ondusky
Gary Rieck

Producers/Directors

...ews Program No. 6
National news highlights.

		15:00
		15:00
		10:00
		:00
		0
		7:00
8617	DNC Johnson/Washington Olympics	1/10/86	7:00
8620	"Lifestyles of the Clean & Famous" Store Sanitation A behind-the-scenes look at store sanitation.	5/1/86	13:00

FIGURE 14-7 Corporate programs are distributed live via satellite or on videotape. (Courtesy of Domino's Pizza Satellite Network)

consultant Nick Ondusky, the idea of a music video evolved as a way of catching and holding the interest of the audience. They then developed the story line. The narrative would be about a famous physician who got his start learning sanitation techniques in a pizza store. A songwriter was hired to write the music and lyrics. In addition to the information presented in the music and action, some explanations of specific procedures were needed, so the character's conscience was added as a voice to give the character something to react to.

To create visual excitement, Rieck planned to use a moving camera, colored lighting, a fog and smoke machine, and plenty of physical action on the part of the main character. In fact, the pizza store set would be trashed in some scenes. The location chosen was one of the company's training facilities. That gave the authentic look of a store, but allowed the crew to lay tracks for the camera dolly and to make other changes called for in the script without disrupting the activities of an actual store.

A professional actor was hired to play the part of the physician. When the budget allows, Rieck prefers to use professionals for lead roles and fill supporting roles with company employees. To make sure that the uniforms worn by the actors were accurate and the dough-making procedure was correct, a veteran store employee provided technical advice on the production. In addition, the executive producer was on the set each day to approve changes made during the production.

The music had been recorded earlier, so lip sync was used for the lyrics during the action sequences. Some narration was done live; some was recorded. The voice of the conscience was recorded and dubbed in during postproduction.

The video footage was shot in three days with a crew of six. The first day's shoot lasted from 7:00 AM until 1:00 AM. The next two days were used to shoot pickups. Two more days were spent editing the final tape at a postproduction facility.

In talking about working in a corporate setting, Rieck pointed out several factors that need to be recognized. One is the approval process that projects go through. In presenting materials for approval, Rieck finds that "selling" the idea is important. He believes it is important to express enthusiasm for the idea and the script, so he often reads the script aloud for the client and acts out some of the parts. The story line for "Lifestyles of the Clean and Famous" was approved before the script was developed. When the script and lyrics for the music were submitted, some changes had to be made because of corporate policies. As mentioned earlier, the executive producer was on the set during the shooting to approve changes. After the final tape was edited, a few insert changes were requested before the tape was released for distribution.

It is also important to be flexible. As Rieck points out, there is no one way to do production. When budget or available equipment makes one approach impossible, he improvises and tries to do things in other ways. As he demonstrated with "Lifestyles of the Clean and Famous," it is possible even on a limited budget to produce training materials that are creative, fun to watch, technically polished, and effective.

SUMMARY

The examples we've included in this chapter offer a limited view of the tremendous range of video production today. We are all familiar with the wide variety of programs that bring us information and entertainment on broadcast television as well as specialized cable channels. We continually see or hear about videos produced to market popular music recordings or how-to videos we can purchase to help us fill out our tax returns or learn a new language.

Artists, too, are exploring the creative potential of video. Works by pioneer video artist Nam June Paik and others are frequently on exhibit in museums and galleries. Video art is even finding its way into television programming in such series as "Alive From Off Center," created for PBS.

At many cable systems, public-access channels are providing an outlet for local citizens. On these channels, it is common to see live, remote coverage of city council or board of education meetings, interview programs produced by community organizations, movies created by high school or college students, and much more. Not only is the general public invited to bring in programs for possible use, but in many cases the cable system provides video equipment and training in how to use it.

Learning to use video involves much more than simply understanding the technology. Technical competence is important. But in approaching any type of video production, you'll be more successful if you begin with a comprehensive understanding of communication as a process. What ideas, emotions, stories do you want to communicate? How can you turn your ideas into sounds and images that will have the impact you want? And then, what equipment and production techniques will allow you to record those sounds and images to share them with your viewers?

Video is a powerful tool for communication. Whether you're interested in a career in broadcast television or want to use video as a means of personal expression, the information covered in this section should help you get started. We hope you'll enjoy the challenge of learning to use video effectively and creatively.

FOR FURTHER READING

NEWCOMB, HORACE and ROBERT S. ALLEY. *The Producer's Medium: Conversations with Creators of American TV* (New York: Oxford University Press, 1983).

VERNA, TONY. *Live TV: An Inside Look at Direction and Producing* (Boston: Focal Press, 1987).

appendix a

Audio Exercises

INTRODUCTION

The exercises in this section are designed to give you experience scripting and producing a variety of materials. All are assignments that you might be asked to work on if you interned for or worked in closed-circuit or broadcast radio stations. They will allow you to practice the principles discussed in Part I of the book.

PUBLIC-SERVICE ANNOUNCEMEMT

Write and produce a 60-second public-service announcement for an organization in your community. A public-service announcement, like a commercial, is intended to change behavior or attitudes. It might persuade us to donate to the United Fund, to visit the health fair to have our hearing checked, or to change our eating habits.

After you have chosen the organization and the specific event or campaign, select a target audience. Then analyze the event or campaign with that target audience in mind. Why should that specific audience donate or attend or change? Using that information, create the theme or specific selling point.

In writing the script, choose the style that's most appropriate—a dramatic scene, a testimonial, a humorous skit, a musical jingle, or a straight presentation of the information. Whichever you choose, think about ways to take advantage of the unique qualities of the audio medium to create vivid mental images. Remember, too, the restrictions imposed by standards of good taste, the policies of individual radio stations, and FCC or Federal Trade Commission (FTC) rules and regulations.

After the script is written, select the sound effects, music, and voices needed to carry out your ideas. Decide how much preproduction needs to be done. For example, you may want to transfer sound effects from record to cartridge for easier cueing. Plan your production strategy based on the facilities available to you. Then, rehearse and record your announcement.

SINGLE-SUBJECT MUSIC CONTINUITY

Music is the main basis for most radio programming, although a few stations specialize only in news or talk. The majority of radio stations play records, tapes, or compact discs selected by the air personality or music director. They usually follow a playlist and carefully select recordings to fit the station's format.

There are occasions, however, when a music program is prepared in a more formal way. These include live broadcasts, spotlight features on performers and composers, and broadcasts on special occasions such as national holidays. Opportunities for these kinds of productions are more numerous on noncommercial stations, but chances are that you might have to write such a program sooner or later regardless of the kind of radio station for which you work. What would you do if you were assigned the job of selecting the recordings and writing the commentary for a music program on twentieth-century English choral music or on jazz pianist Bill Evans? What if you had to make intelligent comments between selections during a live broadcast of a concert of French music for two pianos? How would you go about researching and writing the script? This assignment is designed to give you some experience in researching, writing, and finding the selections for a single-subject music program for radio broadcast.

The Assignment

Write a 60-minute classical music program on a single subject. Select all music cuts and write all continuity. We have chosen classical music because you are less likely to know a great deal about it, and you will have to work in unfamiliar territory to prepare your program. However, the skills you gain by doing this assignment can be easily applied to writing programs about other kinds of music as well. Programs on musical theatre, jazz, folk music, and rock performers can be researched in a similar manner.

Subjects

There is a wide variety of possible topics for single-subject classical music programs. For example, you could do a biographical sketch of a famous composer, illustrating the evolution of his style with selected compositions. You could do a program about the music of a particular country or about music associated with an event, such as the Fourth of July. You could do a program about music for a unique combination of instruments, such as flute and organ, or a program about music that creates a certain kind of mood. Here are some possible titles: "Organ Music for French Cathedrals," "Twentieth-Century English Pastoral Music," "Unfinished Symphonies," or "Music for Halloween."

You will note that these titles are fairly specific. You should avoid broad, general topics that cannot be explored adequately in a short program. Examples of such topics are: "The Life and Times of Beethoven," "Great Classical Violinists," or "The Art of Italian Opera." These topics are more suitable for treatment in a book; they are not for a one-hour radio program. Choose a topic that is very specific and limited in scope.

Research

Where do you go for information? A good place to start is Grove's *Dictionary of Music and Musicians* or Grout's *A History of Western Music*. There are many music-appreciation books, biographies of composers, and books about music of different countries and groups of instruments. Another useful source is the *Schwann Record and Tape Catalogue*. This important publication lists all currently available classical recordings. Its contents are arranged alphabetically by composer. Schwann also makes available an Artist Issue, which groups the recordings by performer. If you are doing a program about the music of Aram Khachaturian, the Schwann catalogue will tell you the titles of his major works and information about the availability of recordings. The Artist Issue would be valuable if you are doing a musical biography of organist E. Power Biggs, for example. Listed under his name are all of his recordings that are still available. Finally, there is no better resource than the knowledgeable staff of a good record store. They can help you find selections and let you read through record jackets.

The Script

Write a script that contains all copy spoken by the announcer and a clear identification of all musical selections, along with their timings. Organize the script in a clear and interesting way, and choose the selections carefully so that they illustrate points made in the copy. In the opening paragraph of the script, state clearly what the program is about and indicate what will occur during the hour. The paragraph must capture and hold the listener's attention. Once the purpose and general structure of the program have been established in the opening paragraphs, the script should proceed with succinct commentary followed by clear musical examples.

The script should lead your listeners to a greater understanding of the subject so that by the end of the program, they have learned something. Avoid dull, dry, or overly esoteric language. Use clear, interesting examples. If possible, include a number of nonmusical references so that listeners with little knowledge of classical music will not feel alienated or lost.

Here are a few paragraphs from a sample script to give you an idea of how a single-subject music program might be introduced (see box, p. 288).

```
┌─────────────────────────────────────────────────────────────────────────┐
│                          Afternoon Concert                                │
│                                                                           │
│     MUSIC: Tschaikovsky: Waltz from Serenade for Strings (establish and   │
│            then under the following introduction)                         │
│ ANNOUNCER: Hello and welcome to ''Afternoon Concert,'' a daily program of │
│            the finest music selected for your listening pleasure. We'll be│
│            back in a moment with today's program.                         │
│                          [COMMERCIAL ANNOUNCEMENT]                        │
│ ANNOUNCER: The place where a piece of music is to be performed often in-  │
│            fluences the way it is written. For centuries, composers have  │
│            written music intended for use in the great interiors of Euro- │
│            pean cathedrals. During the next hour, we'll listen to some    │
│            outstanding examples of music for cathedrals and learn how the │
│            composers purposely wrote the music in certain ways to take ad-│
│            vantage of these magnificent, reverberant interiors. We call   │
│            this program ''Music for Great Spaces.''                       │
│                                                                           │
│            The best place to start our exploration of ''Music for Great   │
│            Spaces'' is at the beginning, with the oldest form of music de-│
│            signed for cathedrals-the sublime musical form known as plain- │
│            chant. For centuries, it was a common form of music for worship│
│            and was heard throughout Europe. Here is an example of plain-  │
│            chant. Listen to how the slow, simple, strong melody takes ad- │
│            vantage of the acoustical space and achieves a power and grace │
│            as it floats through the interior of a cathedral.              │
│     MUSIC: Rorate Caeli                          (2:51)                    │
└─────────────────────────────────────────────────────────────────────────┘
```

RADIO NEWS FEATURE

For this exercise, you are to produce a 3-minute radio news feature using sound bits recorded on location and narration recorded by the reporter either on location or in the studio. Unlike a news story, which must be produced quickly about an event that just occurred or is occurring, a news feature is often scheduled for production well in advance of the air date. Months prior to a local election, it may be obvious which ballot issues are going to be controversial, so well-researched news features might be prepared for airing closer to election day. When the news release about a major traveling art exhibit arrives, a reporter may be assigned to prepare a feature about the exhibit to air the day before the opening. Features on annual community events, such as "heritage days" or amateur golf benefit tournaments, may be common assignments.

In choosing a topic for this exercise, think about the format of the program you'd like to write for and the specific audience that listens to the program. What will they find interesting? What do they want to know about? Issues, events, interesting people, unique places, unusual hobbies, organizations—all could make good news features.

As you gather information about the topic, look for a specific focus or theme for the feature. When you begin scripting, a clear theme will help you organize the material so that ideas flow smoothly from beginning to end. During the research process, try to identify one or more persons willing to be interviewed on tape. Decide which ideas or information you want the reporter to supply in the narration, and which will be more compelling if related by one of the persons interviewed. Then prepare questions that will encourage the person being interviewed to talk about those points. Choose a location for the interview that will provide interesting ambient sound. For example, if you are producing a story about a high school class that is building a house, you might want to interview the instructor at the construction site, with the sounds of saws and hammers in the background.

After the interviews are recorded, decide which sound bits you will use and write the final draft of the script with reporter narration, supplying transitions as needed. Record that narration. Then edit the narration and sound bits together into your finished news feature.

appendix b

Video Exercises

INTRODUCTION

The three exercises in this section introduce you to the techniques of producing and directing simple studio and remote programs. In the first exercise, you direct an opening for a 10-minute studio interview. In the second, you shoot a short feature on location. In the third, you produce and direct a 10-minute studio interview which uses the opening from the first exercise and the feature prepared in the second exercise.

OPENING FOR STUDIO INTERVIEW

Write an opening for a studio interview. Include introductory music, three graphics cards, and a spoken introduction by the program's host. The opening should take approximately 30 seconds. You will need two cameras, either a boom microphone or two lavalieres, two chairs, and a coffee table with a few books on it. You will also need two easel stands for the graphics. You can use either flats or the studio curtain as a backdrop. Feel free to decorate the set in a more elaborate fashion if you see fit.

Floorplan

Your floorplan should show the location of cameras, graphic easels, chairs, curtains, and the boom microphone (if you use one). Here is a sample floorplan (see Fig. B-1).

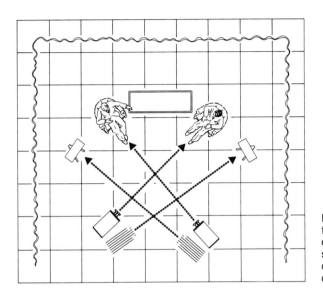

FIGURE B-1 Floorplan. This floorplan shows the location of curtain, talent, sets, easel stands, and cameras. Subjects covered by cameras are indicated by dotted arrows.

Lighting

You will need a key, back, and fill light for each of the performers and separate key lights for each of the graphics easels. (Please refer to Chapter 12 for instructions on how to set up these lights.) You can prepare a lighting plot showing the location of each light on a plastic transparency that can be laid over the floorplan.

Camera Blocking

The two cameras are crossed throughout the show. Camera 1 opens on the first graphic and Camera 2 on the second. Camera 1 shows the third graphic; during this time, Camera 2 pans right to a closeup of the host. While the host makes introductory remarks, Camera 1 pans left to a closeup of the guest. The remainder of the show can continue with these shots, but a creative director will occasionally zoom out to a two shot on either camera.

Graphics Cards

You will need three graphics cards. The first contains the name of the program; the second, the name of the host; and the third, the name of the guest. (Please refer to Appendix C for instructions on how to prepare simple graphics.) The three cards can look something like the sample given in Fig. B-2.

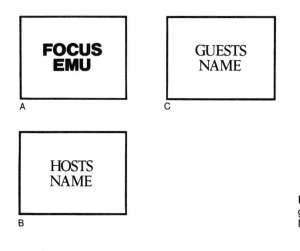

A

C

B

FIGURE B-2 Title cards. Simple graphics cards. (a) Title of show. (b) Name of host. (c) Name of guest.

Script

See p. 293 for a sample script for this opening sequence. It contains the director's commands and the host's introductory remarks.

REMOTE VIDEO FEATURE

For this assignment you are to write, storyboard, and produce a 2-minute video feature to be used during the interview show you'll produce in the third video exercise. This feature might be used in several ways in the interview show. It might serve as a background piece to introduce the general subject area the interview will cover. It might be used during the interview as an example of what the interviewee is saying. It might be used to summarize the topic and provide an ending for the interview. For example, if the interview topic is the Special Olympics, a feature about several of the children who will participate might be a good introduction to the interview. A feature about preparations for the event might be used during the interview to show how volunteers can get involved. A feature highlighting the satisfaction experienced by the sponsors and volunteers working on the event might provide an appropriate ending for the interview.

The video is to be shot on location. (The suggestions in Chapter 9 will help you choose a topic and make decisions about how to approach that topic.) As you are scripting the feature, develop the storyboard to help you shoot the footage you need. (Chapter 13 will help you plan the actual production.) How you shoot will depend on the equipment available to you. If you have editing capabilities, you can shoot out of order and reassemble the scenes in postproduction. If you don't have access to editing equipment, you will have to edit in the camera. That means you must shoot in sequence, stopping and starting the camera for each new shot. If you have planned your storyboard well, you can shoot an inter-

Video	Audio
Standby 30 seconds	
Line in Black	
Ready Roll VTR	
Roll VTR	
Ready Bars and Tone	
Take Bars and Tone	
Ready Slate	
Take Slate	
Ready Fade in Music	
Ready Fade in Camera 1 on Graphic #1	
Fade in Music	
Fade in #1 on graphic	MUSIC: THEME
GRAPHIC #1	
Ready dissolve to #2 on Graphic #2	
Dissolve to #2	
GRAPHIC #2	
Pull Graphic on #1	
Ready dissolve to #1	
Dissolve to #1	
GRAPHIC #3	
Ready Pan right #2 to CU Host	
Pan right #2	
Ready Fade Out Music	
Ready Mike Host	
Ready Cue Host	
Ready Dissolve to #2	
Fade Out Music	
Mike Host	THEME OUT
Cue Host	
Dissolve to #2	
CU HOST	Host: Welcome to today's edition of "Focus EMU." Last week, the university's president announced that the School of Business will relocate . . .

esting feature with a minimum of angle and location changes. Panning to follow action, zooming in or out, and tilting to reveal new objects can be used instead of cuts. If the action moves from one location to another, a fade in and out or a defocus–focus may smooth the transition.

Whether you use editing equipment or edit in the camera, be sure to put a leader with countdown on your tape. You will need it for pre-roll cueing during the interview production.

TEN-MINUTE STUDIO INTERVIEW

Produce and direct a 10-minute studio television interview using a host and one guest. Use the interview opening prepared in the first exercise and the feature from the second exercise. This assignment is designed to teach you basic skills in producing, scripting, and directing.

Producing

You will need the following materials, crew, equipment, and talent for this production:

Materials	recorded music for beginning and end of program, three graphics cards from the first exercise plus one more with the names of producer and director, two chairs, a coffee table with a few books on it, additional set decorations as desired, and two easel stands
Crew	a standard studio crew with at least two camera operators and two floor assistants to pull graphics
Equipment	two cameras, a boom microphone or two lavalieres, standard lighting, VTRs, and control-room equipment
Talent	a host and one guest

Selecting Talent

An important part of your producing job is to locate talent. A good host is someone who feels comfortable on camera and who can ask intelligent questions of the guest. The host must be a good listener and put the guest at ease. Teachers, students of communication, and professional broadcasters often make competent hosts.

A guest should be someone who has an occupation, hobby, cause, or other interest that can be discussed during the show. Students, teachers, community leaders, or local celebrities make interesting guests. It is usually not a good idea to ask relatives. Your Uncle Ed may be a riot at the dinner table but may be totally inarticulate in front of a video camera. Try to select someone who is intelligent, articulate, and experienced in public speaking.

Scripting

You will not need a complete script for an interview show because you want to encourage spontaneity in the conversation between the host and guest. You should prepare a list of questions for the host to use, but with the understanding that they will not be followed slavishly. The host should preinterview the guest and let the guest talk in a relaxed fashion about the subjects that interest her. From this preinterview, the host prepares a number of questions that can be asked during the show. The host's main job is to listen carefully, however, and to let the guest's answers suggest the next question. The host and guest should agree to one last question that will be a signal that the show is about to end. The guest should prepare a short answer to that question.

In addition to the questions that the host asks the guest, the script should contain director's commands and host's copy for all transitions—the opening, the introduction and close of the feature, and the end of the show.

Here is a sample script. (Note that the opening portion is identical to the script for the first video exercise.)

Video	Audio

Standby 30 seconds
Line in Black
Ready Roll VTR
    Roll VTR
Ready Bars and Tone
    Take Bars and Tone
Ready Slate
    Take Slate
Ready Fade in Music
Ready Fade in Camera 1 on Graphic #1	

Fade in Music
    Fade in #1 on graphic
GRAPHIC #1
Ready dissolve to #2 on Graphic #2
    Dissolve to #2
GRAPHIC #2
    Pull Graphic on #1
Ready dissolve to #1
    Dissolve to #1
GRAPHIC #3
Ready Pan right #2 to CU Host
    Pan right #2
Ready Fade Out Music
Ready Mike Host
Ready Cue Host
Ready Dissolve to #2
    Fade Out Music
    Mike Host
    Cue Host
    Dissolve to #2
CU HOST
	MUSIC: THEME
	
	THEME OUT
	
	Host: Welcome to today's edition of "Focus EMU." Last week, the university's president an-nounced that the School of Business will relocate . . .

Video	Audio
CAMERAS STAY ON CLOSEUPS OF GUESTS DURING INTERVIEW	INTERVIEW QUESTIONS HERE
Ready Roll video feature	Host: And now, let's take a moment to view a short feature that was shot yesterday at the site of the new EMU School of Business.
Roll video feature VIDEO FEATURE	
Ready Mike host Ready Cue Host	

Ready #2
    Mike Host
    Cue Host
	Outcue: . . . this is Terry Smith reporting from downtown Ypsilanti.

Take #2 CU OF HOST	Host: That was a very interesting feature. It raised some important issues that perhaps we can address in the last few minutes of our show.
CAMERAS STAY ON CLOSEUPS OF GUESTS DURING THIS SEGMENT	MORE INTERVIEW QUESTIONS HERE
CU HOST	Host: We have time for just one last question. Professor Jones, when do you think the School of Business will actually move to its new location?
CU GUEST	GUEST ANSWERS LAST QUESTION
Ready Pan right #1 to easel for closing graphic	
Ready Dissolve to #1	
Ready Close mike	
Ready Fade in music	
Ready Fade sound and picture out CU HOST	Host: I want to thank our guests for being with us today on "Focus EMU." Next week, we'll be back with another show, and our guest will be John Sizemore, director of Academic Services at EMU. Be sure to join us then.
Pan right #1 to easel	
Dissolve to #1 on CLOSING GRAPHIC	
Close mike	
Fade in music	MUSIC: THEME
Fade sound and picture out	

Directing the Rehearsal and Show

A complete rehearsal will rob the final show of its spontaneity. Therefore, the director should conduct only a partial rehearsal, including the opening, the bridge to the feature, the transition out of the feature, and the ending of the show. These transitions are the most difficult moments in the show for the director, and the script should contain all commands for them.

During the show itself, the director needs to watch the camera monitors and follow the conversation. Cutting back and forth between closeups can become very monotonous, however, and the director can vary this pattern by cutting occasionally to cover shots. Except for the scripted portions of the show, the director should be flexible and follow the action rather than sticking to rigid shot plans.

appendix c _____

Graphics _____

INTRODUCTION

Video graphics include title cards, drawings, diagrams, maps, and photographs. They are an important part of most video productions, and a few simple guidelines should be followed in making them.

Graphics come from three main sources within the video system: They can be (1) placed on easel cards and shot by a studio camera, (2) photographed on slides which are then placed in the film chain, or (3) printed up on a character generator. Many stations today use very elaborate moving graphics that are prepared on digital video effects units. These are usually produced by private production companies and are put on videotape or film for use at the station.

TITLE CARDS

The video exercises described in Appendix A require you to make simple title cards for use at the beginning of your interview. Even if you have a character generator at your studio, it is a good idea to learn how to make title cards. They are still used in many kinds of productions.

Aspect Ratio

In making your title cards, you must keep in mind the size of the video screen on which they will appear. At the present time, the video screen has an aspect ratio (vertical/horizontal dimensions) of 3 units high by 4 units wide. Your title cards should be of the same proportions. A title card that is 4 units high by

3 units wide, for example, will have a vertical border on either side (see illustration). The only way to remove the border is to move the camera closer, but this might eliminate some of the information on the graphic. Either choice leaves something to be desired.

Another possibility is to move the camera horizontally or vertically along the title card. A very tall card containing opening or closing credits is sometimes used in combination with a slow pedestal down to give the effect of a vertical crawl.

Scanning and Essential Areas

Not all of an easel card's area can be used to hold information. Around the perimeter of the card, there should be a border area where numbers, pull tabs, and labels can be attached. This will probably take up about one-sixth of the surface of the card, and it will not be seen by the camera. If you start with a card that is 18 inches by 24 inches, you will have an area 12 inches by 16 inches after subtracting the border.

This remaining area is what will be seen by the camera. It is called the *scanning area*. Most video equipment will not transmit this entire area. What the camera actually sees will be cropped slightly by the electronics of the system so that what finally appears on the monitor is a somewhat smaller area. To allow for this electronic cropping, you should designate an even smaller portion of the scanning area in which all of your graphic information must fall. This is called the *essential area*. If your scanning area is 12 inches by 16 inches, your essential area is about 9 inches by 12 inches. Thus, the area that is actually available for use is approximately 50 percent of the total size of the card.[1]

FIGURE C-1 Aspect ratios. (Left) Grid 3 units high by 4 units wide is in the correct aspect ratio to fit on the video screen. (Right) Grid 4 units high by 3 units wide will not fit on the video screen.

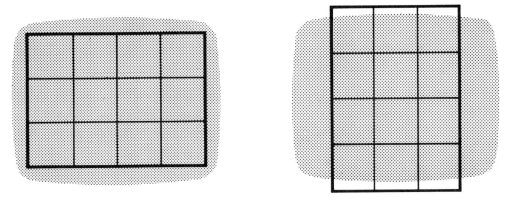

[1]See Thomas D. Burrows and Donald N. Wood, *Television Production: Disciplines and Techniques,* 2nd ed. (Dubuque, Iowa: Wm. C. Brown, 1982), pp. 208–209.

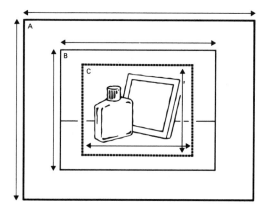

FIGURE C-2 Scanning area. Of the whole easel card A, only area B is actually scanned. Only the essential area C is seen on the monitor.

Amount of Information

Because the video screen is small and has limited resolution, it is best to keep the information on an easel card simple and easy to read. Use bold, plain letters rather than ornate ones. Use only a few words. Don't try to crowd your card with hard-to-read text.

Lettering can be no smaller than approximately one-fifteenth of the height of the screen. If your essential area is 15 inches high, then the letters should be no smaller than 1 inch. This also means that you would be limited to approximately 7 lines of information within that space.[2]

If you have additional information, such as artwork, on the graphic, keep its design simple as well. Remember that small, complicated designs cannot be seen well on the video screen at home. They are likely to confuse and distract the viewer.

Contrast

Avoid sharp contrasts between the background and lettering. Colors should complement one another. For black-and-white graphics, a few moderately contrasting shades of grey plus some white and black for variety make the most effective title cards.

Keying. The only exception to the foregoing rule occurs when cards are going to be keyed. Then, the letters should be white on a black background. This creates a high contrast and ensures that the background will disappear completely, leaving only the letters keyed over.

Size

Title cards should be large enough so that they can be handled easily by crew members. Cards measuring 11 inches by 14 inches are a workable size for most purposes. Students sometimes rely on the fact that a camera can zoom in

[2]Ibid., p. 210.

on a small card and fill the screen with it. Although it is possible to do this, moving in close to a small easel card creates problems. For one, blemishes on the card are magnified along with the lettering and become a distraction. Also, any unsteadiness in the camera is also magnified. It is safer to make the card large and frame it on a looser zoom setting.

Materials

Easel cards can be made from artist's board, which can be cut to various sizes and is available in many colors. You should use matte rather than glossy finishes so that light will not reflect from the easel into the camera lens.

Lettering can be done by hand, although this is difficult for anyone who is not a skilled artist. It can also be done using a variety of ready-to-apply letters, which can be rubbed onto the graphic. Various kinds of mechanical lettering systems are also available.

Glossary _____

A/B ROLL EDITING   In film, the technique of assembling alternate shots on separate reels, rolling the two reels at the same time, and dissolving or cutting between them. In video, segments are divided between two source decks which are fed through a switcher so special effect transitions can be done at the edit points.

ABOVE-THE-LINE COSTS   Fees paid to the creative personnel working on a production.

ACOUSTICAL SPACE   The space in which a sound is heard, such as a studio, room, or concert hall. The acoustical properties of this space influence the quality of the sound generated in it.

ACTUALITIES   The actual sights and sounds of an event recorded on location used as segments in news stories, features, and documentaries.

ADDITIVE PRIMARY COLORS   Red, blue, and green. Combining red, blue, and green light waves produces the full range of colors.

ADDRESS TRACK   A separate track used to record SMPTE time code on the video tape.

AESTHETICS   Principles or standards of artistic beauty.

AMBIENT SOUND   Sound that is naturally present in an acoustical space—for example, sounds of an air conditioner, office, birds singing, wind, and so on.

AMPLIFIER   Device that increases the strength of an electrical signal.

AMPLITUDE   The strength of an electrical or acoustical signal.

ANALOG   A recording process that creates a mechanical analogy (analog) of an incoming electrical signal. Example: The grooves in a phonograph record contain a physical representation of the fluctuations of the incoming signal's strength and frequency.

ANALOG-TO-DIGITAL CONVERTER   Device that converts an analog signal to a digital one.

APERTURE   A variable diameter opening on a camera which regulates the amount of light passing through a lens system.

ARC   The curved movement of a camera around a stationary subject.

ARMED FORCES RADIO AND TELEVISION NETWORK   The radio and television service of the U.S. Armed Forces.

ASCAP   American Society of Composers, Authors, and Publishers. A copyright licensing agency for sheet music, music performances, and recordings.

ASPECT RATIO   The vertical and horizontal dimensions of a video or film screen. The standard aspect ratio for broadcast video is 3 units high by 4 units wide.

ASSEMBLE EDITING   In videotape editing, the mode in which all tracks (audio, video, and control tracks) are transferred from the source tape to the record tape for each shot.

ASSISTANT DIRECTOR   Helps director in timing show, setting up shots, and cueing up inserts, films, slides, and graphics.

ATTACK   The rate at which a sound begins.

ATTENUATE   To gradually reduce the strength of a signal by reducing the output of the amplifier.

ATTENUATION   The rate at which a sound loses its strength and becomes inaudible.

AUDIO BOARD   The console into which input signals feed so that they can be processed and routed out to a transmitter or tape recorder.

AUDIO SYSTEM   A group of electronic components designed to record, store, and reproduce sound.

AUDITION   The circuit in the audio board that allows the audio signal to be monitored before being sent to the output channels.

AUTO-IRIS FUNCTION   A light sensing device which automatically opens or closes the camera's iris to obtain proper exposure for the image.

AUTOMATIC CUEING   A tape which cues itself automatically to the beginning of the recording.

AXIS-OF-ACTION   An imaginary line drawn along a direction of movement or between two people in conversation. Cameras are placed on one side of this line.

BACKLIGHT   A directional light placed above and behind a subject. It separates the subject from the background and provides modelling. One of three lights in the three-point lighting scheme.

BACKTIMING   1. Timing a program element, such as theme music, so that it will end when the program or program segment ends. 2. Counting the time remaining in a program or program segment rather than the elapsed time.

BALANCE   In audio, the relative strength or volume of various sounds that have been mixed together.

BALANCED LINE   A line containing two conductors plus a shield.

BAND PASS FILTER   A filter that does not pass frequencies above or below the selected frequency.

BANDWIDTH   A set of adjacent frequencies assigned for a specific use.

BARN DOORS   Adjustable metal shutters which can be attached to the front of a lighting instrument to control the spread of light.

BASE STATION   A digital camera control unit.

BASS ROLL OFF   Device which helps eliminate low-frequency sounds.

BEAM SPLITTING SYSTEMS   Dichroic mirrors, prisms, or filter strips which separate light into its red, blue, and green components.

BEAT   A regular pulsation in an audio signal caused by the combination of two sounds of slightly different frequencies.

BELOW-THE-LINE COSTS   Expenses related to the actual production, including fees paid to technical personnel, costs of facilities, and equipment.

BETAMAX   A 1/2-inch videotape format developed by the Sony Corporation. Used mostly on consumer units.

BIAS   A high-frequency signal that increases the accuracy of audio tape recording by changing the transfer characteristics of magnetic information.

BIDIRECTIONAL   A microphone pickup pattern which is equally sensitive to sounds directly in front or behind, while rejecting sounds from either side.

BINARY SYSTEM   System of mathematical notations in which all numbers can be expressed as combinations of 1's and 0's.

BINAURAL SOUND   An audio recording process which uses microphones placed on either side of a dummy human head. Headphones are used in playback.

BITS   (Binary Digits) A number on the binary notation system, either a 1 or a 0.

BLACKBODY RADIATION   Light emitted by a blackbody thermal radiator. The intensity and wave length of the light depend solely on the temperature of the body. Used as a standard for comparing the color temperature of various light sources.

BLACK TAPE   A videotape on which a black video signal has been recorded.

BLANK TAPE   A videotape with no video signal recorded on it.

BLANKING LEVEL   The level to which the video signal falls when the beam is turned off to allow the electron gun to retrace to the beginning of the next line.

BLOOMING   A halo effect around bright areas in the video image.

BLUMLEIN   A stereo miking technique which uses a pair of microphones mounted on the same vertical axis.

BMI   Broadcast Music Incorporated, an organization which collects copyright fees and distributes them to composers.

BNC CONNECTOR   A plug used to connect audio and video equipment.

BOOM   A long pole used as a microphone mount. The boom may be hand-held or attached to a wheeled base.

BROAD   A large rectangular floodlight with a panshaped reflector.

BROADCAST QUALITY   A technical standard for video signals set up by the NTSC.

BURN-IN   Damage to the pickup tube caused by bright lights.

BYTES   A sequence of digital numbers (bits).

CAMCORDER   Portable video camera with VTR combined in the same unit.

CAMERA CONTROL UNIT   The controls necessary to adjust video cameras and regulate their operation; usually placed some distance away in master control.

CAMERA HEAD   The part of the camera system containing lenses, pickup tube, monitor, and necessary circuitry.

CAMERA PROCESSING UNIT (Base Station)   A device separate from the camera head that processes signals from digitally controlled cameras.

CAPACITOR   Device that can store an electrical charge.

CAPSTAN   Rotating spindle in the tape transport system which moves the tape forward.

CARDIOID   The heart-shaped pickup pattern of a unidirectional microphone.

CARTRIDGE   Plastic box holding a continuous loop of tape.

CARTRIDGE TAPE RECORDER   Tape recorder which uses a cartridge containing a continuous loop of tape.

CASSETTE RECORDER   Tape recorder which uses a cassette containing tape wound on spindles.

CATV (Cable)   A wired video distribution system that provides original programming, satellite services, and improved reception of broadcast radio and television stations. Originally called community antenna television, now referred to as Cable TV.

CBS GRAY A widely-used neutral color for TV studio curtains.

C-CLAMP A clamp, shaped like the letter "C," which attaches studio light units to the overhead pipe grid.

CHANNEL In audio, the path of a single audio signal. In broadcasting, the bandwidth assigned for transmitting a radio or television signal.

CHARACTER GENERATOR A special-effects device that generates letters and numbers directly onto the television screen.

CHARGE-COUPLED DEVICE A solid state device that is used in place of the conventional vidicon tube.

CHROMA The saturation or purity of a color.

CHROMA CRAWL In video images, the barberpole-like effect that appears on the edges of color areas.

CHROMA KEY COLORS Colors used to trigger the key, usually blue or green, since these colors are not present in skin tones.

CHROMINANCE Color information. The chrominance component in the video signal supplies information about hue and saturation.

CINEMATOGRAPHY CAMERA Video camera designed to resemble the operating characteristics of a motion picture camera. Takes fixed focal length lenses and various filters.

CLIPPING Type of signal distortion which results when an amplifier clips or flattens the top of an overmodulated signal.

CLOSE UP Camera shot showing a close view of the subject.

COERCIVITY The strength of the magnetic field needed to completely erase fully saturated tape.

COLOR BARS A standard reference used to set chrominance levels for cameras and playback units.

COLOR BURST Reference signal used for interpreting the color information encoded in the video signal.

COLOR TEMPERATURE The wave length of a given light source measured in degrees Kelvin.

COMET TAILING The stream of light following the image as the camera moves across the screen.

COMPACT DISC A small record, 4 inches in diameter, upon which audio information is recorded digitally and read off by a laser beam. Compact discs have no surface noise and can reproduce the entire dynamic range of an incoming signal.

COMPONENT VIDEO A video signal in which the chrominance and luminance signals are carried separately rather than encoded into one signal, as in composite video.

COMPOSITE VIDEO An encoded signal which includes a luminance signal, a chrominance signal, and synchronizing signals.

COMPRESSION Reducing the output of an amplifier to prevent distortion.

CONDENSER MICROPHONE Microphone that uses a capacitor as the vibrating element which produces an electrical signal.

CONTINUITY The spoken material linking musical selections on a radio program. Generally, any spoken material linking segments of audio and video programs.

CONTINUITY EDITING An approach to video and film editing designed to ensure a smooth, continuous flow of the visuals.

CONTINUITY SYSTEM An approach to film or video production in which screen direction is maintained, editing made unobtrusive, and space clearly defined. Hollywood's standard production approach from the 1930s through the 1950s.

CONTRAST RANGE (Contrast Ratio)   The difference between the brightest and darkest portions of the picture. For video, the contrast ratio needs to be limited to 30:1 or 20:1.

CONTROL TRACK   Series of timing pulses recorded on videotape which identify the beginning of each frame. During playback, these sync pulses guide the transport speed.

CONTROL TRACK EDITING   In videotape editing, counting the sync pulses on the control track to establish edit points.

CONTROLLER   In videotape editing, the unit which controls the operation of the source and record decks.

CONVERGENCE LINES   Parallel horizontal lines that appear to intersect at a point on the horizon.

CONVERTIBLE   A video camera that can be converted for use in either a studio or remote production situation.

COPYRIGHT   A license issued on creative works such as music, literature, and films, which requires permission from the licensing agency before they can be reproduced in part or in whole.

CORPORATE VIDEO   Video productions, made by corporations, that are intended for internal use.

COUNTERWEIGHT   Weights in a camera pedestal base which counter the weight of the camera head. These permit the pedestal to be moved up or down more easily.

CRAB STEERING   A wheel setting for camera dollies in which front and back wheels are set parallel to one another, thus permitting a side-to-side or parallel movement of the camera.

CRADLE HEAD   A counterbalanced camera head mount that allows the camera to remain in any tilted position without being held by the operator.

CRANE   A large wheeled camera mount which raises or lowers both the camera and its operator at the end of a long boom arm.

CRITICAL FLICKER FREQUENCY   The number of frames per second needed to eliminate the flicker of the image. Usually twice the frequency required to create the illusion of movement.

CROSS-CUTTING   Cutting between two or more simultaneously occurring actions. Also known as parallel editing.

CROSS-LUMINANCE   In video images, a wavy pattern that appears in areas of fine detail, such as checked or tweed patterns in clothing.

CROSS-TALK   Interference between signals on adjacent channels.

CUCALORUS   Metal pattern that can be mounted in an ellipsoidal spot, which will then project that pattern on a curtain, wall, flat, or set.

CUE   1. An indication to begin action or dialogue. 2. To thread up audio/video tape or film to a predetermined point.

CUE TONE   An audio signal outside the audible range which triggers the stop mechanism in the cartridge tape recorder.

CUTAWAY   Shots of things or actions that are peripheral to the main action. An editor can cut away to these shots to provide a smooth bridge between mismatched shots.

CUTTING BLOCK   Metal or plastic block with a channel to hold audio tape and grooves to act as cutting guides when splicing tape.

CUTTING LATHE   Machine that cuts an analog audio signal onto the surface of a master recording disc.

CYCLORAMA   A large, smooth curtain that can be stretched along 2 or 3 sides of a studio. It provides a continuous, neutral background upon which patterns can be projected.

DBX NOISE REDUCTION SYSTEM System for processing the audio signal to reduce the levels of noise in the audio system.

DEAD AIR Unintended silence in a program.

DEAD POT Playing a tape with the fader or pot closed.

DEAD SPOT A place in an acoustical space where sound waves arrive out of phase, thus canceling some frequencies.

DECAY The rate at which a sound becomes inaudible.

DECIBEL A unit of measure of a sound's perceived intensity. Every 10 decibel increase is perceived as approximately twice as loud.

DECODING Reconstructing an analog signal from digital information.

DEFOCUS/FOCUS A transition between shots, in which the end of one scene is defocused and the beginning of the new scene is brought into focus.

DEGAUSS To erase or demagnetize an audio or videotape using a strong electromagnetic field produced by a degausser or bulk eraser.

DEMOGRAPHICS Broad categories describing the audience in terms of age, gender, education, marital status, economic status, and so on.

DEPTH OF FIELD The area from near to far in front of the camera lens in which all objects are in acceptable focus.

DIAPHRAGM The vibrating element in a microphone.

DIGITAL The process of using binary numbers to represent audio or video information.

DIGITAL AUDIO RECORDER An audio recorder that records information digitally rather than in analog form.

DIGITAL EFFECTS GENERATOR Device that converts video frames to digital information and manipulates it mathematically to produce flips, twists, rotating cubes, page turns, and other elaborate video effects.

DIMMER Device that controls the amount of electricity that flows to a lighting instrument. The operator can control the instrument's brightness in this way.

DIRECT BROADCAST SATELLITE Satellite that sends a signal directly to the viewer's home antenna.

DIRECTOR Member of the production crew who is in charge of the entire production.

DISSOLVE A transition between shots in which the end of one shot gradually fades out as the beginning of the next one simultaneously fades in.

DISTORTION An alteration of sound or video that causes the output signal to differ from the input signal.

DOLLY 1. A wheeled camera mounting device that permits the camera to be rolled smoothly about the studio. 2. Camera movement in which the camera moves in toward a subject or out away from it.

DOUBLE REENTRY SWITCHER A switcher that permits its output to be reentered for additional manipulation; for example, camera 2 keyed over camera 1 can be reentered as a single source and dissolved to camera 3.

DOWNSTREAM KEYING Device that permits keying over the line output of a video switcher.

DRAG A control on the camera mount that places resistance on the panning and tilting movements.

DURATION The length of time a sound lasts.

DUTCH ANGLE   A camera angle in which the camera is tilted sideways. Horizontal and vertical lines then appear diagonal.

DYNAMIC MICROPHONE   Microphone that uses a conductor moving in a magnetic field to produce an electrical signal. The conductor may be a coil of wire attached to the diaphragm or a thin ribbon of metal foil.

DYNAMIC RANGE.   The range of frequencies generated by a sound source.

ECHO   Repetition, or repetitions, of a sound caused by sound waves reflecting off a nearby surface.

EDIT POINTS   In audio and videotape editing, the point on the tape at which an edit will begin or end.

EDITING   Changing the content of a recording by cutting and splicing segments in the desired order.

ELAPSED TIME   Length of time which has passed since the beginning of the program or recording.

ELECTROMAGNETIC ENERGY   Energy generated when the electrons in the atoms begin to reorient themselves in relationship to the nuclei.

ELECTROMAGNETIC FIELD   The magnetic field surrounding a conductor when a current is flowing through it.

ELECTRON GUN   Device which scans the target area of the pickup tube, releasing the electrical signal created by the reaction of light and the photo-sensitive material on the face of the pickup tube.

ELECTRONIC EDITING   Rerecording program elements in their final order.

ELECTRONIC FIELD PRODUCTION   Shooting a carefully planned production on location with portable equipment.

ELECTRONIC NEWS GATHERING   In video, reporting a news event from the place in which it is occurring, using lightweight, portable cameras and recorders.

ENCODING   To convert analog information into digital form.

ENG/EFP CAMERA   Video camera designed for field operation and used in electronic news gathering and electronic field production.

ENG/EFP ZOOM   Zoom lens especially designed for an ENG/EFP camera.

EQUALIZATION   To alter the audio signal by increasing or decreasing the volume of selected frequencies.

ESTABLISHING SHOT   A wide angle shot that shows the location in which the action of a scene takes place.

EXTERNAL MICROPHONE   A microphone separate from the camera which is connected to the external microphone jack on the video recorder or camera.

FADE IN   Gradual transition from black to an image often used at the beginning of a program.

FADE OUT   Gradual transition from an image to black, often used at the end of a program.

FAIR USE   Use of short examples from copyrighted material in ways that do not require paying copyright fees, such as reviews.

FALL-OFF   Rate at which the light portions of an image turn into the darker portions. A slow fall-off is a gradual change with many gradations inbetween bright and dark; a rapid fall-off is a more abrupt transition.

FEATURE   Program or segment which provides information in an interesting way. In style, it is less serious than news or a documentary.

FEEDBACK   An audio or video signal output which is routed back in the channel as an input.

FERRIC OXIDE   Metallic compound used in the manufacture of audio and video tape.

FIBER OPTICS   Method of changing electrical signals into light waves which are sent through glass fibers.

FIELD   1. The area viewed by a camera and reproduced on a video or film screen. 2. One complete sweep of the electron beam over the video screen. Two sweeps are required to make a complete frame because in the NTSC system alternate lines are scanned with each sweep of the electron beam down the face of the screen.

FIELD OF VIEW   The entire area seen by a camera.

FIELD ZOOM LENS   Zoom lens designed for use on location shooting. Usually has a wide zoom range.

FILL LIGHT   Floodlight placed 90° from the key light in front of the talent to soften harsh shadows created by the key light.

FILM CHAIN/TELECINE   A piece of video production equipment consisting of a film projector, slide projector, and video camera. It allows the use of slides and film in a video production.

FILM SCRIPT FORMAT   Script format in which each shot is described separately. Description includes location, time of day, and action. Dialogue then follows.

FILTER (High Pass–Low Pass)   An equalizer designed to reduce the level of selected frequencies.

FISHEYE LENS   An extreme wide angle lens.

FISHPOLE   A lightweight pole on which a microphone is mounted so that it can be held close to the sound source.

FISHPOLE MIKE   Microphone, usually a unidirectional one, mounted on a fishpole.

FLATS   Moveable walls used in the construction of studio sets.

FLIP-FLOP CONTROLS   A control on the switcher that allows the operator to place the preview image on line by pressing a single button (cut bar). What appeared on preview now appears on line, and vice versa. (The line and preview images are flip-flopped.)

FLOODLIGHTS   Large, lensless studio lights that produce a diffused beam of light over a large area. Used for general illumination and to soften shadows.

FLOOR MANAGER   Studio crew member who gives directions to talent and carries out the director's other instructions.

FLOORPLAN   A scale diagram showing the location of flats, props, set pieces, and cameras for a studio production.

FLUTTER   A high-frequency speed change in an audio signal.

FOCAL LENGTH   The distance from the optical center of a lens to the plane upon which the image falls in focus.

FOLLOW FOCUS   Changing the focus of a lens to keep a moving object in focus as it moves toward or away from the camera.

FOOTCANDLE   A measurement of light intensity defined as the amount of light falling on 1 square foot of surface from 1 candle located 1 foot away.

FOREGROUND REFERENCE   An object placed in the foreground of a scene to give some idea of distance and size. Also suggests depth.

FRESNEL   Spotlight using a planoconvex lens.

F-STOP   Numerical designation indicating the aperture opening. The F-stop number varies inversely with the diameter of the aperture. Thus, the larger the F-stop number, the smaller the aperture; the smaller the F-stop number, the larger the aperture opening.

GAIN   The strength of the audio signal.

GEL   A color filter placed in front of a light source.

GENERATIONS   Copies. The first generation is the original recording, the second, a copy of that tape, and so on.

GENRE   Particular class of motion pictures or television programs, such as science fiction, musicals, and so on.

GRAPHICS   Television visuals such as titles, charts, and graphs. They can be prepared by artists or generated by electronic devices.

GRAY SCALE   Chart that provides a standard reference for shades of brightness from television white (60% reflectance) to television black (3% reflectance).

HDTV (High Definition Television)   Television system using more than 1,000 scan lines and a wide screen format.

HEAD-ON/TAIL-AWAY   A shot sequence showing a subject approaching the camera and then moving away from it. Used to reverse screen direction without confusing the viewer.

HEADS (Erase, Record, Playback)   The components of a tape recorder that act as transducers. The erase head produces an electromagnetic signal to demagnetize the tape. The record head produces an electromagnetic field in response to the audio signal that magnetizes the tape. The playback head responds to the magnetic information on the tape to reproduce the audio signal.

HELICAL SCAN   Tape recording format in which the head moves in a diagonal path across the tape.

HERTZ (Hz)   Cycles per second.

HIGH HAT   A camera mounting device, resembling a tall formal hat, that can hold a camera just above the floor.

HILL AND DALE   An older method of recording signals on a phonograph record in which the stylus rides up and down rather than from side to side.

HUE   Color.

ICON   A representation which resembles the thing it represents. A photograph is an icon of the subject photographed. All video and film images function at a basic iconic level in that they resemble the subject photographed. (See also Index; Symbol.)

IMAGE-ORTHICON   A type of camera pickup tube used in older studio monochrome cameras.

INCIDENT LIGHT   Light falling on a subject directly from its source. An incident light reading is taken by pointing the light meter directly at the light source.

IN CUE   The first word or sound of a program segment.

INDEX   An image which represents a larger set of similar images; for example, a locomotive wheel is an index of a larger class of images associated with transportation technology. (See also Icon; Symbol.)

IN POINT   In videotape editing, the frame at which the edit will begin.

INPUTS   Signals coming into the audio board.

INSERT EDITING   In videotape editing, the mode which uses a tape with a continuous control track as a master tape and transfers only video and audio from the source tape.

INTENSITY   The characteristic of sound perceived as loudness.

INTERGROOVE DISTORTION   An alteration of a signal on a phonograph recording caused when wide swings in a groove press on adjacent grooves and change their shape.

INTERLACE SCANNING   The process by which the video screen is scanned. Odd numbered lines are scanned first, followed by the even numbered lines. Each scan makes up one field, and two scans make up a complete frame. The NTSC standard is 1/60 of a second per field and 1/30 of a second per frame.

INSTRUCTIONAL VIDEO   Video programs used to teach a specific body of knowledge, often for academic credit.

INVISIBLE EDITING   An approach to editing in the continuity system in which edits are made less noticeable by having them occur on action, or between matched shots. A standard approach in Hollywood films and later on television; it ensures a smooth, unobtrusive, editing style.

IRIS   Another name for the aperture on a camera.

ISO (isolated camera)   A production method in which each video camera feeds its own separate videotape recorder.

JACK   Sockets used to connect various pieces of equipment or in a patch bay to route signals.

KEY   Special video effect in which an image (usually lettering) from one source is electronically placed into another.

KEY LIGHT   The principal light source falling on a subject. Usually supplied by a spotlight.

KICKER LIGHT   A light placed to the rear and side of a subject, usually below eye level.

KILO   A prefix meaning "thousand." A kilohertz is 1,000 hertz, for example.

KINESCOPE   Film made directly off a television monitor. This was the only way to record television programs prior to the introduction of videotape.

KISS BLACK/TOUCH BLACK   A quick fade to black between two shots.

LAG   Retention of the image after the camera has moved to another shot.

LARYNX   Organ in the human throat that contains folds of tissue which vibrate with the passage of air, producing sounds.

LAVALIERE   Small microphone that can be hung around the neck or clipped to a performer's clothing.

LEAD SPACE   Empty space in the video frame ahead of or leading a moving object.

LEADER   Information recorded at the beginning of a tape, usually bars and tone as a reference to set playback units, a slate to identify the program, and a countdown for cueing the tape.

LEADER TAPE   Nonmagnetic tape that precedes, follows, or separates segments of an audio recording tape.

LEAKAGE   An unwanted sound or signal affecting (leaking into) the desired sound or signal.

LED DISPLAYS   Light-emitting diodes used to monitor the peaks or high levels in an audio signal.

LENS FLIP   Rotating or flipping a lens turret to put the desired lens in place. Prior to the zoom lens, this required separate instructions from the director. The rotating turret often made noise, and camera operators were cautioned to make lens flips quiet.

LENS TURRET   Rotating device that holds several different lenses in front of older video cameras.

LENSLESS SPOT   Spotlight that produces a strong directional light without using a focusing lens.

LEVEL   Amplitude of the audio signal.

LIGHTING GRID   Pipe work suspended just below a studio ceiling, from which lighting instruments are hung.

LINE LEVEL   Amplitude of signals from sources such as audio tape recorders and turntables.

LINE MONITOR   A video monitor that shows what is being sent to the master VTR or to the transmitter.

LIVE-ON-TAPE   Production method in which a video program is recorded on videotape without interruption as though it were live.

LOCALIZATION   Our perception of the location or the source of a sound.

LOCATION SHOOTING   Recording done outside the studio.

LONG SHOT   A shot which shows a subject from a distance. Also referred to as establishing shot or cover shot.

LOOK SPACE   Empty space in the video frame on the side toward which the subject is looking.

LOUDNESS   The impression of a sound's amplitude or intensity.

LUMINANCE   Brightness or intensity of light.

MACRO LENS   Lens that allows the camera to get close-up views of very small objects.

MACRO ZOOM   Setting on a zoom lens that allows it to get close views of small objects. It is an extension beyond the closest normal zoom position.

MASTER GAIN   Potentiometer that controls the volume of the output of the entire audio board.

MEDIUM OF TRANSMISSION   The substance, such as air or water, through which sound waves are transmitted.

MEDIUM SHOT   A shot midway between a long shot and a closeup.

MEGA   Prefix meaning "million." One megahertz is 1 million hertz.

MIC-LEVEL   The amplitude of signals generated by microphones.

MICROPHONE   Device which acts as a transducer to convert acoustical energy into electrical energy.

MICROPROCESSOR   A small digital computer.

MICROWAVE   High-frequency directional electromagnetic signals used to relay electronic information across short distances in a straight line.

MISE-EN-SCÈNE   French theatrical term meaning "the things in the scene," used also to describe the objects in the film or video frame.

MIX   1. In audio, to combine two or more audio signals. 2. In video, a dissolve between images.

MIXER   The audio control board.

MODULATION   Variations in the strength of the audio signal.

MONAURAL   A sound recorded with one channel of information.

MONITOR   High-quality audio and video receivers used in production studios and control rooms to listen to and watch the audio and video signals.

MONOCHROME   Black and white video.

MONTAGE   1. Approach to film editing developed by the Soviet filmmaker Serge Eisenstein. 2. A quick succession of shots.

MULTIDIRECTIONAL MICROPHONE   Microphone which can be switched from one pickup pattern to another.

MULTIPLEXER   In video, a device containing a series of mirrors used to direct the light from various projectors into one video camera.

MUSIC BED   Music played in the background to help create mood or atmosphere.

MUSIC BRIDGE   Music used as a transition between program segments.

NANOMETER   A measure 1-billionth of a meter in length.

NARROW ANGLE 1. A close-up view of a subject. 2. A close-up lens.

NATIONAL PUBLIC RADIO (NPR) Non-commercial radio network funded by the Corporation for Public Broadcasting.

NOISE Unwanted electrical signals that are heard as noise in audio and seen as a grainy texture in video.

NOISE REDUCTION SYSTEM Device that processes the audio signal to reduce noise levels.

NON-BROADCAST QUALITY Video that does not meet NTSC broadcast standards of resolution, contrast range, and color reproduction.

NON-BROADCAST VIDEO Video that does not meet NTSC technical standards and therefore is unsuitable for broadcast.

NORMAL ANGLE 1. A view similar to what the eye would see through an opening of the same size. 2. A lens that does not distort space but renders objects as the eye would see them.

NTSC STANDARDS The technical standards for American television; 525 scan lines, 60 fields per second, 30 frames per second, and so on.

OCTAVES Whole number multiples of a fundamental pitch. They appear 8 notes up the scale from the fundamental.

OFF-BEAM Placing the source of the sound outside of the most sensitive area of the microphone's pickup pattern.

OFF-LINE EDITING Editing lower quality, non-broadcast copies of master tapes. Masters are then conformed to the edited copies.

OMNI-DIRECTIONAL Microphone pickup pattern that is equally sensitive to sounds coming from all directions.

ON-BEAM Placing the source of the sound directly in the most sensitive area of the microphone's pickup pattern.

ON-LINE Audio or video signals being sent to tape recorders or the transmitter.

ON-LINE EDITING Editing the original high-quality master tapes.

ONE-EIGHTH INCH MINI A plug used as a connector for audio and video equipment.

ONE-FOURTH INCH PHONO A plug used as a connector for audio and video equipment.

ONE-HUNDRED EIGHTY DEGREE RULE A practice of the continuity system which requires that all cameras be placed on the same side of a line of action or conversation.

OPEN REEL RECORDER Tape recorder which uses tape wound on open reels rather than cassettes or cartridges.

OPERATING LIGHT LEVEL Minimum amount of light needed to produce an acceptable video signal. Most video cameras produce a good image with 100-250 foot candles of illumination.

ORGAN OF CORTI Spiral-shaped organ of the ear that converts sound vibrations into nerve impulses.

OSCILLATOR Signal generator that produces a pure sine wave at a selected frequency.

OUT CUE The last words, sounds, or images in a program segment.

OUT POINT In videotape editing, the frame at which the edit will end.

OUTER EAR Visible portion of the ear.

OUTPUT MODULE On the audio board, the module that routes the signal to the tape recorder or transmitter.

OUTTAKE Audio or video material that is discarded in the editing process.

OVERLOAD Distortion that occurs when a signal is overmodulated.

OVERMODULATION   Allowing a signal to increase beyond the maximum level the system is designed to reproduce.

PAL (Phase Alternate Line)   Video standard of 625 scan lines and 25 frames per second used in Europe.

PAN   To rotate the video camera horizontally around its vertical axis to obtain a panoramic view of a subject.

PAN CONTROL   Routing device which sends the audio signal to the left or right channels.

PANTOGRAPH   Adjustable hanging device for studio lights.

PARABOLIC REFLECTOR   A parabolic-shaped shield which reflects sound waves into a microphone mounted facing the center of the shield.

PARALLAX VIEWFINDER   A video viewfinder that sights along a lens rather than through it. There is a slight discrepancy between what the viewfinder and the camera see.

PARTIAL SCRIPT   Script containing only portions of written dialogue, with other portions left unscripted to be filled in at air time. Useful for interviews and other kinds of programs in which spontaneity is desired.

PATCH BAY   Panel containing multiple jacks for routing signals.

PEAK WHITE SIGNAL LEVEL   Video signal which reads 100 IRE units.

PEAKING   Allowing the audio signal level to reach 0 dB or 100 percent modulation on the VU meter.

PEDESTAL   A wheeled device upon which studio cameras can be placed. It can be moved up and down by raising or lowering a central column.

PERSISTENCE OF VISION   A lag in the retina's retention of an image so that one image lingers long enough for another to take its place. Rapidly flashing images therefore appear to be continuous (see also Phi-phenomenon).

PHANTOM POWER   Electrical power fed from the audio console to a microphone via the microphone cable.

PHI-PHENOMENON   The illusion that makes a row of lights flashing in sequence appear to be a continuously moving light. Explains the apparent motion of moving pictures and video images. (See also Persistence of vision.)

PHOTO CONDUCTOR   Substance that produces an electrical charge when struck by light.

PHOTON   Quanta or particles of energy radiating from a light-emitting body.

PHOTORECEPTORS   Cells in the eye that are stimulated by light.

PICKUP PATTERN   Area around a microphone which is sensitive to sound. Common pickup patterns are unidirectional, bidirectional, and omnidirectional.

PICKUP TUBE   The tube in a video camera that converts light energy to electrical energy.

PITCH   The impression or perception of a sound's frequency.

PLANO-CONVEX LENS   Lens that is smooth on one side and curved outward on the other.

POINT OF VIEW   The person represented by the camera. Usually, it represents an anonymous viewer who can see everything and be everywhere; this is third-person-omniscient point of view. Sometimes, the camera represents the view of a person in the story; this is first-person point of view.

POLAR RESPONSE PATTERN   Graph representing the sensitivity of a microphone to sounds within a 360-degree radius of the pickup element.

POSTPRODUCTION   All the work that follows the recording of audio and video program segments to complete the program. This may include editing, mixing, adding special effects, and so on.

POTENTIOMETER   A volume control device.

POTTING IN   Using the potentiometer to increase the volume of the audio signal.

PRE-PRODUCTION   The planning stages of a production up to actual taping or broadcast.

PRE-ROLL   Starting a tape shortly before the playback point to ensure that the machine is fully up to speed.

PRESENCE   The impression that the source of the sound is close to the listener. Presence is affected by the pickup pattern of the microphone, the placement of the microphone, and room acoustics.

PREVIEW BUSS   Row of buttons on a video switcher which permits the operator to put any video source on the preview monitor.

PRINT THROUGH   Changes in the magnetic signal on one section of audio tape produced by the magnetic patterns on the adjacent layer of tape.

PROCESSING   Manipulating the electrical signal generated by a microphone or a video camera.

PRODUCER   Member of the production team who is responsible for organizing and coordinating the production prior to taping.

PROGRAM   A unit of audio or video material with a clearly defined beginning, middle, and end.

PROGRAM BUSS   Row of buttons on a video switcher that allows the operator to put any video source on the program monitor and send it out of the switcher.

PROMO   Short announcement used to persuade the audience to tune in to a specific program.

PSYCHOGRAPHICS   Information about the audience's values, attitudes, lifestyle, and behaviors such as buying habits and voting patterns.

PUBLIC DOMAIN   Material on which the copyright has expired is said to be in the public domain and can be used without payment to the author or composer.

PUBLIC SERVICE ANNOUNCEMENT   Spot announcement for a nonprofit organization.

QUADRAPHONIC   Four- channel audio recording. Two front channels record a normal stereo signal. Two rear channels pick up ambient and reflected sound of the recording hall.

QUANTA   Particles of energy radiating from a light-emitting body.

QUANTIZING   Assigning discrete numerical values to digitally sampled sections of a wave form.

RANGE EXTENDERS   Lenses added to a zoom lens system that extend the zoom range.

RATING   Measurement of the audience for a particular program.

RCA PHONO   A plug used in connecting various pieces of audio and video equipment.

READIES   Preparatory video commands as in "ready one, take one" or "ready mic talent, mic talent."

REAR PROJECTION   Projecting film or slides from a projector mounted behind a screen. Used to make backgrounds for studio productions.

RECEIVER   Device that tunes in broadcast signals, amplifies them, and converts them into images and sounds.

RECORD CUEING   Placing the stylus at the beginning of a selection so that the sound will begin immediately.

RECORD DECK   In videotape editing, the deck used to record the master tape.

REFERENCE TONE   A single frequency recorded at the beginning of a tape to provide a reference for adjusting equipment for playback.

REFLECTED LIGHT   Light which is reflected from the surface of an object.

REFLEX VIEWFINDER   Viewfinder that looks at a scene through the lens of the camera. What the operator and the camera see are identical.

REFRACTION   Deflection or bending of light waves as they pass through objects of varying density.

REGISTRATION   The process of aligning the images from the RGB tubes in a video camera so they overlap precisely.

RESOLUTION   The degree to which a video system reproduces the fine detail of an image.

RETENTIVITY   Ability to retain magnetism when the current is turned off.

RETINA   Light-sensitive portion of the eye.

REVERBERATION   Many closely spaced repetitions of a sound.

REVERBERATION SYSTEM   Device used to simulate the acoustical characteristics of large rooms.

RIBBON MICROPHONE   Type of dynamic microphone which uses a thin ribbon of metal foil suspended within a magnetic field as the vibrating element.

RING FOCUS   Ringlike focus control on a spotlight. By turning the ring, the light beam can be spread or pinned.

RISERS   Wooden platforms used in studios to elevate talent and props.

ROLL FOCUS   To adjust a camera's focus so that a portion of a scene is brought into focus while another goes out of focus.

RUNDOWN SCRIPT   List of the program segments with notations about the running time of each segment, where it originates, and in and out cues for each.

RUNDOWN SHEET   A rundown script.

SAMPLING RATE   Rate at which an analog signal is sampled to determine its frequency and amplitude at a particular instant. Sampling is a step in the process of converting analog signals to digital form.

SATURATION   Point at which a tape is fully magnetized.

SCANNING   Process by which a video raster or image is read by the stream of electrons hitting its inner surface. In the American NTSC system, the gun reads across from left to right and top to bottom. It reads the odd-numbered lines and then returns to read the even-numbered. Each scan takes 1/60 of a second. This means that there are 60 separate scans making 30 complete images per second. The process is called interlace scanning.

SCENE   1. A view in front of a camera. 2. A group of related shots.

SCREEN DIRECTION   Direction in which a subject moves on the screen. In the continuity system, screen direction is maintained from one shot to another.

SCRIM   Translucent filter or screen placed in front of a spot or floodlight to soften the beam.

SECAM (Sequential Couleur a Memorie)   Television standard used in France and several other countries.

SEGMENT TIME   Individual timings for separate portions of a video program.

SEGUE   Beginning one sound or record as soon as the preceding one ends.

SEQUENCE   A group of related scenes. (See Shot and Scene.)

SESAC   European copyrighting agency.

SHOT   A single uninterrupted run of a camera.

SHOT BOX   Device that allows the video operator to preset several zoom positions and locate them by means of buttons.

SHOT SHEET   List of shots in a program for each individual camera.

SIDE LIGHT   Spotlight directed at a subject from the side.

SIGNAL-TO-NOISE RATIO   Ratio between the strength of an audio or video signal and the background noise in the equipment.

SILHOUETTE LIGHT   Arrangement of lights producing a bright background against which an unlighted subject appears outlined.

SINE WAVE   The waveform produced by a single frequency. It is symmetrical and regular in form.

SLATE   1. A marker which makes a noticeable audio and video starting point for a program. 2. A clear identification of a program's content.

SLIP CUEING   Method for cueing the record by locating the first sound, holding the record stationary while the turntable rotates and releasing the record on cue.

SMPTE TIME CODE   Method of assigning a specific number (in hours: minutes: seconds: frames) to each frame of video.

SOLID STATE SENSOR   In video cameras, a chip storage device that is used instead of a pickup tube to change light energy into electrical energy.

SOLO SWITCH   Switch that isolates an individual audio input channel for monitoring.

SOUND BITS   Segment of recorded sound, usually a portion of an interview or other spoken comments recorded on location.

SOUND EFFECTS   Sounds other than music or speech added to a program to suggest environment or action. Sound effects may be recorded or produced manually.

SOUND TRACK   The audio portion of a video or film program.

SOURCE DECK   In videotape editing, the deck used to playback the raw footage.

SPEAKER (LOUDSPEAKER)   Cone-shaped device which moves back and forth in response to signals fed into an electromagnetic coil at its base. Used to reproduce sounds from electrical signals.

SPECIAL EFFECTS   Wipes, keys, split screens, and other creative manipulations of the video image.

SPECIAL EFFECTS GENERATOR   Device in a video switcher that allows the operator to create special effects.

SPECTRUM   The complete range of frequencies of electromagnetic energy.

SPLICING TAPE   Tape with adhesive on one side, used in audio tape editing to join two sections of tape.

SPLIT SCREEN   A special effect in which the video screen is divided by a vertical or horizontal line.

SPOTLIGHT   A studio lighting unit that produces a strong focusable beam of illumination. Some spotlights use lenses, others do not.

STANDING WAVES   An audio wave that appears to be stationary. Caused when a wave is reflected back to its source. Various points of the wave will alternately cancel and reinforce each other.

STATUS DISPLAY MONITOR   In videotape editing, the video monitor that provides a read-out of all the controller settings, including such things as edit mode, pre-roll time, in and out points, and so on.

STEADICAM   A camera mounting device attached to the operator's body. It permits a steady image while the operator moves about. This is made possible by a combination of springs and counterweights.

STEREO MICROPHONE   Microphone which has two diaphragms mounted in one case. The output of one feeds into the left channel, the other into the right.

STEREOPHONIC   Two-channel audio sound.

STEREOPHONIC SEPARATION   The degree of separation between the right and left channels of a stereo signal.

STORAGE   Converting electrical signals into magnetic patterns on tape or physical shapes on a record or compact disc so that the original signal can be reproduced later.

STORYBOARD   Outline of a video program, commercial, or PSA using a series of drawings or photographs to illustrate the sequence of visuals.

STUDIO CAMERA   Large, high-quality video camera designed for use in a television studio. It usually requires a tripod or pedestal mount.

STUDIO ZOOM LENS   A zoom lens designed for use on a studio camera. It usually has a smaller zoom ratio than lenses intended for field cameras.

STYLUS   The needle mounted in the cartridge of the tone arm of a turntable which vibrates as it follows the grooves in a record.

SUBMASTER   On the audio console, an output channel ahead of the master output to which several inputs can be assigned.

SURFACE NOISE   Noise caused by imperfections, dust, or scratches on the surface of an audio recording.

SWEEP FOCUS   A spotlight focus control consisting of a lever that can be moved back and forth.

SWITCHER   Device that selects from several video inputs, provides various transitions between them, and sends the selected signal out.

SYMBOL   Something that represents something else. Visual images can represent things other than the objects which they resemble; for example, an American flag symbolizes the United States.

SYNC GENERATOR   The device which generates a series of timing pulses which serve to keep all units in the video system scanning the image in unison.

SYNC PULSE   Pulses read by various units in the video system and used to time the scanning of the image.

SYNTHESIZER   A signal generator which can be programmed to produce wave forms imitating acoustical signals.

TAIL OUT   A reel of tape stored without rewinding so that the end of the tape, rather than the beginning, is out.

TALLY LIGHT   A light on a video camera that indicates to the operator and talent when the camera's signal is on line.

TAPE LIFTER   Device that holds the tape away from the tape heads during fast forward or rewind.

TAPE NOISE   Extraneous signals created by the magnetic recording process. On playback, these are heard as tape hiss.

TAPE TRANSPORT MECHANISM   A series of reels, guides, and rotating shafts that move a tape across the recording and playback heads at a uniform speed.

TEASER   A short segment at the beginning of a program designed to capture attention and create interest in the program that follows.

TELEPHOTO   A lens capable of close views of objects from a great distance.

TENSILIZE   A process in manufacturing audio tape which stretches the plastic base material to minimize stretching during use.

THREE-POINT LIGHTING SCHEME   A method of studio lighting that uses three principal lighting positions—the key, back, and fill lights.

TILT   A vertical movement of the camera head achieved by swivelling it up or down around the horizontal axis.

TIMBRE   The quality of a particular sound caused by the unique pattern of overtones (upper harmonics), attack, and decay.

TIME BASE CORRECTOR   A device which corrects timing errors caused by variations in videotape speed by storing a field or frame of video and reading it out in sync with other components of the system.

TONE ARM   A device that holds a phonograph cartridge so that it can track the grooves of an audio recording.

TONE GENERATOR   A device that produces pure sine waves at designated frequencies.

TONGUE   A camera movement accomplished by moving a camera back and forth horizontally by means of the crane arm on a panorama dolly or studio crane.

TRACK   A strip of magnetic information recorded on a tape.

TRANSDUCER   A device that converts one form of energy into another form of energy.

TRANSMITTER   A device that generates electromagnetic signals and broadcasts them out into space.

TRANVERSE SCAN   The scanning pattern used by quadraplex videotape recorders in which the signal is recorded across the tape at a 90° angle from the path of the tape.

TREATMENT   A narrative description of the proposed production project, including the purpose of the project, what the final program will be like, and the resources needed to complete the production.

TRIPOD   A three-legged camera mount.

TRUCK   Moving a camera parallel to a moving object.

TUNEABLE ACOUSTICAL SPACE   An acoustical space in which the reverberation time can be adjusted by moving baffles and sound absorbing surfaces.

TWO-FOLDS   Scenery flats that fold into two parts.

TYPE-B FORMAT   Videotape format where each pass of the record head lays down only a portion of the video field.

TYPE-C FORMAT   Videotape format in which each pass of the video record head across the tape records one complete field of video information. Freeze frame is possible with this format, since each pass of the playback head generates one complete frame of information.

UNBALANCED LINE   A cable which usually contains only one conductor with the shield acting as a ground.

UNIDIRECTIONAL   A microphone pickup pattern which is most sensitive to sounds directly in front while rejecting those from other directions. Depending upon the angle of sensitivity, these may also be referred to as cardioid, super-cardioid, or hyper-cardioid.

UPLINK   Transmitter that sends signals from earth to a satellite.

USIA (United States Information Agency)   A government organization that produces films, video and audio tapes, and printed materials for distribution to other countries.

VARIABLE FOCAL LENGTH LENS   A lens system that can be adjusted from wide angle to very closeup views by changing the distance among internal optical elements. Also known as a zoom lens.

VCR   A videocassette recorder usually of the VHS or Betamax format and intended primarily for home use.

VERTICAL BLANKING INTERVAL   The time that the video electron beam is shut off as it moves from the bottom of a field to the top of the next.

VIDEO   Electronically reproduced images.

VIDEO NOISE   Snow or other electrical interference in a video signal.

VIDICON   A common type of camera pickup tube often designated by a manufacturer's trade name such as Plumbicon, Saticon, Newvicon.

VOICE-OVER   In video or film, a voice from an offscreen source, often used for narration.

VOLUME   The perceived loudness of a sound.

VU METER   A device which gives a visual rendering of an audio signal's average strength in discrete volume units.

WATT   Unit of electrical power.

WAVE FORM MONITOR   A device that provides a visual display of the video signal.

WAVELENGTH   The distance between crests of successive energy waves.

WEDGE MOUNT   A device used to attach a camera head to a camera base. A wedge on the base of the camera fits into a slot on the top of the camera pedestal or tripod.

WHITE BALANCE   Balancing the strength of the three primary colors (red, green, blue) of a video image to give an accurate rendering of white.

WIDE ANGLE   1. A distant view of a scene. 2. A lens of short focal length which shows a wide view of a scene.

WIDE SCREEN TECHNOLOGIES   Various combinations of lenses, film stocks, and projection techniques designed to produce wide screen film images—for example, Cinerama, Cinemascope, Vistavision, Todd A-O.

WINDSCREEN   Foam or mesh covers placed on microphones to minimize noise created by the rush of air from wind or explosive speech sounds.

WIRELESS MICROPHONE   Microphone equipped with a low power transmitter which relays the microphone's output to a receiver. From the receiver, the signal travels via cable to the audio board.

WORK PRINT   A copy of the master recording used for viewing during off-line editing to protect the master from unnecessary wear.

WOW   A low-pitched variation in an audio signal.

XLR CONNECTOR   A plug used to connect audio and video equipment.

Y- CONNECTOR   A Y-shaped connector that allows one electrical signal to be split to feed two channels.

ZOOM FOCUS PRESET   Setting a zoom lens so that everything is in focus throughout the entire zoom range. Accomplished by zooming in to the closest setting and focusing the lens. Focus must be reset for each different position of the camera.

Bibliography

Chapter 1

APPLBAUM, RONALD L., et. al *Fundamental Concepts in Human Communication* (New York: Canfield Press, 1973).

DANCE, FRANK E. X. *Human Communication Theory* (New York: Harper & Row, Pub., 1982).

DeFLEUR, MELVIN L. and SANDRA BALL-ROKEACH. *Theories of Mass Communication*, 4th ed. (New York: Longman, 1982).

HODGES, DONALD A. *Handbook of Music Psychology* (Lawrence, Kans.: National Association for Music Therapy, 1980).

ROCK, IRVIN. *The Logic of Perception* (Cambridge, Mass.: The MIT Press, 1983).

ROSS, RAYMOND. *Speech Communication: Fundamentals and Practice* (Englewood Cliffs, N.J.: Prentice-Hall, 1986).

SANDERS, DEREK H. *Auditory Perception of Speech* (Englewood Cliffs, N.J.: Prentice-Hall, 1977).

SCHUBERT, EARL D. *Hearing: Its Function and Dysfunction* (New York: Springer-Verlag Wien, 1980).

SCHWARTZ, TONY. *The Responsive Chord* (New York: Anchor Press, 1973).

ZETTL, HERBERT. *Sight, Sound, Motion: Applied Media Aesthetics* (Belmont, Calif.: Wadsworth, 1973).

Chapter 2

CHEDD, GRAHAM. *Sound: From Communication to Noise Pollution* (Garden City, N.Y.: Doubleday, 1970).

OSTWALD, PETER F. *Soundmaking: The Acoustic Communication of Emotion* (Springfield, Ill.: C Thomas, 1963).

PIERCE, JOHN R. *The Science of Musical Sound* (New York: Scientific American Library, 1983).

STEVENS, S. S., FRED WARSHOFSKY, and the Editors of Time-Life Books, *Sound and Hearing* (Alexandria, Va.: Time-Life Books, 1980).

WORAM, JOHN M. *The Recording Studio Handbook* (Plainview, N.Y.: ELAR, 1982).

Chapter 3

ALTEN, STANLEY R. *Audio in Media*, 2d ed. (Belmont, Calif.: Wadsworth, 1981).

BARTLETT, BRUCE. *Introduction to Professional Recording Techniques* (Indianapolis, Ind.: Howard W. Sams & Co., Inc., 1987).

CLIFFORD, MARTIN. *Microphones: How They Work and How to Use Them*, 2d ed. (Blue Ridge Summit, Pa.: TAB Books, 1982).

NISBETT, ALEC. *The Technique of the Sound Studio*, 4th ed. (Boston: Focal Press, 1979).

NISBETT, ALEC. *The Use of Microphones*, 2d ed. (Boston: Focal Press, 1983).

ORINGEL, ROBERT. *Audio Control Handbook*, 5th ed. (New York: Hastings House, 1983).

WELLS, THOMAS H. *The Technique of Electronic Music* (New York: Schirmer, 1981).

WORAM, JOHN M. *The Recording Studio Handbook* (Plainview, N.Y.: ELAR, 1982).

Chapter 4

BIAGI, SHIRLEY. *Interviews That Work: A Practical Guide for Journalists* (Belmont, Calif.: Wadsworth, 1985).

HILLIARD, ROBERT L. *Radio Broadcasting*, 3d ed. (White Plains, N.Y.: Longman, 1985).

HILLIARD, ROBERT L. *Writing for Television and Radio,* 4th ed. (Belmont, Calif.: Wadsworth, 1984).

JOSEPHSON, LARRY, ed. *Telling the Story: The National Public Radio Guide to Radio Journalism* (Dubuque, Iowa: Kendall/Hunt, 1983).

KEITH, MICHAEL C. *Production in Format Radio Handbook* (Lanham, Md.: University Press of America, 1984).

O'DONNELL, LEWIS B., PHILIP BENOIT, and CARL HAUSMAN. *Modern Radio Production* (Belmont, Calif.: Wadsworth, 1986).

ORLIK, PETER B. *Broadcast Copywriting* (Boston: Allyn & Bacon, 1986).

Chapter 5

KEITH, MICHAEL C. and JOSEPH M. KRAUSE, eds. *The Radio Station* (Boston: Focal Press, 1986).

MCLEISH, ROBERT. *The Technique of Radio Production*, 2d ed. (Boston: Focal Press, 1988).

O'DONNELL, LEWIS B., PHILIP BENOIT, and CARL HAUSMAN. *Modern Radio Production* (Belmont, Calif.: Wadsworth, 1986).

STEPHENS, MITCHELL. *Broadcast News*, 2d ed. (New York: Holt, Rinehart & Winston, 1986).

WHETMORE, EDWARD JAY. *The Magic Medium: An Introduction to Radio in America* (Belmont, Calif.: Wadsworth, 1981).

Chapter 6

BUROWS, THOMAS D. and DONALD N. WOOD, *Television Production: Disciplines and Techniques*, 3d ed. (Dubuque, Iowa: Wm. C. Brown, 1986).

GREGORY, R. L. *Eye and Brain: The Psychology of Seeing* (New York: McGraw-Hill, 1966).

KAUFMAN, LLOYD. *Sight and Mind: An Introduction to Visual Perception* (New York: Oxford University Press, 1974).

KINDEM, GORHAM. *The Moving Image: Production Principles and Practices* (Glenview, Ill.: Scott, Foresman, 1987).

MADSEN, ROY PAUL. *The Impact of Film: How Ideas Are Communicated Through Cinema and Television* (New York: Macmillan, 1973).

MONACO, JAMES. *How to Read a Film: The Art, Technology, Language, History and Theory of Film and Media* (New York: Oxford University Press, 1984).

NEWCOMB, HORACE, ed. *Television: The Critical View*, 3d ed. (New York: Oxford University Press, 1982).

PATTERSON, RICHARD and DANA WHITE, eds. *Electronic Production Techniques* (American Cinematographer Reprint, 1986).

PRIMEAU, RONALD. *The Rhetoric of Television* (New York: Longman, 1979).

WOLLEN, PETER. *Signs and Meaning in the Cinema*, 2d ed. (New York: Viking Press, 1972).

WURTZEL, ALAN. *Television Production*, 2d ed. (New York: McGraw-Hill, 1983).

ZETTL, HERBERT. *Sight, Sound, Motion: Applied Media Aesthetics* (Belmont, Calif.: Wadsworth, 1973).

———. *Television Production Handbook*, 4th ed. (Belmont, Calif.: Wadsworth, 1984).

Chapter 7

GREGORY, RICHARD L. *Eye and Brain: The Psychology of Seeing* (London: World University Library, 1972).

HABER, RALPH NORMAN and MAURICE HERSHENSON. *The Psychology of Visual Perception*, 2d ed. (New York: Holt, Rinehart & Winston, 1980).

INGRAM, DAVE. *Video Electronics Technology* (Blue Ridge Summit, Pa.: TAB Books, 1983).

MATHIAS, HARRY and RICHARD PATTERSON. *Electronic Cinematography* (Belmont, Calif.: Wadsworth, 1985).

NOLL, EDWARD M. *Broadcast Radio and Television Handbook*, 6th ed. (Indianapolis, Ind.: Howard W. Sams & Co., 1983).

OVERHEIM, R. DANIEL and DAVID L. WAGNER. *Light and Color* (New York: John Wiley, 1982).

WALDMAN, GARY. *Introduction to Light: The Physics of Light, Vision, and Color* (Englewood Cliffs, N.J.: Prentice-Hall, 1980).

Chapter 8

BURROWS, THOMAS D. and DONALD N. WOOD. *Television Production: Disciplines and Techniques*, 3d ed. (Dubuque, Iowa: Wm. C. Brown, 1986).

GROSS, LYNNE SCHAFER. *The New Television Technologies* (Dubuque, Iowa: Wm. C. Brown, 1983).

KINDEM, GORHAM. *The Moving Image: Production Principles and Practices* (Glenview, Ill: Scott, Foresman, 1987).

MILLERSON, GERALD. *The Technique of Television Production* (London: Focal Press, 1981).

PATTERSON, RICHARD and DANA WHITE, eds. *Electronic Production Techniques* (An American Cinematographer Reprint, 1986).

STASHEFF, EDWARD and RUDY BRETZ. *The Television Program: Its Direction and Production* (New York: Hill & Wang, 1962).

WURTZEL, ALAN. *Television Production*, 2d ed. (New York: McGraw-Hill, 1983).

ZETTL, HERBERT. *Television Production Handbook*, 4th ed. (Belmont, Calif.: Wadsworth, 1984).

Chapter 9

BLUM, RICHARD A. *Television Writing: From Concept to Contract*. (New York: Hastings House, Publishers, 1980).

HILLIARD, ROBERT L. *Writing for Television and Radio*, 3d ed. (New York: Hastings House, Publishers, 1976).

KINDEM, GORHAM. *The Moving Image: Production Principles and Practices* (Glenview, Ill: Scott, Foresman, 1987).

MILLER, WILLIAM. *Screenplay Writing for Narrative Film and Television*. (New York: Hastings House, 1980).

WILLIS, EDGAR E. and CAMILLE D'ARIENZO. *Writing Scripts for Television, Radio, and Film* (New York: Holt, Rinehart & Winston, 1981).

Chapter 10

BOGGS, JOSEPH M. *The Art of Watching Films* (Menlo Park, Calif.: Benjamin/Cummings, 1978).

BORDWELL, DAVID and KRISTIN THOMPSON. *Film Art: An Introduction* (Reading, Mass.: Addison-Wesley, 1979).

BURROWS, THOMAS D and DONALD N. WOOD. *Television Production: Disciplines and Techniques*, 3d ed. (Dubuque, Iowa: Wm. C. Brown, 1986).

STROMGREM, RICHARD L. and MARTIN F. NORDEN. *Movies: A Language in Light* (Englewood Cliffs, N.J.: Prentice-Hall, 1984).

WURTZEL, ALAN. *Television Production*, 2d ed. (New York: McGraw-Hill, 1983).

ZETTL, HERBERT. *Sight, Sound, Motion: Applied Media Aesthetics* (Belmont, Calif.: Wadsworth, 1973).

———. *Television Production Handbook*, 4th ed. (Belmont, Calif.: Wadsworth, 1984).

Chapter 11

BOGGS, JOSEPH M. *The Art of Watching Films* (Menlo Park, Calif.: Benjamin/Cummings, 1978).

BORDWELL, DAVID, JANET STAIGER, and KRISTIN THOMPSON. *The Classical Hollywood Cinema: Film Style and Mode of Production to 1960* (New York: Columbia University Press, 1985).

BORDWELL, DAVID and KRISTIN THOMPSON. *Film Art: An Introduction* (Reading, Mass.: Addison-Wesley, 1979).

BURROWS, THOMAS D and DONALD N. WOOD. *Television Production: Disciplines and Techniques*, 3d ed. (Dubuque, Iowa: Wm. C. Brown, 1986).

MASCELLI, JOSEPH V. *The Five Cs of Cinematography: Motion Picture Filming Techniques Simplified* (Hollywood: Cine/Grafic Publications, 1965).

STROMGREN, RICHARD L. and MARTIN F. NORDEN. *Movies: A Language in Light* (Englewood Cliffs, N.J.: Prentice-Hall, 1984).

WURTZEL, ALAN. *Television Production*, 2d ed. (New York: McGraw-Hill, 1983).

ZETTL, HERBERT. *Television Production Handbook*, 4th ed. (Belmont, Calif.: Wadsworth, 1984).

Chapter 12

ARMER, ALAN A. *Directing Television and Film* (Belmont, Calif.: Wadsworth, 1986).

BELLMAN, WILLARD F. *Lighting the Stage: Art and Practice* (New York: Chandler, 1974).

BORDWELL, DAVID, JANET STAIGER, and KRISTIN THOMPSON. *The Classical Hollywood Cinema: Film Style and Mode of Production to 1960* (New York: Columbia University Press, 1985).

BURROWS, THOMAS D and DONALD N. WOOD. *Television Production: Disciplines and Techniques*, 3d ed. (Dubuque, Iowa: Wm. C. Brown, 1986).

WURTZEL, ALAN. *Television Production*, 2d ed. (New York: McGraw-Hill, 1983).

ZETTL, HERBERT. *Television Production Handbook*, 4th ed. (Belmont, Calif.: Wadsworth, 1984).

Chapter 13

ANDERSON, GARY H. *Video Editing and Post-Production: A Professional Guide* (White Plains, N.Y.: Knowledge Industry Publications, 1984).

BROWNE, STEVEN E. *The Video Tape Post-Production Primer* (Burbank, Calif.: Wilton Place Communications, 1982).

COMPESI, RONALD J. and RONALD E. SHERRIFFS. *Small Format Television Production: The Technique of Single-Camera Television Field Production* (Boston: Allyn & Bacon, 1985).

FULLER, BARRY J., STEVE KANABA, and JANYCE BRISCH-KANABA. *Single-Camera Video Production: Techniques, Equipment, and Resources for Producing Quality Video Programs* (Englewood Cliffs, N.J.: Prentice-Hall, 1982).

HUBATHA, MILTON C., FREDERICK HULL, and RICHARD W. SANDERS. *Audio Sweetening for Films and TV* (Blue Ridge Summit, Pa.: TAB Books, 1985).

LeTourneau, Tom. *Lighting Techniques for Video Production* (White Plains, N.Y.: Knowledge Industry Publications, 1987).

Millerson, Gerald. *TV Lighting Methods*, 2d ed. (London: Focal Press, 1982).

Shook, Frederick. *Television Field Production and Reporting* (New York: Longman, 1988).

Yoakam, Richard D. and Charles F. Cremer. *ENG: Television News and the New Technology* (New York: Random House, 1985).

Chapter 14

Diamond, Edwin and Stephen Bates. *The Spot: The Rise of Political Advertising on Television* (Cambridge, Mass.: The MIT Press, 1984).

Newcomb, Horace and Robert S. Alley. *The Producer's Medium: Conversations with Creators of American TV* (New York: Oxford University Press, 1983).

Verna, Tony. *Live TV: An Inside Look at Direction and Producing* (Boston: Focal Press, 1987).

Ward, Hiley H. *Professional Newswriting* (San Diego, Calif.: Harcourt Brace Jovanovich, Inc., 1985).

Index